Transgender Rights and Politics

To date, the media has focused on the gay community's call for the end of discrimination and for marriage equality. Likewise, most of the scholarship on gay politics and policy has focused on the morality debates over sexual orientation and the legal aspects of rights for nonheterosexuals. With the intense focus on gay and lesbian rights, transgender concerns have received little attention, from either the media or researchers in political science. However, as transgender activism has become more visible, policymakers, both in the United States and around the world, have begun to respond to demands for more equitable treatment.

In this volume, Jami K. Taylor and Donald P. Haider-Markel bring together new research employing the concepts and tools of political science to explore the politics of transgender rights. Volume contributors address the framing of transgender rights in the United States and in Latin America. They discuss transgender interest groups, the inclusion of transgender activists in advocacy coalitions, policy diffusion at the state and local levels, and, importantly, the implementation of transgender public policy. This volume sets the standard for empirical research on transgender politics and demonstrates that the study of this topic can contribute to the understanding of larger questions in the field of political science.

Jami K. Taylor is Associate Professor of Political Science and Public Administration at the University of Toledo.

Donald P. Haider-Markel is Professor of Political Science and Chair at the University of Kansas.

Transgender Rights and Politics

Groups, Issue Framing, and Policy Adoption

Edited by Jami K. Taylor and
Donald P. Haider-Markel

UNIVERSITY OF MICHIGAN PRESS

Ann Arbor

First paperback edition 2015
Copyright © by the University of Michigan 2014
All rights reserved

Published in the United States of America by the
University of Michigan Press
Manufactured in the United States of America
⊚ Printed on acid-free paper

2018   2017   2016   2015   5   4   3   2

A CIP catalog record for this book is available from the British Library.

Library of Congress Cataloging-in-Publication Data

Transgender rights and politics : groups, issue framing, and policy adoption /
edited by Jami K. Taylor and Donald P. Haider-Markel.
       pages   cm
    Includes bibliographical references and index.
    ISBN 978-0-472-07235-4 (hardcover : alk. paper) — ISBN 978-0-472-05235-6 (pbk. : alk.
paper) — ISBN 978-0-472-12060-4 (e-book)
    1. Transgender people—Civil rights.   2. Transgender people—Legal status, laws, etc.
3. Sex and law.   I. Taylor, Jami K., editor of compilation.   II. Haider-Markel, Donald P.,
editor of compilation.
HQ77.9.T7173   2014
306.76'8—dc23
                                                              2014018293

Contents

Beyond Nondiscrimination Policy

Jami K. Taylor and Donald P. Haider-Markel

Introduction to Transgender Rights and Politics

Over the past few decades, gay civil rights have been center stage in American politics. Incessant battles over issues such as same-sex marriage, gays in the military, and legislation banning discrimination have been waged. Regardless of one's position on these issues, it is difficult to deny the impact of the lesbian, gay, bisexual, and transgender (LGBT) civil rights movement on American politics and society. However, when we speak of LGBT issues, there is a tendency to focus on policy based on one's sexual orientation. This ignores an important segment of the LGBT community, transgender people. Despite being an afterthought, which, politically, it often has been for the LGBT movement, the transgender community raises important concerns for governance and our theoretical understandings of the democratic process (Taylor 2007; Johnson 2011).

To address these issues, this edited volume brings together needed scholarship on transgender advocacy and policy. Its goal is to provide a clear and penetrable exploration of transgender issues in politics. This is certainly needed given that a recent issue of the *Journal of Public Affairs Education* (Johnson 2011) identified transgender rights as a topic that public affairs programs should address. This volume brings together experts on administration, public policy, public opinion, and state politics to examine the phenomenon of transgender advocacy in largely democratic political systems. Importantly, this compilation departs from existing queer theory and legal approaches to the topic and applies empirical testing and examination of questions related to transgender rights. Collectively, the authors provide new insights on this increasingly salient policy area.

Transgender-Related Policy in the United States

As of 2013, as shown in figure 1, fifteen states and the District of Columbia had passed hate crimes laws that protect on the basis of gender identity

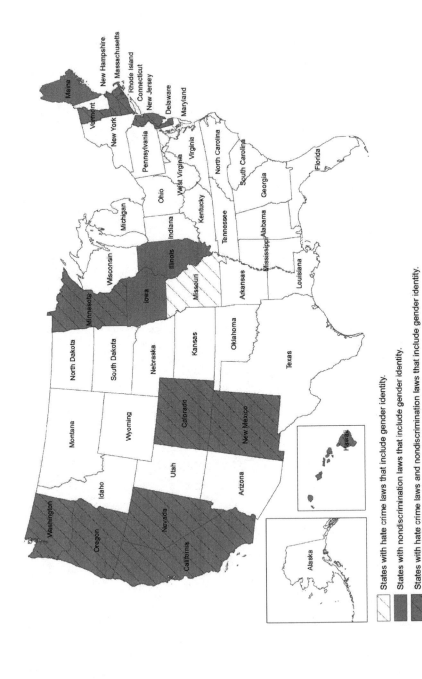

Fig. 1. Map of states with transgender inclusive hate crimes and nondiscrimination laws, as of June 2013. (Data compiled from National Gay and Lesbian Task Force and Human Rights Campaign.)

States with hate crime laws that include gender identity.

States with nondiscrimination laws that include gender identity.

States with hate crime laws and nondiscrimination laws that include gender identity.

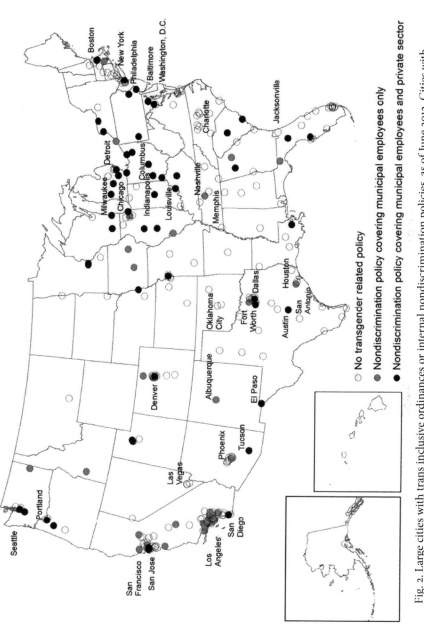

Fig. 2. Large cities with trans inclusive ordinances or internal nondiscrimination policies, as of June 2012. Cities with populations greater than 100,000 as of 2010. Census CDPs not included. (Data compiled by the authors and the Transgender Law and Policy Institute.)

○ No transgender related policy

◉ Nondiscrimination policy covering municipal employees only

● Nondiscrimination policy covering municipal employees and private sector and sexual orientation (National Gay and Lesbian Task Force 2012a; Human Rights Campaign 2013). In 2009, Congress followed the lead of states such as Illinois and Maryland and enacted a fully LGBT-inclusive federal hate crimes statute. Furthermore, as shown in figure 1, seventeen states and the District of Columbia banned employment discrimination against transgender individuals as of 2013 (National Gay and Lesbian Task Force 2012b). Even where statutes have not explicitly mandated employment protections based on gender identity, some governors have extended these protections to public sector workers via executive orders. Additionally, the courts, in cases such as *Smith v. City of Salem Ohio* (2004) or *Glenn v. Brumby* (2011) have sometimes extended existing Title VII sex discrimination protections to transgender workers. Also, half of the states have statutes that specifically authorize transgender individuals to amend their birth certificates in the event of sex reassignment. Similarly, the State Department, Social Security Administration, and most if not all state motor vehicle agencies allow the sex marker to be changed on key identification documents (Taylor 2007). Finally, as shown in figure 2, many local jurisdictions have enacted various transgender-inclusive ordinances and policies (Transgender Law and Policy Institute 2012).

Despite these advances, there have also been important setbacks. Transgender identity related issues were singled out by Congress for exclusion from coverage under the Americans with Disabilities Act (Committee on Education and Labor 1991). Decisions in court cases such as *Ulane v. Eastern Airlines* (1984) and *Oiler v. Winn-Dixie* (2002) have hurt the ability of transgender people to seek redress through the courts when they have suffered from alleged employment discrimination. The failures of state courts to legally recognize a transgender person's identity in cases such as *Littleton v. Prange* (1999) and *In re Estate of Gardiner* (2002) have also dealt setbacks to the movement. The issue of transgender inclusion has also blocked some LGBT rights bills in state legislatures. As witnessed in local-level battles over nondiscrimination ordinances in Anchorage, Alaska, and Gainesville, Florida, attacking transgender rights has become a useful tactic for opponents of LGBT rights. Sometimes, and as demonstrated in Delaware in 2009 or New York in 2003, LGBT movement activists and their legislative allies have elected to advance nondiscrimination bills without gender-identity-inclusive language in the belief that including trans protections would endanger the passage of legislation.

Although this list of advances and setbacks to the transgender rights movement is not exhaustive, it does show that the legal framework for transgender people in the United States is best described as "thin, heterogeneous and ad hoc" (Dasti 2002, 1742). A patchwork of laws protect transgender people from discrimination. However, some policies, such as the Department of Defense's regulations that forbid openly transgender servicemembers, also sanction bias. Additionally, the "statutes that define one's legal sex are vague, contradictory, and inadequate" (Taylor 2007). In this incoherent framework, administrators and the courts are left to implement or interpret laws that have often provided insufficient legislative or executive guidance. Administrators and the courts are also frequently exercising discretion on transgender issues that they repeatedly conflate, and often mistakenly, with sexual orientation. There are important unresolved civil rights and equity issues in this environment.

Despite all of this policy activity and despite the importance of equity in their profession (Frederickson 1971), political scientists and public administration scholars have paid little attention to these issues (Taylor 2007; Johnson 2011). With few exceptions, such as Colvin's (2007) research on the implementation of gender-identity-inclusive nondiscrimination policies and Nownes's (2010) study of the transgender interest group system, much of the existing work (e.g., Currah, Juang, and Minter 2006; Stryker and Whittle 2006) approaches transgender policy with a normative lens, via queer theory, deconstructive interpretive analysis, or through legal analysis. There have also been historical treatments of the topic (e.g., Stryker 2008) and works centered on legal advocacy (e.g., Levi 2012). Although certainly important and needed, those techniques and approaches often ignore many of the primary empirical avenues of inquiry in political science, nor do they contribute to broader social science theories. Indeed, this is a criticism of much of the discipline's existing LGBT research (Novkov and Barclay 2010). Specifically related to this topic, scholars have not sufficiently studied the framing of transgender issues as part of the policy process (but see chapters 2 and 3 in this volume). There has also been inadequate attention paid to the factors that affect policy adoption across types of transgender-inclusive legislation (but see chapters 6 to 9 in this volume).

Although morality politics models explain LGBT rights policy in some contexts (Haider-Markel and Meier 1996), it might not always apply to transgender policies. For example, laws that allow transsexual individuals to amend their birth certificates in the event of sex reassignment exist in half of the southern states and in Utah. This type of distribution is not indicative of the typical morality politics pattern (Mooney and Lee 1995). What explains this anomaly?

This edited volume explores those issues and it provides needed scholarship on other aspects of transgender advocacy and policy. Before we turn our attention to these topics, we provide a brief discussion of transgender identity, the transgender social movement, and some of its legal advocacy. The inclusion of this material helps to situate our contributors' work within the context of transgender rights policy and policymaking. After providing this important background information, we describe the organization of the book and introduce the chapters.

The Concept of Transgender

When a baby is born, it is classified as male or female according to the child's external genitalia (Bishop and Myricks 2004). A person's secondary sex characteristics, hormone levels, reproductive organs, and genetic makeup provide additional clues regarding an individual's sex (Greenberg 1999). Gender identity, an internal sense of being male or female, is another marker of one's sex (Bullough 2000). It is a continuum that is influenced by how society constructs gender, but it is likely "hardwired into the brain at birth" (Rudacille 2005, 292). When a person's gender identity is not congruent with the other markers of one's sex, that person might be described as transgender. Transgender is "used to refer to individuals whose gender identity or expression does not conform to the social expectations for their assigned birth" (Currah, Juang, and Minter 2006, xiv). However, transgender is an informal term. As Ryan Combs (2014) notes later in this volume, there is no precise definition of this concept. Different academic disciplines have various understandings of the term and what is interpreted as gendered behavior varies over time and by place.

In the United States and in many other Western nations, transgender is often conceived of as a "collective political identity" (Currah, Juang, and Minter 2006, xv). It is an umbrella term that is inclusive of different identities. Although not an exhaustive list of identities, this includes the gender queer, those who cross-dress, and transsexual individuals. Those who are gender queer reject the binary gender system and offer "a third gendered or non-gendered identity and presentation" (Combs 2014). Individuals who cross-dress are sometimes known as transvestites. These individuals may occasionally adopt the dress of the opposite birth sex and they might also have a dual male and female identity. People with a "strong and persistent cross-gender identification" (American Psychiatric Association 2000) are said to have gender identity dysphoria. In public discourse, they are sometimes referred to as transsexual individuals. The etiology of this state is uncertain. Leading theories include prenatal exposure to abnormal levels of sex hormones that affect the development of certain brain structures that determine gender identity (Zhou et al. 1995; Kruijver et al. 2000) or a possible genetic cause (Green 2000; Henningsson et al. 2005; Bentz et al. 2008).

Zucker and Lawrence (2009) note that rigorous epidemiological studies on the prevalence of gender identity disorders have not been conducted. Many of the studies that exist focus only on those who have received medical treatment for transsexualism (e.g., Olsson and Möller 2003). Often, these studies commonly address samples within a single country (e.g., van Kesteren, Gooren, and Megens 1996). Methodological differences, social stigma, and differences in treatment access make comparison across this body of research difficult (Cohen-Kettenis and Gooren 1999). As such, it is not surprising that a review of the literature on transsexualism (De Cuypere et al. 2007) noted estimates that range from 1:2,900 to 1:100,000 for adults born male and 1:8,300 to 1:400,000 for adults born female. In the United States, the study of prevalence rates for transsexual individuals is hampered by a lack of governmental data. One must rely on limited service provider data and self-reporting (Zucker and Lawrence 2009). With regard to prevalence rates for the larger category of transgender, Rudacille (2005, 14) states that any estimates are "mere guesswork."[1] Regardless of origin or prevalence, there are a number of treatments available when there is severe impairment associated with gender dysphoria. However, such care must be individualized because of personal circumstances and varying degrees of discomfort with one's gender dysphoria (World Professional Association for Transgender Health 2012). For those with severe gender identity dysphoria, sex reassignment surgery and related procedures are often an effective treatment (Cohen-Kettenis and Gooren 1999). The cost of surgeries, hormones, psychotherapy, and other related procedures can reach upwards of $100,000 (Dasti 2002). Access to these treatments varies by country. In the United States, insurance companies rarely provide coverage and individuals normally pay the full amount out of pocket for these services. Despite the need for medical treatment and counseling by some portions of the transgender community, the medicalization and treatment of gender-identity-related conditions is contentious (Combs 2014).

The Transgender Social Movement

The recognition of transsexualism as a medical issue in the 1950s and the increasing availability of clinical treatment in the 1960s and 1970s was a necessary but not sufficient condition for the rise of the transgender movement (Minter 2006). The subgroups and individuals associated with the transgender movement face rampant violence, discrimination in employment and housing, and they sometimes lack access to restrooms (Grant, Mottet, and Tanis 2011). In the 1990s, these types of deprivations and injustices, combined with high-profile murders (e.g., Gwen Araujo and Brandon Teena), and seminal writings by authors such as Holly Boswell, Leslie Feinberg, and Kate Bornstein, led to the development of today's transgender movement (Wilchins 2004; Denny 2006). This separate movement was in large part necessary because the gay and lesbian rights movement had increasingly viewed gender-variant individuals as outsiders who had no claims to gay rights advocacy (Minter 2006). This shift occurred despite the historical involvement of gender-variant individuals in gay and lesbian communities (Denny 2006, 173) and the appropriation of cross-gendered identities into gay rights history (Minter 2006). In context, the exclusion of the gender variant was likely part of what Rimmerman (2002; 2008) described as the gay movement's shift in the 1970s and early 1980s from sexual minority-focused liberation and outsider politics to one whose goal was assimilation into the mainstream along with the utilization of insider-based political strategies to achieve rights. Indeed, during the late 1960s and early 1970s, the gay movement, like many other social movements, saw their more liberationist wing fall into deep disagreements over goals, the need for coalition building, structure, and the role of women and minorities (Rimmerman 2008).[2] With their decline, gender-variant individuals were commonly excluded because it was feared that their presence could hamper the ability of more assimilationist gays and lesbians to gain rights (Minter 2006; Gallagher 1994).

The development of the transgender rights movement was a direct challenge to the marginalization of gender-variant individuals in gay and lesbian communities and in the larger society. Like other identity based social movements (Button, Rienzo, and Wald 1997, 5), such as those based around race, gender, and sexual orientation, the transgender social movement is centered around a shared trait (gender nonconformance) and it has broad social (e.g., greater acceptance) and political goals (e.g., laws against discrimination and health care access). Along with achieving the types of civil rights policy gains made by other identity based movements, this movement also arose out of a desire to shed the stigma associated with being a transsexual (Bornstein 1994; Minter 2006). Although the individuals and groups that loosely comprise this movement remain diverse and are sometimes at odds, Currah, Juang, and Minter (2006, xvi) note that those in this social movement share an interest in a fight for "a right to gender self-determination."

Social movements, and the individuals and interest groups that comprise them, are faced with a political opportunity structure that shapes what types of activities are likely to produce social and policy change. Because social movements have many goals, they also often utilize a variety of tactics (Button, Rienzo, and Wald 1997, 5–6). In the American context, groups can lobby or otherwise engage the executive, legislative, or judicial branches. The federal system expands these access points further, given a similar institutional makeup in each of the 50 states. States additionally provide their local jurisdictions with various degrees of policymaking authority. Interest groups and social movements can also attempt to affect public opinion. They can try to alter the actions of private entities such as corporations or nonprofit groups. Although the laws and regulations that affect how groups engage in political activity may vary across jurisdictions, it is clear that those who advocate for transgender rights have many potential avenues to pursue social and policy change.

However, a movement's resources, such as wealth, social status, organizational capacity, and leadership, affect whether it is able to achieve viable actions and outcomes (McCarthy and Zald 1978; Button, Rienzo, and Wald 1997). Groups that lack social status and resources, such as the transgender movement in its earliest days, might be confined to outsider tactics like picketing and protest. As a movement matures and spawns interest groups, these resource endowments continue to drive the tactical decision making for specific policy goals. Inside lobbying, electoral activity, testifying before committees, litigating, and other ways to affect policy require different resources (Wright 2003). Groups also engage in venue shopping to find the most favorable policymakers and institutional structures (Schattschneider 1960). This brings us to one of the important routes for transgender advocacy, the courts.

Advocacy and the Courts

As shown in cases like *Brown v. Board of Education, Romer v. Evans,* and *Craig v. Boren,* the courts have long been a central battleground in the fight for minority rights. Particularly at the federal level, judges and justices are somewhat insulated from majoritarian pressures. Indeed, the Founders, as discussed in Federalist No. 47, envisioned the courts as a bulwark against abuses by the other branches. As such, it is no surprise that the transgender movement and its allies have followed in the footsteps of other identity politics based movements by utilizing the courts as an instrument for social and policy change. Judicial protection of rights empower minority communities to combat discriminatory acts and symbolically convey full inclusion in society (Rimmerman 2002; Broadus 2006). In short, the courtroom is a venue for achieving policy gains and for forcing outsider groups into the mainstream (Rimmerman 2002, 47).

The transgender movement has several entities that engage in protransgender litigation; although not an exhaustive listing, this includes the National Center for Lesbian Rights, Gay & Lesbian Advocates & Defenders, the American Civil Liberties Union, and the Transgender Law Center. To create policy change, these groups can file friend of the court briefs if they determine that a case has implications for transgender rights. They might be particularly prone to do so if there is a transgender individual who is a plaintiff or defendant in a case. Groups might also choose to represent transgender clients. Through the strategic selection of cases for litigation, advocacy groups can also advance their policy goals. The outcomes of these actions set legal precedents that later courts might follow. This is particularly true when precedents are set by the Supreme Court or at the appellate level. Precedents are also set within state court systems.

With respect to transgender-specific law, employment discrimination, education, birth certificates, family law, and the treatment of transgender prisoners are policy areas that have seen significant litigation. Because this volume is not centered on legal analysis, we will only provide a cursory examination of a legal topic that is central to several of the chapters in the book, employment discrimination law.

Employment Law and Legal Advocacy

At the federal level, transgender individuals are not explicitly covered under the Civil Rights Act of 1964's Title VII prohibition on sex discrimination. Decisions in early cases testing whether transgender people could be covered under this law were not encouraging for the movement. In *Holloway v. Arthur Andersen* (1977), the 9th Circuit Court of Appeals held that discrimination against transsexuals was based on gender and that Title VII must be narrowly interpreted so as to only protect against sex discrimination. Similarly, in *Ulane v. Eastern Airlines* (1984), the 7th U.S. Circuit Court of Appeals held that discrimination was permissible under Title VII if it occurs because of a person's transsexual identity. The precedents formed during these earlier transgender employment cases have been challenged by application of the core findings in *Price Waterhouse v. Hopkins* (1989). In this case, the Supreme Court expanded Title VII sex discrimination protections to cover sex stereotyping. Although *Price Waterhouse* did not involve a transgender plaintiff, the finding that sex-stereotype-based discrimination is impermissible under Title VII has been a useful legal weapon in combatting gender identity based discrimination. Indeed, the 9th Circuit Court of Appeals in *Schwenk v. Hartford* (2000) noted that *Price Waterhouse* overturned Title VII precedents from those earlier cases. This line of Title VII reasoning has been utilized in cases like *Smith v. City of Salem, Ohio* (2004) and *Barnes v. City of Cincinnati, Ohio* (2005) by the 6th Circuit, *Glenn v. Brumby* (2011) by the 11th Circuit, and *Schroer v. Billington* (2008) by the U.S. District Court for the District of Columbia. In a move that might influence other litigation in this area, the U.S. Equal Employment Opportunity Commission ruled, in *Macy v. Department of Alcohol, Tobacco, Firearms and Explosives* (2012), that transgender people are covered under existing Title VII protections (American Civil Liberties Union 2012). However, in *Oiler v. Winn-Dixie* (2002) a district court in Louisiana elected not to take this approach. It dismissed a Title VII claim by a man who was fired for cross-dressing while off duty. To date, the Supreme Court has not ruled directly on transgender inclusion under Title VII. However, in some instances, trans individuals might find shelter under the Court's decision in *Oncale v. Sundowner Offshore Services* (1998). In *Oncale*, the justices unanimously held that Title VII's sexual harassment protections also cover unwanted and improper activity between members of the same sex.

Having briefly addressed federal employment law as it relates to transgender individuals, we turn our attention to the states. The courts in some states, such as New Jersey, New York, and Connecticut, have chosen to use the logic of the *Price Waterhouse* decision in their rulings on transgender employment discrimination cases (Broadus 2006). Additionally, Levi and Klein (2006) note that some trans individuals have been able to find shelter from discrimination under disability laws in a few states. However, more clearly defined statutory protections are desirable. As noted previously, seventeen states and the District of Columbia had statutes that banned discrimination against transgender employees as of 2013.[3] Statutory inclusion is often obtained by adding the terms "gender identity" or "gender expression," or both, to the relevant nondiscrimination law. This addition is necessary because unless the statutory definition of sexual orientation is explicitly transgender inclusive, the courts have generally found that transgender individuals are not covered under gay friendly policies (e.g., *Maffei v. Kolaeton Industry, Inc., et al.* 1995; *Underwood v. Archer Management Services, Inc.* 1994). In an effort to be even more expansive in their legal protections, some state statutes contain provisions based on "actual or perceived" gender identity.

Overview of the Book

It is here, with discussion of state statutes, that we turn our attention from the courts. What factors affect passage of these laws? Who advocates for them and what internal pressures do these coalitions face? Our contributors address these questions and more. The chapters are grouped into four areas. These include the framing of transgender rights, advocacy coalitions and interest groups, the diffusion and implementation of transgender-inclusive nondiscrimination laws, and work in other policy areas. We start with framing because this topic is fundamental to the earliest stages of the policy process (Kingdon 1984). Framing is often done by advocacy groups or related social movements. Thus, works related to interest groups and advocacy coalitions comprise our second section. Section three focuses on one of the key policy areas deemed most important by transgender people, laws banning gender identity based discrimination (Grant, Mottet, and Tanis 2011). In section four, attention turns to two other policy areas deemed important by the trans community, health care and vital records laws.

Framing in the United States and Abroad

In chapter 1, Barry Tadlock explores the framing of transgender rights in the United States. To do this, he uses a sample of newspaper articles and investigates interest group websites. This piece discusses how framing of transgender rights issues differs from those of sexual orientation. Tadlock finds that the sides in the debate over transgender rights use safety/security, education, and equality frames. He also touches upon the limited polling data on transgender rights. This chapter provides important insights on agenda setting and transgender advocacy.

Jacob Longaker and Don Haider-Markel (chapter 2) step away from the policy fights in the United States to provide a comparative perspective on transgender rights in Latin countries and on the framing of trans-related legislation in selected Latin countries. To do this, they focus on policy proposals allowing trans individuals to legally change their name in Brazil, Argentina, and Chile. Similar to Tadlock's U.S.-focused piece in chapter 1, they find that these Latin American countries use equality, discrimination, and education frames. They also find evidence that these policies are shaped by policy learning from other countries.

Advocacy and Interest Groups

Interest groups often do the real work of framing. Building on his earlier work published in *Social Science Quarterly*, Anthony Nownes (2010) explores the transgender interest group system and its relationship with their gay and lesbian allies (chapter 3). Using data on the formation of transgender advocacy groups and when gay rights groups incorporated transgender rights into their organizations' missions, he addresses the role of legitimation and competition in the transgender interest group system. Nownes notes that transgender and gay rights groups have become political allies but that they often compete over similar organizational resources. While the expansion of historically gay and lesbian interest groups into the realm of transgender politics has been important in obtaining policy goals, it has also raised challenges for groups that focus solely on transgender rights. Nownes discusses the future of the movement in light of these issues and a backlash by political opponents.

Related to the development of a more inclusive LGBT rights movement is how these entities work together in a coalition. Given resource scarcity faced by all organizations, whose policies are prioritized by a coalition? As noted by Grant, Mottet, and Tanis (2011), nondiscrimination laws are extremely important policy goals for the transgender community. In their chapter on advocacy coalition framework and transgender rights (chapter 4), Jami Taylor and Daniel Lewis focus on how these nondiscrimination policies are prioritized by LGBT rights coalitions. Through interviews with activists, review of newspaper articles, and quantitative modeling, they explore how LGBT coalitions deploy their scarce political resources in ways that have occasionally dismayed transgender rights advocates. Sometimes, when faced with tough political realities, LGBT coalitions and their legislative allies have removed transgender inclusion from proposed nondiscrimination legislation. At other times, and rather than passing gender-identity-inclusive nondiscrimination laws, the movement has then switched to issues such as same-sex marriage. In large part, these distributional concerns over movement priorities are due to the transgender community's small size, stigma, and lack of resources. However, the authors note that transgender activists have been much more successful at avoiding this fate in the past decade.

The Diffusion and Implementation of Transgender-Inclusive Policy

Given the poverty and discrimination that afflicts much of the transgender community, it is no wonder that policies to ban gender identity related discrimination are key policy priorities for transgender rights advocates (Grant, Mottet, and Tanis 2011). As such, this volume focuses much attention on these policies. Local-level laws against gender identity discrimination are the focus of a chapter by Jami Taylor, Barry Tadlock, Sarah Poggione, and Brian DiSarro (chapter 5). In addition to being a priority for transgender activists, the local level is where some of the earliest transgender rights advances were made. These authors use event history analysis and case studies to explore adoption of city level gender-identity-inclusive ordinances against discrimination. Much of their research is grounded in Elaine Sharp's (2005) excellent primer on local-level morality policy. They find support for Sharp's assertions about the role of the local political subculture. They also find that subculture interacts with the form of local government in ways that might be instructive to transgender rights advocates.

State-level laws against discrimination are the focus of the chapter by Daniel Lewis, Jami Taylor, Brian DiSarro, and Matthew Jacobsmeier (chapter 6). By incorporating some state-level case studies, this piece builds upon their article (Taylor et al. 2012) on policy complexity and policy diffusion in *State Politics & Policy Quarterly*. Unlike other chapters in this book, they look at the adoption of both sexual orientation and gender-identity-inclusive statutes. Importantly, they look at the content of these laws rather than just their passage. As such, their analysis extends beyond employment nondiscrimination to other important issues such as public accommodations and housing. Using a novel statistical approach, they find that the factors that influence state-level adoption of these laws against discrimination vary by *who* and *what* is covered.

Nondiscrimination statutes are not the only way for transgender people to receive legal protections. Executive orders can also provide limited nondiscrimination coverage in public employment. Mitchell Sellers (chapter 7) uses event history analysis on state-level data covering 1999 through 2010 to explain the strategic deployment or removal of these measures by governors. He finds that Democratic governors sometimes have incentives to enact these measures. This is more likely to occur when there is divided government and these orders also tend to happen when there is a change in party control of the governor's mansion.

Regardless of how nondiscrimination policies are enacted, implementation of these directives is important. To address implementation of local nondiscrimination ordinances, Mitchell Sellers and Roddrick Colvin (chapter 8) build upon their work in the *Review of Public Personnel Administration* (Colvin 2007) and *Administration & Society* (Sellers 2014). Using an ordered logistic regression, they find that transgender-inclusive ordinances passed more recently have more precise definitions and more enforcement mechanisms than do earlier policies. Precise legal definitions reduce ambiguity for those charged with enforcing or interpreting an ordinance. With respect to these definitions, Sellers and Colvin discuss trends in the preferred language to use in statutory construction. At this time and related to the goal of expanding legal protections to as many individuals as possible, "actual or perceived gender identity and gender expression" are the legal language preferred by many in the LGBT activist community.

Beyond Nondiscrimination Policy

Although nondiscrimination laws are policy priorities for the transgender community, there are other important policy areas of interest. One key area is access to health care and the treatments related to gender identity. Ryan Combs addresses these topics in the United Kingdom (chapter 9). Using an inductive qualitative approach, he explores the provision of gender identity health care with service providers and with transgender individuals. Combs finds that service providers and transgender patients struggle with inadequate resources and with whether gender dysphoria should be pathologized. While the latter is often unpopular with transgender individuals, depathologizing gender dysphoria would remove the impetus for medical interventions. This is particularly troublesome in nations with government-provided or government-funded health care services.

In the last research-focused chapter, Jami Taylor, Barry Tadlock, and Sarah Poggione (chapter 10) address the intersection of medical care and vital records laws by looking at state laws that allow transsexual individuals to amend their birth certificates in the event of sex reassignment. These documents are important in determining one's legal identity. Given current legal prohibitions (as of 2013) on same-sex marriage in many jurisdictions, the sex marker on the birth certificate may also determine the type of partner one can marry in many states. Unlike transgender-inclusive nondiscrimination statutes or laws allowing same-sex marriage (as of 2013), many conservative states allow trans individuals who have undergone prescribed treatment protocols to change the name and sex marker on their birth certificate. This piece, which is a follow-up to their article in the *American Review of Politics* (Taylor, Tadlock, and Poggione 2014), uses a Cox nonproportional hazards model to explore the vertical diffusion of similar policy recommendations made by the Centers for Disease Control and Prevention to the states.

Future Directions

This volume brings together much of the existing empirical political science and public administration work on transgender rights and transgender-focused policy. It connects the study of these topics to questions in the broader fields of political science and public administration. Collectively, the contributors to this edition show that transgender rights is not solely a topic of interest for transgender individuals but that it can be used to learn about politics and policy more generally. These authors also show how existing social science theory can be effectively used to understand the development of transgender rights policy.

However useful these insights, there are many unanswered questions. Also, some policy areas are not fully addressed. Unfortunately, space limitations do not allow us to further incorporate policymaking in the executive branch. In particular, this volume is unable to address important policy advances made by the Obama administration in the area of housing nondiscrimination. His administration is also notable for the appointment of the first openly transgender individual, Amanda Simpson, to serve in any federal-level administration. Additional research on national policy and representation on trans-related issues, in the United States and elsewhere, is clearly needed.

We do not address of the American military's medical and psychiatric regulations that exclude openly transgender people from service. This policy, as enforced, also leads to veterans having difficulty obtaining health care from the Department of Veterans Affairs. With the removal of the ban on gay servicemembers, some LGBT rights activists have started to target these regulations. Indeed, the OutServe—Servicemembers Legal Defense Network and the Transgender American Veterans Association have recently been active on this front. While this policy has important impacts on transgender servicemembers and veterans, we felt that there was not enough data or sufficient ripeness to include a chapter that did not amount to a critical examination of the issue. Although such a treatment is warranted and needed, it was not within the purview of this volume given its empirical focus.

The important area of transgender individuals and criminal justice is also left for another day. Prior to the Obama administration, transgender rights advocates had succeeded in obtaining hate crimes protections in several states. They also fought for and obtained passage of the transgender-inclusive Matthew Shepard Hate Crimes Act of 2009. This law was the first federal-level transgender-inclusive policy. With regard to state-level policies, event history analysis or explorations of policy content are possible ways for other scholars to address discipline-specific questions. With a single federal law, a case study exploring passage might provide interesting insights about the legislative process, coalition building, and interest group strategy.

Also relevant to criminal justice are administrative policies and court rulings that affect how transgender individuals are treated while incarcerated. We believe that other scholars should critically examine these policies. Like with the regulations barring openly transgender servicemembers, we felt that this type of approach is best addressed in another venue.

There have been a few openly trans candidates for public office, and a few appointed openly trans officials. The number of these public servants appears to be on the increase at the state and local level (Haider-Markel 2010). Furthermore, in a cross-national comparative study that finds a positive relationship between LGBT representation and gay rights, Reynolds (2013, 260) notes that between the years 1976 and 2011 there have been three transgender members of various national legislatures. However, even though it is likely, because the paucity of transgender representatives and due to the way that Reynolds (2013) operationalized his dependent variable, we cannot say whether descriptive representation of transgender people leads to policy gains by transgender people. Whether and to what extent the representation of the trans community will occur without descriptive representation remains an open question. Future research on trans-related policy should examine these issues in the context of democratic theory.

It is our hope that the chapters in this volume will encourage greater interest and effort in empirically exploring the political and policy issues related to the transgender community. This is important because as the broader gay civil rights movement continues to compile milestone victories, it seems more likely that the sometimes forgotten T element of LGBT will increasingly become salient in political and policy debates.

NOTES

1. Estimates from a recent Pew Research Center poll of LGBT American adults suggests that about 5 percent of LGBT respondents identify primarily as transgender, and this would be consistent with estimates that put less than .05 percent of American adults as identifying as transgender; this is roughly consistent with other estimates of the proportion of the LGBT population that is transgender. http://www.pewsocialtrends.org/2013/06/13/a-survey-of-lgbt-americans/.

2. This debate continues today as a recent Pew Research poll indicates; in the poll of LGBT American adults "About half of survey respondents (49%) say the best way to achieve equality is to become a part of mainstream culture and institutions such as marriage, but an equal share say LGBT adults should be able to achieve equality while still maintaining their own distinct culture and way of life." http://www.pewsocialtrends.org/2013/06/13/a-survey-of-lgbt-americans/.

3. Maryland became the 18th state to enact a comprehensive transgender inclusive law against discrimination, doing so on May 15, 2014 (and occurring while this book was in press).

REFERENCES

American Civil Liberties Union. 2012. "EEOC Breakthrough: Anti-Transgender Discrimination Is Unlawful." Retrieved January 25, 2013, from http://www.aclu.org/blog/lgbt-rights-womens-rights/eeoc-breakthrough-anti-transgender-discrimination-unlawful.

American Psychiatric Association. 2000. *Diagnostic and Statistical Manual of Mental Disorders DSM-IV-TR.* 4th ed., rev. Washington, DC: APA.

Barnes v. City of Cincinnati, 401 F.3d 729, 735 (6th Cir. 2005).

Bentz, Eva, Lukas Hefler, Ulrike Kaufmann, Johanness Huber, Andrea Kolbus, and Clemens Tempfer. 2008. "A Polymorphism of the CYP17 Gene Related to Sex Steroid Metabolism Is Associated with Female-to-Male but Not Male-to-Female Transsexualism." *Fertility and Sterility* 90 (1): 56–59.

Bishop, E. P., and Noel Myricks. 2004. "Sex Reassignment Surgery: When Is a He a She for the Purpose of Marriage in the United States?" *American Journal of Family Law* 18 (1): 30–35.

Bornstein, Kate. 1994. *Gender Outlaw: On Men, Women, and the Rest of Us.* New York: Routledge.

Broadus, Kylar. 2006. "The Evolution of Employment Discrimination Protections for Transgender People." In *Transgender Rights,* ed. Paisley Currah, Richard Juang, and Shannon Price Minter, 93–101. Minneapolis: University of Minnesota Press.

Bullough, Vern. 2000. "Transgenderism and the Concept of Gender." *International Journal of Transgenderism* 4 (3). Retrieved January 18, 2013, from http://www.wpath.org/journal/www.iiav.nl/ezines/web/IJT/97–03/numbers/symposion/bullough.htm.

Button, James, Barbara Rienzo, and Kenneth Wald. 1997. *Public Lives, Public Conflicts: Battles over Gay Rights in American Communities.* Washington, DC: CQ Press.

Cohen-Kettenis, P. T., and Louis Gooren. 1999. "Transsexualism: A Review of Etiology, Diagnosis, and Treatment." *Journal of Psychosomatic Research* 46 (4): 315–33.

Colvin, Roddrick. 2007. "The Rise of Transgender-Inclusive Laws: How Well Are Municipalities Implementing Supportive Nondiscrimination Public Employment Policies?" *Review of Public Personnel Administration* 27 (4): 336–60.

Combs, Ryan. 2014. "Key Issues in Transgender Healthcare Policy and Practice." In *Transgender Rights and Politics,* ed. Jami Taylor and Don Haider-Markel, 231–51. Ann Arbor: University of Michigan Press.

Committee on Education and Labor, U.S. House of Representatives, 101st Congress. 1991. *Legislative History of Public Law 101–336, The Americans With Disabilities Act.* Washington, DC: Government Printing Office.

Currah, Paisley, Richard Juang, and Shannon Price Minter, eds. 2006a. *Transgender Rights.* Minneapolis: University of Minnesota Press.

Currah, Paisley, Richard Juang, and Shannon Price Minter. 2006b. Introduction to *Transgender Rights, ed.* Paisley Currah, Richard Juang, and Shannon Price Minter, xiii–xxiv. Minneapolis: University of Minnesota Press.

Dasti, Jerry. 2002. "Advocating a Broader Understanding of the Necessity of Sex-Reassignment Surgery under Medicaid. *New York University Law Review* 77 (6): 1738–75.

De Cuypere, G., M. Van Hemelrijck, A. Michel, B. Carael, G. Heylens, R. Rubens, and S. Monstrey. 2007. "Prevalence and Demography of Transsexualism in Belgium." *European Psychiatry* 22 (3): 137–41.

Denny, Dallas. 2006. "Transgender Communities of the United States in the Late Twentieth Century." In *Transgender Rights,* ed. Paisley Currah, Richard Juang, and Shannon Price Minter, 171–91. Minneapolis: University of Minnesota Press.

Frederickson, H. George. 1971. "Toward a New Public Administration." In *Toward a New Public Administration: The Minnowbrook Perspective,* ed. Frank Marini, 309–31. Scranton, PA: Chandler.

Gallagher, John. 1994. "For Transsexuals, 1994 Is 1969: Transgendered Activists Are a Minority Fighting to Be Heard within the Gay and Lesbian Community." In *Witness to Revolution: The Advocate Reports on Gay and Lesbian Politics, 1967–1999,* ed. Chris Bull. Los Angeles: Alyson Books.

Glenn v. Brumby et al. 663 F. 3d 1312 (11th Cir. 2011).

Grant, Jaime, Lisa Mottet, and Justin Tanis. 2011. *Injustice at Every Turn: A Report of the National Transgender Survey.* Washington, DC: National Gay and Lesbian Task Force. Retrieved March 28, 2012, from http://www.thetaskforce.org/downloads/reports/reports/ntds_full.pdf.

Green, Richard. 2000. "Family Co-occurrence of 'Gender Dysphoria': Ten Sibling or Parent–Child Pairs." *Archives of Sexual Behavior* 29 (5): 499–507.

Greenberg, Julie. 1999. "Defining Male and Female: Intersexuality and the Collision between Law and Biology." *Arizona Law Review* 41:265–78.

Haider-Markel, Donald P. 2010. *Out and Running: Gay and Lesbian Candidates, Elections, and Policy Representation.* Washington, DC: Georgetown University Press.

Haider-Markel, Donald P., and Kenneth J. Meier. 1996. "The Politics of Gay and Lesbian Rights: Expanding the Scope of Conflict." *Journal of Politics* 58 (May): 332–49.

Henningsson, Susanne, Lars Westberg, Staffan Nilsson, Bengt Lundström, Lisa Ekselius, Owe Bodlund, Eva Lindström, Monika Hellstrand, Roland Rosmond, Elias Eriksson, and Mikael Landén. 2005. "Sex Steroid Related Genes and Male-to-Female Transsexualism." *Psychoneuroendocrinology* 30 (7): 657–64.

Holloway v. Arthur Andersen 566 F.2d 659 (9th Cir. 1977).

Human Rights Campaign. 2013. "Nevada's Hate Crimes Protections Now Include Transgender Community." Retrieved June 5, 2013, from http://www.hrc.org/press-releases/entry/nevadas-hate-crimes-protections-now-include-transgender-community.

In re Estate of Gardiner, 42P.3d 120 (Kan. 2002).

Johnson, Richard. 2011. "Social Equity in the New 21st Century America: A Case for Transgender Competence within Public Affairs Graduate Programs." *Journal of Public Affairs Education* 17 (2): 169–85.

Kingdon, John W. 1984. *Agendas, Alternatives, and Public Policies.* Boston: Little, Brown.

Kruijver, Frank, Jiang-Ning Zhou, Chris W. Pool, Michel A. Hofman, Louis J. G. Gooren, and Dick F. Swaab. 2000. "Male to Female Transsexuals Have Female Neuron Numbers in a Limbic Nucleus." *Journal of Clinical Endocrinology Metabolism* 85 (2): 818–27.

Levi, Jennifer. 2012. *Transgender Family Law: A Guide to Effective Advocacy.* Bloomington, IN: AuthorHouse.

Levi, Jennifer, and Bennett Klein. 2006. "Pursuing Protection for Transgender People through Disability Laws." In *Transgender Rights,* ed. Paisley Currah, Richard Juang, and Shannon Price Minter, 74–92. Minneapolis: University of Minnesota Press.

Littleton v. Prange, 9 S.W.3d 233 (Tex. App 1999).

Macy v. Department of Alcohol, Tobacco, Firearms and Explosives. Appeal No. 0120120821 (United States Equal Employment Opportunity Commission 2012). Retrieved January 25, 2013, from http://www.eeoc.gov/decisions/0120120821%20Macy%20v%20DOJ%20ATF.txt.

Maffei v. Kolaeton Industry, Inc., et al. 626 N.Y.S.2d 391 (NY Sup. 1995).

McCarthy, John, and Mayer Zald. 1978. "Resource Mobilization and Social Movements: A Partial Theory." *American Journal of Sociology* 82 (6): 1212–41.

Minter, Shannon. 2006. "Do Transsexuals Dream of Gay Rights?" In *Transgender Rights,* ed. Paisley Currah, Richard Juang, and Shannon Price Minter, 141–70. Minneapolis: University of Minnesota Press.

Mooney, Christopher Z., and Mei-Hsien Lee. 1995. "Legislating Morality in the American States: The Case of Pre-*Roe* Abortion Regulation Reform." *American Journal of Political Science* 39:599–627.

National Gay and Lesbian Task Force. 2012a. "Hate Crimes Laws in the U.S." Retrieved January 14, 2013, from http://www.ngltf.org/downloads/reports/issue_maps/hate_crimes_03_12_color.pdf.

National Gay and Lesbian Task Force. 2012b. "State Nondiscrimination Laws in the U.S." Retrieved January 14, 2013, from http://www.ngltf.org/downloads/reports/issue_maps/non_discrimination_1_12_color.pdf.

Novkov, Julie, and Scott Barclay. 2010. "Lesbians, Gays, Bisexuals, and the Transgendered in Political Science: A Report on a Discipline Wide Survey." *PS: Political Science & Politics* 43 (1): 95–106.

Nownes, Anthony. 2010. "Density Dependent Dynamics in the Population of Transgender Interest Groups in the United States 1964–2005." *Social Science Quarterly* 91 (3): 689–703.

Oiler v. Winn-Dixie La., Inc., No. 00-3114, 2002 U.S. Dist. LEXIS 17417.

Olsson, Stig-Eric, and Anders Möller. 2003. "On the Incidence and Sex Ratio of Transsexualism in Sweden, 1972–2002." *Archives of Sexual Behavior* 32 (4): 381–86.

Oncale v. Sundowner Offshore Services, 523 U.S. 75 (1998).

Price Waterhouse v. Hopkins, 490 U.S. 228 (1989).

Reynolds, Andrew. 2013. "Representation and Rights: The Impact of LGBT Legislators in Comparative Perspective." *American Political Science Review* 107 (2): 259–74.

Rimmerman, Craig. 2002. *From Identity to Politics: The Lesbian and Gay Movements in the United States*. Philadelphia: Temple University Press.

Rimmerman, Craig. 2008. *The Lesbian and Gay Movements: Assimilation or Liberation?* Boulder: Westview Press.

Rudacille, Deborah. 2005. *The Riddle of Gender: Science, Activism, and Transgender Rights*. New York: Pantheon Books.

Schattschneider, Elmer E. 1960. *The Semi-Sovereign People: A Realist's View of Democracy in America*. New York: Holt, Reinhart and Winston.

Schroer v. Billington, 577 F. Supp.2d 293 (D.D.C. 2008)

Schwenk v. Hartford, 204 F.3d 1187 (9th Cir. 2000).

Sellers, Mitchell Dylan. 2014. "Discrimination and the Transgender Population: Analysis of the Functionality of Local Government Policies That Protect Gender Identity." *Administration & Society* 46 (1): 70–86.

Sharp, Elaine. 2005. *Morality Politics in American Cities*. Lawrence: University Press of Kansas.

Smith v. City of Salem Ohio, 378 F.3d 566 (6th Cir. 2004).

Stryker, Susan. 2008. *Transgender History*. Berkeley, CA: Seal Press.

Stryker, Susan, and Stephen Whittle, eds. 2006. *The Transgender Studies Reader*. New York: Routledge.

Taylor, Jami. 2007. "Transgender Identities and Public Policy in the United States: The Relevance for Public Administration." *Administration & Society* 39 (7): 833–56.

Taylor, Jami, Daniel C. Lewis, Matthew L. Jacobsmeier, and Brian DiSarro. 2012. "Content and Complexity in Policy Reinvention and Diffusion: Gay and Transgender-Inclusive Laws against Discrimination." *State Politics &Policy Quarterly* 12 (1): 75–98.

Taylor, Jami, Barry Tadlock, and Sarah Poggione. 2014. "State LGBT Rights Policy Outliers: Transsexual Birth Certificate Laws." *American Review of Politics* 34 (Winter): 245–70.

Transgender Law and Policy Institute. 2012. "Nondiscrimination Laws That Include Gender Identity and Expression." Retrieved January 30, 2013, from http://www.transgenderlaw.org/ndlaws/index.htm.

Ulane v. Eastern Airlines, 742 F.2d 1081 (7th Cir. 1984).

Underwood v. Archer Management Services, Inc., 857 F. Supp 96 (DDC. 1994).

van Kesteren, Paul, Louis Gooren, and Jos Megens. 1996. "An Epidemiological and Demographic Study of Transsexuals in the Netherlands." *Archives of Sexual Behavior* 25 (6): 589–600.

Wilchins, Riki. 2004. *Queer Theory, Gender Theory: An Instant Primer.* Los Angeles: Alyson Books.

World Professional Association for Transgender Health. 2012. "Standards of Care for the Health of Transsexual, Transgender, and Gender-Nonconforming People, Version 7." *International Journal of Transgenderism* 13 (4): 165–232.

Wright, John. 2003. *Interest Groups and Congress: Lobbying, Contributions, and Influence.* New York: Longman.

Zhou, Jiang-Ning, Michel A. Hofman, Louis J. G. Gooren, and Dick F. Swaab. 1995. "A Sex Difference in the Human Brain and Its Relation to Transsexuality." *Nature* 378 (6552): 68–70.

Zucker, Kenneth, and Anne Lawrence. 2009. "Epidemiology of Gender Identity Disorder: Recommendations for the Standards of Care of the World Professional Association for Transgender Health." *International Journal of Transgenderism* 11 (1): 8–18.

Framing in the United States
and Abroad

Barry L. Tadlock

1 | Issue Framing and Transgender Politics

An Examination of Interest Group Websites and Media Coverage

A July 14, 2009, *Boston Globe* article about transgender-inclusive legislation pending before the Massachusetts General Court (the state legislature) highlights two frames of discourse that are often used in news coverage about transgender politics.[1] One frame is equality and it is revealed in a quote from a transgender woman: "I want people to know we're no different than anyone else. We have families. We have jobs. We contribute in meaningful, lasting ways, and we need protection." Another frame, that of safety and security, is voiced by Massachusetts Family Institute's Kris Mineau, who refers to the proposed legislation as "the bathroom bill." He argues that the bill "would open up single-sex bathrooms and locker rooms to 'anyone who simply says they feel like that gender.'" He adds, "the bottom line is we want safety, privacy and modesty" (English 2009, B1).

Americans cherish values like liberty, equality, security, majority rule, and minority rights. The *Boston Globe* article incorporates the values of equality and security in the form of news frames. The *Globe* is not unique in this respect. These frames are used repeatedly by political actors to shape the debate about transgender rights.

In this chapter, I investigate the framing of transgender politics in the United States. I first discuss the concept of framing and how it applies to transgender politics, and I briefly review the history of the transgender movement (including the issues of naming and mobilization). I continue with a content analysis of interest group websites and of newspaper articles. My goal is to understand the frames used by political elites and the extent to which news coverage incorporates these frames. I find that group naming has evolved over the last two decades and that the issue frames used by interest groups and in news coverage center around three key frames. These frames include equality, safety/security, and education. I also find that news coverage tends to be favorable toward transgender issues and that the frames tend to be embedded within an individualistic perspective.

Issue Framing

Issue frames represent the multiple conceptualizations of an issue. Framing theory suggests that different statements of equivalent information, or frames, affect individuals' perceptions of issues (Tversky and Kahneman 1981, 1986). If an issue is new, one way that individuals make sense of it is to rely on a cherished value like equality. They use frames to connect the value to a political issue (Brewer 2001). A framing strategy proves useful for a social movement, especially for its leaders (Fetner 2008; Snow and Benford 1988). For elites to influence individuals' opinions about an issue, individuals must recognize that the issue is relevant to them. A movement's framing strategy helps to ensure that this happens.

Framing effects represent changes in judgment brought about by repackaging an issue (Iyengar 1987). With a newspaper article, a framing effect is evident when the author's emphasis on a subset of relevant considerations causes readers to focus on these considerations in their opinion formation (Druckman and Nelson 2003). Framing effects have been identified in various contexts, including poverty programs (Iyengar 1990), government programs following Hurricane Katrina (Haider-Markel, Delehanty, and Beverlin 2007), and same-sex marriage (Tadlock, Gordon, and Popp 2007). Elites connected with social movements introduce frames in hopes of influencing nonelites' opinions regarding so-called public facts about these issues. Elites seek frame alignment between their social movement organizations and individuals' opinions (Snow et al. 1986). Alignment comprises distinct processes, including one in which a social movement organization bridges individuals' opinions with that organization's pursuit of those shared interests.

Framing effects have limitations. Zaller (1992) argues that individuals' opinions reflect elites' messages received, accepted, and sampled. This means that acceptance of an argument rests upon one's exposure to that argument, its alignment with previous beliefs, and a relationship with contemporaneous issues and arguments. Hull (2001) suggests that elites' frames do not always resonate with nonelites. At times, competing frames limit the impact of a single frame (Brewer 2002). Additionally, the public's existing predispositions limit the effectiveness of elites' framing strategies (Price, Nir, and Cappella 2005; Benford and Snow 2000; Brewer 2003). News sources matter as well. In a study that contrasts the impact of unattributed and attributed sources, Joslyn and Haider-Markel (2006) find that an attributed source can limit a frame's impact (as compared to content that includes no attributed source). Finally, Druckman (2001) cautions against overstating frames' impact on individual opinions, given that research methods sometimes inadequately consider social contact and context.

Groups that successfully frame their issues in newspapers are more likely to reap policies reflecting their beliefs (Schram and Soss 2001). This is important because a newspaper such as the *New York Times* sets the issue agenda for other media, including television. Repetition of a frame across multiple media platforms creates familiarity with the frame and, more important, repetition creates familiarity with the position that the frame supports. Elite competition over issues occurs in distinct rhetorical contexts. One context concerns framing with respect to individualistic and systemic understandings of an issue. Individualistic understandings focus on an individual or group, while a systemic understanding focuses on broad, societal factors. What impact does this have? Iyengar (1987) demonstrates that explanations for poverty differ according to whether someone is presented with descriptions framed in societal versus particularistic terms. In addition, evidence suggests that differences exist with respect to education levels. Specifically, those with lower levels of education more likely utilize individualistic explanations; those with higher levels of education more likely use systemic explanations (Joslyn and Haider-Markel 2013).

Transgender Politics: The Development of a Social Movement

Transgender politics receives little attention from political scientists. This coincides with the relatively marginalized status of transgender issues within the broader lesbian, gay, bisexual and transgender (LGBT) movement throughout the years. Following the Stonewall riots, "gender nonconformity and homosexual erotic desire were often perceived as being" part of the same identity (Spade and Currah 2008, 1). During that time, the framing rhetoric that emerged from group leaders focused on liberation, incorporating issues such as police brutality and freedom of assembly. However, subgroups within the movement started questioning its goals. This occurred as the "gay and lesbian" tag assumed a prominent place in the nation's vernacular (e.g., in news coverage and within popular culture). In essence, transgender individuals' interests became increasingly invisible as the LGBT movement matured. As noted by Spade and Currah (2008), this invisibility manifested itself in the work of lesbian and gay organizations:

> "When our lesbian and gay leaders call for unity, quite often it's really a call for conformity," says Mr. Bunch. He (says) the movement is relegating them to crazy-uncle status, in an effort to convince mainstream America that homosexuals are as "straight" as heterosexuals. It's an ironic twist, given that transvestites started the gay-rights movement 24 years ago with riots to protest police raids on a gay bar in New York's Greenwich Village. (Jefferson 1993)

The AIDS epidemic and "transphobia within progressive political" movements exacerbated this impulse toward conformity (Currah 2008, 93).

Due to this invisibility, those not conforming to society's gender norms began to solidify their own movement. During the last two decades this movement has led to the development of groups solely devoted to transgender policy and it has caused many LGB groups to reconsider transgender interests. Furthermore, the transgender movement has "gained particular momentum from the Internet, with its ability to connect far-flung people and afford them a sense of safety" (Goldberg 1996). Movement leaders increasingly emphasize its multi-issue orientation, member diversity, and the movement's intersection with race and class issues. On the other hand, some argue that LGB leaders focus on a single issue (same-sex marriage) and are divorced from other social justice issues (Currah 2008).

It is possible to understand the transgender movement's growth by seeing how transgender individuals have entered into the public consciousness. For example, a transgender character was introduced on a soap opera (Zarf on *All My Children*). Transgender advocate Chaz Bono participated in the reality show *Dancing with the Stars*. Felicity Huffman won great acclaim for her performance in the 2005 film *Transamerica,* as a preoperative male-to-female transsexual who learns that she fathered a son. Does such "contact" matter? Research in the field of communication studies suggests it does (Schiappa, Gregg, and Hewes 2005). Public consciousness of transgender concerns is raised even further in some locales due to high-profile crimes committed against transgender people. Recent examples include the 2008 murder of Angie Zapata in Greeley, Colorado, and the 2011 attack on a 22-year-old transgender woman in a McDonald's restaurant in Baltimore County, Maryland (Frosch 2008; Fenton and Bishop 2011).

With any social movement, decisions related to its naming can affect citizens' understanding of movement goals as well as movement success. Both the women's rights movement (Costain 1980) and the lesbian and gay rights movement (Gay & Lesbian Alliance Against Discrimination 2010) provide evidence of the importance of naming. To further understand this, consider an example unrelated to transgender politics. In 2005, U.S. Senate Republicans recast the so-called nuclear option as the "constitutional option," by shedding favorable light on their effort to end filibusters of judicial nominees by a majority, instead of a supermajority, vote. This fostered positive public opinion. Naming clearly influences the public's understanding of a social movement or an issue.

As do other authors in this book, I use the name "transgender" to refer to individuals with gender dysphoria. What is its meaning and how does it differ from "transsexual"? Christine Jorgensen once famously stated, "sexuality is who you sleep with, but gender is who you are" (*Appeal-Democrat*/Associated Press 1982). This statement prefigured an evolution in these two terms' usage. In today's parlance, "transgender" is an umbrella term (National Center for Transgender Equality 2009). It refers to transsexuals (those who have transitioned and those who are transitioning), genderqueer, nadleeh (a Native American word for two-spirit), drag queens, drag kings, cross-dressers, transvestites, and others. Evidence presented later in this chapter illustrates the degree to which usage of "transgender" and "transsexual" has changed over recent decades.

Identity Politics and a Focus on Rights

Given the increased discussion of transgender-related issues in the media, it is important to investigate transgender identity. Davidson (2007) distinguishes among the various constituent communities that fall under the transgender umbrella, including transsexual separatists, intersex activists, genderqueer activists, and gender rights activists. This distinction highlights "differences that are often elided in public consciousness by the category *transgender*" (79, italics in original). Given the wide variety of subgroups with which individuals may identify, to what extent is transgender identity analytically useful? Engel (2007) argues that the transgender concept is slippery. He notes that identity is used to explain how LGBT movements emerge, how movements maintain themselves, how identity impacts interest group structure, and how identity impacts both group tactics and the strategic deployment of group resources. Identity "could also *limit the political options available to a group*" (74; italics added), including "interest group elites' preference formation and strategic selection of institutional venues" (90).

Not only is identity conceptually uncertain, but ongoing debate exists within the scholarly and interest group communities as to the function of identity politics within a social movement. Some suggest that identity serves as a useful resource during a social movement's development, but it constrains actions once the movement matures (Engel 2007). Others "argue that identity politics reduces politics to a disparate set of parochial group struggles at the expense of transcendent, 'universal' values" (Mucciaroni 2011, 17). Davidson (2007, 76) echoes this point: "Constructing the organizing options available as either identity politics or a broader agenda against oppression—as either identities or issues—is a falsely circumscribed set of options."

Rimmerman's (2008, 10) assessment of the lesbian and gay movements builds on these points. He sees the movements' rights-based perspective as being based in identity politics; he asserts that it has been "largely unquestioned and unchallenged by mainstream contemporary lesbian and gay movements, especially those who dominate politics and public policy at the national level." Similarly, Vaid (1995, 3) sees a rights-based model as incapable of delivering "genuine freedom or full equality." Currah and Spade (2007, 2) argue that "simply articulating a human rights claim based on gender identity or gender expression will have little, if any, short-term impact."

In spite of these critiques of rights-based politics, evidence exists, such as the myriad of works in this volume, that transgender interest groups focus on rights and that their framing strategies serve as the vehicle through which such a focus occurs. However, the array of issues can differ or these issues could be prioritized differently between the transgender and the gay and lesbian movements. For example, the lesbian and gay movement has focused on police harassment, HIV/AIDS funding, employment discrimination, and military service. The transgender movement has focused on these issues, but also on identity documentation, use of public facilities, and others (Grant et al. 2011). Consider the issue of identity documentation. A driver's license is a document that many of us possess. If it lists a gender different from how we identify, a seemingly mundane document not only masks reality but it could be used to limit our rights. An assimilationist LGB movement[2] may not focus on such an issue, so the need for a transgender rights movement becomes apparent.

Other aspects of transgender politics are not easily captured by the principle of human rights. As mentioned above, Chaz Bono competed on *Dancing with the Stars*. For a few months, he was the transgender community's public face. He was seen weekly during ABC's prime-time lineup, and he also was a regular topic of conversation on shows such as *Entertainment Tonight* and in printed news coverage. Yet, we know little about the framing of this transgender-related coverage. Alternatively, we know quite a bit about the framing of lesbian and gay rights issues. For example, Brewer (2008) finds that four frames are used in gay rights policy: anti-gay-rights morality and equality frames and pro-gay-rights morality and equality frames (see also Tadlock, Gordon, and Popp 2007). Similarly, in the case of same-sex marriage, the two most common frames include equal rights and traditional values (Pan, Meng, and Zhou 2010). It is possible, if not likely, that frames used in the LGB movement are quite similar to those used in the transgender movement. A desire to better understand the transgender movement's framing guides the work in this chapter.

The transgender rights movement includes groups that are broadly focused on the spectrum of LGBT-related politics and policy, such as the Human Rights Campaign (HRC) and the National Gay and Lesbian Task Force, and those that focus solely on transgender politics. This latter category includes the National Center for Transgender Equality. The largest groups are comparable in scope, although not in size, to the nation's most successful lobbying groups. Also, it comes as no surprise that opposition groups have formed in response to the transgender movement. This pattern of group formation by supporters and opponents mirrors that found in the battle over gay rights.

Given both the overlap and the points of departure between the LGB and transgender movements, it is useful to question the extent to which LGB and transgender movement elites use similar frames. A long line of scholars identify equality and morality as being the two predominant frames used by LGB elites and represented in media coverage about LGB issues (Wald, Button, and Rienzo 1996; Brewer 2008, Pan, Meng, and Zhou 2010, Tadlock, Gordon, and Popp 2007). However, there is no similar body of literature in the area of transgender politics. As such, I rely on the LBG literature to guide my expectation that interest groups on both sides of the transgender politics movement will frame their arguments in terms of equality or morality. Further, I expect that news coverage will reflect these dominant frames. The sections that follow provide analyses of interest groups' websites and media coverage in order to understand the ways in which transgender political issues are framed.

Framing and the Struggle over Transgender Rights: The Role of Interest Groups

To understand the frames utilized in transgender politics, I reviewed websites for both pro- and antitransgender rights groups. Among prorights groups, I reviewed 22 websites.[3] One group focused its operations at the regional level, one at the state level, one at the local level, and the remaining 19 at the national level. I investigated the websites of 10 antirights groups. Three of these operated at the state level and seven operated at the national level. For both pro- and antirights groups, some focused on numerous issues, with transgender politics being only one area of interest, while others concentrated solely on transgender issues. Groups represented in my study include traditional advocacy groups, law centers, individual churches, and religious denominations.

My objective in reviewing groups' websites was to ascertain the frame(s) used to explain transgender issues. Most often, I derive this from the mission statement, an "About Us" description, or a statement of welcome, or a combination of these. Occasionally, I had to search elsewhere in the site to locate the group's primary frame. These groups are listed in the appendix for chapter 1.

Equality is the most common frame utilized by prorights groups. Three of the groups that highlight this frame are large LGBT groups: HRC, the National Gay and Lesbian Task Force, and Parents, Families and Friends of Lesbians and Gays (PFLAG). For example, PFLAG's Transgender Network "focuses on issue advocacy to ensure equal rights for the transgender community" (PFLAG 2012). The *equality* frame is also manifested through the related concept of marginalization. That frame was utilized by the Point Foundation. Another common frame is a call for understanding the uniqueness of transgender people; I refer to this as the *education* frame. Two of the groups that highlight this frame are PFLAG and the American Civil Liberties Union. The ACLU's website notes that "transgender people face a range of legal issues that LGB people rarely do" (American Civil Liberties Union 2012). The *education* frame is manifested through the related concept of cultural competence, utilized by HRC. *Safety/security* is another frame utilized by pro-rights groups. The Anti-Violence Project

(AVP) calls attention to the "high rates of violence" that "transgender and gender non-conforming people experience." A manifestation of this *safety/security* frame is community wellness. It was utilized by the Audre Lorde Project. *Empowerment* is a frame found on numerous groups' websites. As an example, "the Sylvia Rivera Law Project (SRLP) works to guarantee that all people are free to self-determine their gender identity" (Sylvia Rivera Law Project 2012). *Visibility*, especially in terms of positive media coverage, is another frame utilized by some prorights groups. For example, the Gay & Lesbian Alliance Against Defamation (GLAAD) "speaks out against transphobia in ways that educate Americans about who transgender people are" (GLAAD 2009).[4]

Among opponents of transgender rights, a *safety/security* frame was prominent. Sometimes, the frame stands alone. At other times it is linked to privacy. The Alliance Defense Fund asserts that "privacy rights specifically protect individuals in their use of restroom facilities and having their bodies exposed to members of the opposite sex" (Alliance Defense Fund 2012). Similarly, the Massachusetts Family Institute argues that women and children would be put at risk if any changes are put in place with respect to gender-specific facilities such as bathrooms (Massachusetts Family institute 2011). *Majoritarian rights* constitute a common frame; "our laws should not be changed to encourage a disorder at the expense of 99.05% of the population" (Massachusetts Family Institute 2011). *Freedom* is another frame used by opposition groups. One group places this frame in its name, as evidenced by the Ethics and Religious Liberty Commission of the Southern Baptist Convention. Finally, *pathology* is a frame favored by opposition groups. This is expressed in various forms, including "transgenderism" (Focus on the Family 2012), "mental illness" (Family Research Council 2012), and "gender confusion" (Massachusetts Family Institute 2011).

Representation of Frames in the Media

To understand the extent to which the media utilize these frames, I conducted a content analysis of newspaper articles. The articles were published during the years 1992–2011. I chose 1992 as the starting point because it precedes passage of the first statewide transgender-inclusive nondiscrimination law (in Minnesota in 1993). Newspapers reviewed included the following: *New York Times, Washington Post, Wall Street Journal, USA Today, Chicago Tribune, Los Angeles Times, Denver Post, Seattle Post-Intelligencer, Atlanta Journal-Constitution,* and the *Boston Globe.* National and major regional newspapers are included because the fight for transgender rights occurs at the national and subnational levels of government. During these years, there were 1,453 articles containing the word transgender and 627 articles containing the word transsexual within the headline or the article's text, or both.[5] I distinguish between these two categories when I report the findings, by separating the discussion of articles that mention "transsexual" from the discussion of articles that mention "transgender." I reviewed 10 percent of all articles, using ProQuest to access the papers, selecting every tenth article for content analysis.[6] Where ProQuest did not archive the article's entire text, I used newspapers' archives.

I focused on various factors, including the frame(s) utilized and whether there was a clear pro- and/or antirights orientation. I also investigated the rhetorical context within which frames were embedded, specifically whether the article featured an individualistic or a systemic orientation. All types of articles were analyzed, including news stories, op/ed pieces, and letters to the editor. I include this diverse range of articles because of their cumulative impact on the public debate. This impact is perhaps most debatable when it concerns letters to the editor. However, evidence from journalists and political scientists suggest that letters are heavily read, that their content is often influenced by interest groups, and that they influence politicians' agendas (Cooper, Knotts, and Haspel 2009). A line was not drawn between overtly political pieces and others; therefore, stories about cultural and community events were analyzed. The impact of ostensibly nonpolitical information on political issues is demonstrated in communications studies literature (Schiappa, Gregg, and Hewes 2005). Additional anecdotal evidence of the impact comes from Michael Schiavi, who said of film historian and AIDS activist Vito Russo, "he also realized that mainstream movies weren't representing him and his kind. He realized that the more negative images of gay people on film, the harder it was for them to get rights" (Piepenburg 2012).

Issue Frames in Newspaper Articles

Figure 1.1 notes that among the articles that highlight *transsexual* politics, the clearly predominant frame is *education* (36 articles; 59%), distantly followed by the *safety/security*[7] and *equality* frames (six articles each; 9.8%), and the *liberty* and *pathology* frames (two articles each).[8] This does not comport with findings in the LGB literature. As noted above, framing of

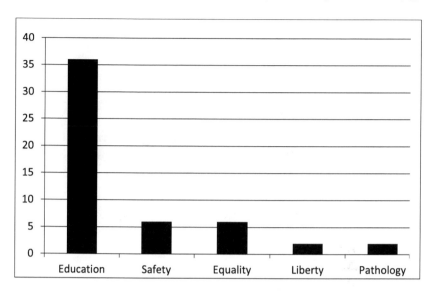

Fig. 1.1. Frames used in newspaper articles including the term "transsexual" (*n* = 61). (Figures 1.1–1.6 are based on articles from the following sources: *New York Times, Washington Post, Wall Street Journal, USA Today, Chicago Tribune, Los Angeles Times, Denver Post, Seattle Post-Intelligencer, Atlanta Journal-Constitution,* and *Boston Globe.* Years include 1992–2011.)

lesbian and gay rights issues typically revolves around equality and traditional values (also referred to as morality).

It is useful to see precisely how articles about transsexual politics utilized the frames of *education, equality, liberty, safety/security,* and *pathology.* An article in the May 15, 2005, issue of the *Washington Post* highlights the frame of *education* in a discussion of a new medical development: "Even with that development, making a decision to transition—and to have expensive gender reassignment surgery—remains a daunting process" (Irvine 2005). This article discusses Uzel, a young woman in Iowa who says she used the Internet in order to understand the meaning of who she was, in this case a transsexual. An October 25, 1998, article in the *Atlanta Journal-Constitution* demonstrates the *equality* frame in its discussion of "laws protecting (them) from . . . discrimination" (Konigsmark 1998). An October 9, 2004, *New York Times* article uses the *pathology* frame, describing a film's character as being toxic, predatory, and kicking off "social and psychological constraints" (Holden 2004). An April 20, 1999, *Los Angeles Times* article uses a *liberty* frame in its discussion of a transsexual woman who was awarded $750,000 as a result of being "strip-

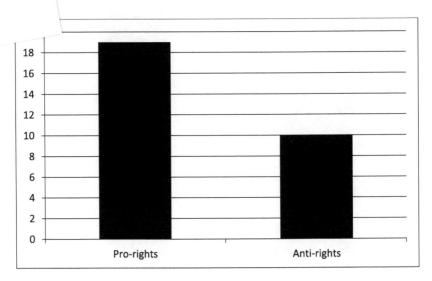

Fig. 1.2. Pro-/anti-rights orientation: Articles including the term "transsexual" (n = 61)

searched by sheriff's deputies to confirm her gender" (Associated Press 1999). A June 4, 2002, *Denver Post* article uses a *safety* frame: "A 19-year-old Farmington man received a 40-year prison sentence Monday for the bludgeoning death last June of a relative stranger, a 16-year-old Navajo boy who sometimes wore makeup, curled his hair and carried a purse" (Draper 2002).

In nearly one-half of the articles (29 out of 61) that include the word transsexual, there is an explicit positive or negative perspective, or both, articulated about rights. In those 29 cases where the perspective is explicit, there is a nearly 2:1 ratio in terms of a prorights to an antirights orientation (see fig. 1.2).

A September 26, 1999, *New York Times* article that references the Anti-Violence Project provides an example of a prorights perspective (Kirby 1999). The article uses an equality frame as a way to document the movement's need for legislative protection. In a slight majority of cases, however, the article makes no explicit pro or con argument about rights. For example, a March 16, 2004, *Atlanta Journal-Constitution* article speculates that the murder of a transsexual woman was connected to a statewide discussion about gay marriage; the article takes no stand on transgender rights (Ahmed 2004).

In terms of the rhetorical context, figure 1.3 notes that framing is nearly

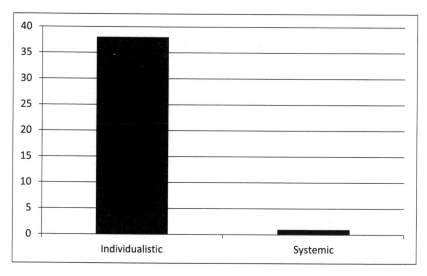

Fig. 1.3. Rhetorical context: Articles including the term "transsexual" (*n* = 61)

always embedded within an individualistic perspective (38 articles; 62.3%) rather than a systemic one (one article; 1.7%). The individualistic perspective is used in an April 20, 1999, *Los Angeles Times* article about the strip search of a transsexual man while the systemic perspective is used in a June 4, 2000, *Los Angeles Times* article about the impact of the large number of sex reassignment operations that occur in Trinidad, Colorado (Associated Press 1999; Arrillaga 2000).

Among the articles that highlight *transgender* politics, the predominant frame is also *education* (49 articles; 34%). Again, this does not align with the LGB literature that finds that the morality and equality frames are most prominently used. However, figure 1.4 shows that the predominance of the education frame is not nearly as strong as was the case with articles discussing transsexual politics. Use of other frames is common. This includes the frames of *equality* (37 articles; 25.7%), *safety/security* (18 articles; 12.5%), *liberty* (9 articles; 6.3%), and *pathology* (2 articles; 1.4%).

Education frames a May 10, 2011, *Los Angeles Times* article written by television critic Mary McNamara about *Becoming Chaz:* "the transgender experience is actually one of the few human conditions almost completely without cultural, literary or artistic landmarks." A September 1, 2011, *USA Today* article provides an example of an *equality* frame: "substantial inequality [is] still faced by gay and transgender Americans who live in an

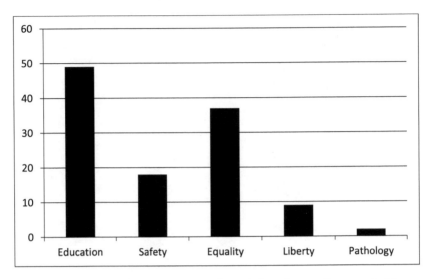

Fig. 1.4. Frames used in newspaper articles including the term "transgender" (*n* = 144)

increasingly two-tiered system, depending largely on where they reside" (Mushovic 2011). A March 30, 1999, *Denver Post* article uses a *liberty* frame in its discussion of a Supreme Court case on "whether students at state universities can be forced to pay fees that are used to fund campus groups with a political agenda" (Savage 1999). A January 5, 2003, *Los Angeles Times* article uses a *pathology* frame in its discussion of parents "pleading for a dress code that would require all adults who interact with students to 'dress in what a 9- or 10-year-old perceives as normal clothes for a man or a woman'" (Simon 2003). A July 17, 2011, *Chicago Tribune* article about homeless LGBT people uses a *safety/security* frame: "some speakers complained they were fearful of the loitering youths" (Meyer 2011).

Figure 1.5 finds that articles that include a prorights orientation of transgender politics (96 articles; 66.7%) outdistance those that use an antirights orientation (30 articles; 20.8%). By way of comparison between transgender and transsexual framing, I would note that this pro/anti orientation ratio is greater than 3:1, whereas among the articles pertaining to transsexual politics, the ratio is not quite 2:1.

In terms of the rhetorical context, figure 1.6 shows that there is a nearly 4:1 ratio in terms of an individualistic perspective (92 articles; 63.9%) versus a broader systemic one (25 articles; 17.4%). An individualistic context is used in a March 12, 2010, *Washington Post* article about the film *Prodigal*

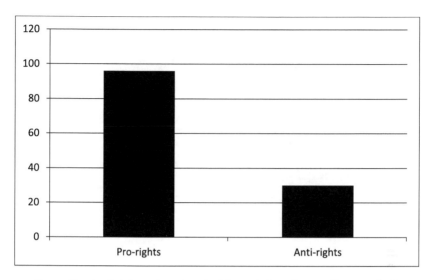

Fig. 1.5. Pro-/anti-rights orientation: Articles including the term "transgender" ($n = 144$)

Sons; the article focuses on the transgender documentary filmmaker Kimberly Reed and her life journey (O'Sullivan 2010). A *USA Today* article published on September 1, 2011, demonstrates the systemic orientation: "Yet such advances can obscure the substantial inequality still faced by gay and transgender Americans who live in an increasingly two-tiered system" (Mushovic 2011).

A final issue concerns frames that oppose each other. If exposed to multiple news sources, it is probable that individuals are subjected to competing frames in stories about transgender politics. However, I would note that within the sample investigated here, it is atypical for a single article to utilize competing frames. In fact, among the 61 articles that include the term "transsexual," only three utilize frames in opposition to each other. Among the 144 articles that mention "transgender," 12 feature competing frames.

A June 6, 1998, *Atlanta Journal-Constitution* article concerns a transsexual applicant to become a police officer in San Francisco. The applicant, Christiana Rivas, was rejected for failing a psychological test, which led the police force to declare Rivas unfit for service. This usage of the *pathology* frame is accompanied by both the *equality* and *education* frames. The *equality* frame is used when a spokesperson for the police asserts that the force does not discriminate; the *education* frame is used when Rivas is

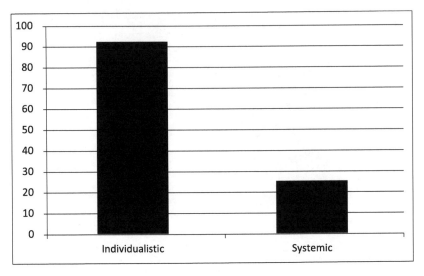

Fig. 1.6. Rhetorical context: Articles including the term "transgender" (*n* = 144)

quoted as saying "the department obviously doesn't understand transgender issues" (*Atlanta Journal-Constitution* 1998, A05). This article embeds its frames with an individualistic perspective, but it utilized no explicit pro- or antirights orientation.

A commentary on the front page of the November 11, 2007, Metro section of the *Washington Post* also demonstrates the use of competing frames. This somewhat lengthy piece (907 words) discusses the Montgomery County (Maryland) Council's consideration of a transgender-inclusive nondiscrimination bill. The proposed legislation included a provision that would allow transgender individuals to use the public restrooms of their choice. The article uses an *equality* frame. This is most evident when one of the article's sources, a supporter of transgender rights, is quoted as saying "adding a protected class for transgendered individuals is common sense" (Fisher 2007). *Safety/security* operates as a competing frame. A local physician states that "the county council should not force or legislate shared nudity" and said the proposal would not protect "Montgomery County residents from unforeseen consequences" (Fisher 2007). With respect to the restroom component of the bill, Marc Fisher, the commentary's author, takes the side of the proposal's opponents. He does this partly by adopting the opponents' safety/security frame, yet also by using the supporters' equality frame in a way that undermines the supporters' argument. Fisher writes that "the restroom provision reached too far, putting the comfort of the few over the rights of the many. People who enter a locker room reserved for members of one sex have the right to expect that everyone in the room shares the same equipment" (Fisher 2007).

Public Opinion

Ultimately, do frames affect individuals' opinions? We know relatively little about citizens' views on transgender rights. Over the last decade, only a few national polls have addressed the topic. According to a 2002 HRC poll, 67 percent agree that it is possible for a person to be born as one sex, but inside feel like another sex; 53 percent believe it is "all right" for a person to be transgender (Human Rights Campaign 2002). From a 2011 Public Religion Research Institute survey, we learn that: (1) 89 percent agree that transgender people should have the same general rights and legal protections as others; and (2) approximately 67 percent report being well informed about transgender politics. The poll includes questions about both federal hate crime and job discrimination legislation. The findings reveal differences in support between Democrats and Republicans and among those associated with various religious denominations. However, even among the presumably more conservative individuals (i.e., Republicans, white, evangelical Protestants), support for protections exceeds 50 percent (Public Religion Research Institute 2011).

These polls do not tell us how these opinions are formulated. We cannot know from these poll results whether respondents were exposed to news coverage about transgender people. If they were exposed to such coverage, we cannot learn from these polls whether framing affected respondents' opinions. A task for those involved in transgender politics research is to elucidate the relationship among groups' framing strategies, media coverage, and public opinion.

Discussion and Conclusion

The analysis in this chapter provides some interesting insights. First, there has been a transformation in the naming of those involved in the transgender movement. Newspaper articles during the 1990s commonly used the term transsexual (if not transvestite). Since 2001, the term most commonly used is transgender. This has had both positive and negative implications. In the United States, where religiously informed "traditional values" have a powerful impact on politics, deemphasis of sex is politically defensible. However, this means that the transgender movement fights some battles previously waged by the LGB movement, involving issues such as hate crimes, family recognition, and employment discrimination (Spade and Currah 2008). As evidence of this fight, Focus on the Family's website makes it clear that they see gender identity as new turf on which to struggle. This ongoing battle consumes time and resources.

Second, despite the large number of groups that lobby on both sides of transgender rights, each side coalesces around a few frames that they use to articulate their arguments. These include *safety/security, education,* and *equality.* These do not precisely overlap with the frames used in LGB politics. Among these three frames, the only one that is also regularly a part of the framing of gay rights is the equality frame. Also of note is the fact that the morality frame—also known as the traditional values frame—which is so prominent in the gay rights debate is relatively absent in the transgender rights debate. Within transgender politics, some frames are used on both sides of the political divide. For example, a frame of safety/security is utilized by groups on each side. However, prorights groups emphasize transgender individuals' safety while antirights groups focus on the safety of women and children as users of public facilities. Of course, one should never lose sight of frames' limitations, including barriers caused by citizens' existing predispositions and the limiting effect of competing frames.

Third, most newspaper articles sampled in this study positively portrayed transgender issues; few articles presented an exclusively negative discussion of such issues. Articles that presented both positive and negative sides of the issue were also relatively few. For example, one-third of the *transsexual*-related stories that included a positive treatment of the subject also included a negative treatment; among the *transgender*-related stories, the percentage was smaller (20%).

Fourth, findings regarding the strength of the safety/security frame are insightful. With his "hierarchy of needs," Maslow instructs us that the need for safety is secondary only to physiological needs (Maslow 1943). Therefore, the safety frame's relevance should not be too surprising. Safety is a fundamental human need. However, what this research does not tell us is how competing safety frames, those within a single newspaper article, might affect citizens' attitudes about transgender politics. That is an important concern for future researchers to investigate.

In conclusion, this chapter reveals a divide. On one hand there exists newspaper coverage that is largely positive in its discussion of transgender rights. Similarly, recent national-level public opinion polls, though few in number, indicate majority support for transgender rights. On the other hand, transgender individuals experience persistent, significant challenges. For example, we know that transgender individuals' safety is often threatened, in both public and private spaces. We know that each group under the transgender umbrella is often misunderstood and therefore champions their uniqueness. We know that transgender individuals continue to seek equal rights, the lack of which is well documented by groups such as the National Center for Transgender Equality. This divide between favorable news coverage and public opinion versus ongoing challenges related to safety, understanding, and equality comes as little surprise. After all, acts of violence, acts of discrimination, legislative failure, and other negative occurrences result from individual actors' actions, not from something as amorphous as public opinion. Furthermore, instances of violence and discriminatory behavior occur in political environments that vary from state to state and from city to city. They occur in political environments where interest groups seek to frame news coverage in ways favorable to their particular interests. So what can political scientists do? We can build upon lessons learned in other contexts, where topics such as issue framing, social movements, and identity politics have been investigated. We can use our discipline's tools to investigate the challenges that transgender individuals face in legislative chambers, in homes, in workplaces, and in public areas. In so doing, we will contribute to an enhanced understanding of transgender politics.

APPENDIX: INTEREST GROUPS' WEBSITES CONSULTED FOR ISSUE FRAMES

Pro-Transgender Rights Groups

American Civil Liberties Union: http://www.aclu.org/
Anti-Violence Project: http://www.avp.org/
Audre Lorde Project: www.alp.org
Gay & Lesbian Alliance Against Defamation: http://www.glaad.org/
Gay, Lesbian and Straight Education Network:
    http://www.glsen.org/cgi-bin/iowa/all/home/index.html
Human Rights Campaign: http://hrc.org/
Immigration Equality: http://www.immigrationequality.org/
Lambda Legal: http://www.lambdalegal.org/
Lesbian, Gay, Bisexual and Transgender Political Alliance of Massachusetts: http://
    www.library.neu.edu/archives/collect/findaids/m91findbioghist.htm
National Center for Transgender Equality: http://transequality.org/

National Gay and Lesbian Task Force: http://ngltf.org/
National Lesbian & Gay Journalists Association: http://www.nlgja.org/
Parents, Families and Friends of Lesbians and Gays TNET (PFLAG's Transgender
    Network): http://community.pflag.org/page.aspx?pid=380
Point Foundation: http://www.pointfoundation.org/index10.html
Survivor Project: http://www.survivorproject.org/
Sylvia Rivera Law Project: http://srlp.org/
TransFamily: http://www.transfamily.org/
Transgender at Work: http://www.tgender.net/taw/
Transgender Database: http://www.transgenderdatabase.com/
Transgender Center: http://www.tgctr.org/tg-center/
Transgender Legal Defense & Education Fund: www.transgenderlegal.org
Williams Institute: http://williamsinstitute.law.ucla.edu/

Anti-Transgender Rights Groups

Alliance Defense Fund: http://www.alliancedefensefund.org/
American Family Association of Michigan: http://www.afamichigan.org/
Christian Coalition of America: http://www.cc.org/
Colorado for Family Values: http://www.coloradoforfamilyvalues.org/CFV_Home.
    html
Ethics & Religious Liberty Commission of the Southern Baptist Convention:
    http://erlc.com/
Family Research Council: http://www.frc.org/
Focus on the Family http://www.focusonthefamily.com/
Massachusetts Family Institute: http://www.mafamily.org/
Saddleback Church http://www.saddleback.com/
Thomas More Law Center: http://www.thomasmore.org/

Note: Groups' websites accessed April-December 2012.

NOTES

1. A previous version of this paper was presented at the 2012 meeting of the Midwest Political Science Association.

2. Assimilationists make the case that lesbian and gay men are no different from straight people and deserve the same rights, including marriage (Rimmerman 2008). To connect this with Currah (2008), assimilationists are divorced from other social justice issues.

3. I use a purposive (i.e., nonprobability) sample. As such, I do not capture all possible elements of the universe of groups that work for or against transgender rights. This type of sampling sacrifices generalizability. However, it does foster the creation of a rich description of groups' framing efforts. My goal was not to precisely enumerate website content, but rather to generate a general comparison between pro-and antirights groups.

4. An example of GLAAD's educational efforts comes in the form of their annual report about diversity on television. In 2007–08 GLAAD reported that during the televi-

sion season "the introduction of these few (transgender) characters is a move . . . toward a more diverse and accurate range of representation" (Gay & Lesbian Alliance Against Defamation 2008).

5. I divided the 20-year period into 5-year increments. Use of "transgender" increased and use of "transsexual" decreased over the years, from a 1:5 to a 9:1 ratio.

6. Given resource constraints, I confronted a trade-off between analyzing all articles within a brief time frame versus a sample of articles within a long time frame. I chose the latter because I wanted to understand the full trajectory of the transgender movement.

7. Note that all frames, but especially the safety/security frame, can be utilized in a positive or negative manner; this counting of frames includes both fashions.

8. Intercoder reliability demonstrated high levels of reliability in coding.

REFERENCES

Alliance Defense Fund. 2012. "ADF: Colorado Legislature Should Reject Sexual 'Non-Discrimination Bill.'" Accessed April 3, 2012. http://www.alliancedefensefund.org/Home/ADFContent?cid=4493.

Ahmed, Saeed. 2004. "Vigil Honors Slaying Victim." *Atlanta Journal-Constitution*, March 16.

American Civil Liberties Union. 2012. "Discrimination against Transgender People." Accessed April 3, 2012. https://www.aclu.org/lgbt-rights/discrimination-against-transgender-people.

Appeal-Democrat/Associated Press. 1982. "News from California: 'Transgender.'" May 11, A2.

Arrillaga, Pauline. 2000. "Onetime Coal-Mining Town Bolstered by Changing Economy." *Los Angeles Times*, June 4.

Associated Press. 1999. "Transsexual Awarded $755,000 Over Strip-Search." *Los Angeles Times*, April 20.

Atlanta Journal-Constitution. 1998. "Nation in Brief: Transsexual Denied Police Job Sues City." June 6.

Benford, Robert D., and David A. Snow. 2000. "Framing Processes and Social Movements: An Overview and Assessment." *Annual Review of Sociology* 26:611–39.

Brewer, Paul R. 2001. "Value Words and Lizard Brains: Do Citizens Deliberate about Appeals to Their Core Values?" *Political Psychology* 22:45–64.

Brewer, Paul R. 2002. "Framing, Value Words, and Citizens' Explanations of Their Issue Opinions." *Political Communication* 19:303–16.

Brewer, Paul R. 2003. "Values, Political Knowledge, and Public Opinion about Gay Rights: A Framing-Based Account." *Public Opinion Quarterly* 67: 173–201.

Brewer, Paul R. 2008. *Value War: Public Opinion and the Politics of Gay Rights*. Lanham, MD: Rowman and Littlefield.

Cooper, Christopher, H. Gibbs Knotts, and Moshe Haspel. 2009. "The Content of Political Participation: Letters to the Editor and the People Who Write Them." *PS: Political Science and Politics* 42:131–37.

Costain, Anne N. 1980. "The Struggle for a National Women's Lobby: Organizing a Diffuse Interest." *Western Political Quarterly* 33:476–91.

Currah, Paisley. 2008. "Stepping Back, Looking Outward: Situating Transgender Activism and Transgender Studies—Kris Hayashi, Matt Richardson, and Susan Stryker Frame the Movement." *Sexuality Research & Social Policy* 5:93–105.

Currah, Paisley, and Dean Spade. 2007. "The State We're In: Locations of Coercion and Resistance in Trans Policy, Part I." *Sexuality Research & Social Policy* 4:1–6.

Davidson, Megan. 2007. "Seeking Refuge under the Umbrella: Inclusion, Exclusion, and Organizing within the Category *Transgender*." *Sexuality Research & Social Policy* 4:60–80.

Draper, Electra. 2002. "Cortez Teen's Killer Gets 40 Years." *Denver Post*, June 4.

Druckman, James N. 2001. "Using Credible Advice to Overcome Framing Effects." *Journal of Law, Economics, and Organization* 17:62–82.

Druckman, James N., and Kjersten R. Nelson. 2003. "Framing and Deliberation: How Citizens' Conversations Limit Elite Influence." *American Journal of Political Science* 47:729–45.

Engel, Stephen M. 2007. "Organizational Identity as a Constraint on Strategic Action: A Comparative Analysis of Gay and Lesbian Interest Groups." *Studies in American Political Development* 21:66–91.

English, Bella. 2009. "Discovering, and Protecting, Their True Selves: Antibias Law Sought for Transgender People." *Boston Globe*, July 14.

Family Research Council. 2012. "Testimony by Peter Sprigg in Opposition to SB 212." February. Accessed April 3, 2012. http://www.frc.org/testimony/testimony-by-peter-sprigg-before-the-maryland-state-senate.

Fenton, Justin, and Tricia Bishop. 2011. "Suspect in McDonald's Attack to Face Hate Crime Charge." *Baltimore Sun*, May 16. Accessed August 26, 2012. http://articles.baltimoresun.com/2011-05-16/news/bs-md-co-mcondalds-hate-crime-20110516_1_crime-charge-sandy-rawls-baltimore-county-grand-jury.

Fetner, Tina. 2008. *How the Religious Right Shaped Lesbian and Gay Activism*. Minneapolis: University of Minnesota Press.

Fisher, Marc. 2007. "Montgomery County Wisely Keeps Anti-Discrimination Law for Transgender People out of Public Restrooms." *Washington Post*, November 11, C1. Accessed December 13, 2012. http://www.washingtonpost.com/wp-dyn/content/article/2007/11/10/AR2007111001526.html.

Focus on the Family. 2012. "Our Position (Transgenderism)." Accessed August 26, 2012. http://www.focusonthefamily.com/socialissues/social-issues/transgenderism/our-position.aspx.

Frosch, Dan. 2008. "Death of a Transgender Woman Is Called a Hate Crime." August 2. Accessed August 26, 2012. http://www.nytimes.com/2008/08/02/us/02murder.html.

Gay & Lesbian Alliance Against Defamation. 2009. "Where We Are on TV Report: 2007–2008." Accessed November 8, 2012. http://www.glaad.org/files/whereweareontv2007-2008.pdf.

Gay & Lesbian Alliance Against Defamation. 2010. "Media Reference Guide." Accessed December 13, 2012. http://www.glaad.org/files/MediaReferenceGuide2010.pdf?id=99.

Gay & Lesbian Alliance Against Defamation. 2012. "Voices of the Transgender Community." Accessed April 3. http://www.glaad.org/programs/transgender.

Goldberg, Carey. 1996. "Shunning 'He' and 'She,' They Fight for Respect." *New York Times*, September 8. Accessed April 1, 2012. http://www.nytimes.com/1996/09/08/us/shunning-he-and-she-they-fight-for-respect.html?pagewanted=all&src=pm.

Grant, Jaime M., Lisa A. Mottet, Justin Tanis, Jack Harrison, Jody L. Herman, and Mara Keisling. 2011. "Injustice at Every Turn: A Report of the National Transgender Discrimination Survey." Washington, DC: National Center for Transgender Equality and National Gay and Lesbian Task Force.

Haider-Markel, Donald P., William Delehanty, and Matthew Beverlin. 2007. "Media Framing and Racial Attitudes in the Aftermath of Katrina." *Policy Studies Journal* 35:587–605.

Holden, Stephen. 2004. "Lured by Stories and an Ambiguous Femme Fatale." *New York Times,* October 9.

Hull, Kathleen E. 2001. "The Political Limits of the Rights Frame: The Case of Same-Sex Marriage in Hawaii." *Sociological Perspectives* 44:207–32.

Human Rights Campaign. 2002. "HRC Releases Ground-Breaking Public Opinion Research on Transgender Issues." Accessed April 4, 2012. http://www.genderadvocates.org/News/HRC%20Poll.html.

Irvine, Martha. 2005. "In Chicago, a Haven for Young Transsexuals." *Washington Post,* May 15.

Iyengar, Shanto. 1987. "Television News and Citizens' Explanations of National Affairs." *American Political Science Review* 81:815–32.

Iyengar, Shanto. 1990. "Framing Responsibility for Political Issues: The Case of Poverty." *Political Behavior* 12:19–40.

Jefferson, David J. 1993. "Some Marchers in Suits May Consider Fetishists and Male 'Nuns' a Real Drag." *Wall Street Journal,* April 23.

Joslyn, Mark R., and Donald P. Haider-Markel. 2006. "Should We Really 'Kill' the Messenger? Framing Physician-Assisted Suicide and the Role of Messengers." *Political Communication* 23:85–103.

Joslyn, Mark R., and Donald P. Haider-Markel. 2013. "The Politics of Causes: Mass Shootings and the Cases of the Virginia Tech and Tucson Tragedies." *Social Science Quarterly* 94:410–23.

Kirby, David. 1999. "Neighborhood Report: Chelsea; For Transsexual, Small Election Victory Is a 'Big Step.'" *New York Times,* September 26.

Konigsmark, Anne Rochell. 1998. "Live-and-Let-Live City." *Atlanta Journal-Constitution,* October 25.

Maslow, Abraham. 1943. "A Theory of Human Motivation." *Psychological Review* 50:370–96.

Massachusetts Family Institute. 2011. "FAQ: Isn't the 'Bathroom Bill' Just about Fighting Discrimination." Accessed April 3, 2012. http://www.nobathroombill.com/faqs/.

McNamara, Mary. 2011. "Television Review: 'Becoming Chaz.'" *Los Angeles Times,* May 10.

Meyer, Erin. 2011. "Young, Homeless Gays Wander Streets of Boystown." *Chicago Tribune,* July 17.

Mucciaroni, Gary. 2011. "The Study of LGBT Politics and Its Contributions to Political Science." *PS: Political Science and Politics* 44:17–21.

Mushovic, Ineke. 2011. "Progress Obscures Gay Inequality." *USA Today,* September 1.

National Center for Transgender Equality. 2012. "Transgender Terminology." Accessed August 15, 2012. http://transequality.org/Resources/NCTE_TransTerminology.pdf.

O'Sullivan, Michael. 2010. "Past and Present Reconciled." *Washington Post,* March 12.

Pan, Po-Lin, Juan Meng, and Shuhua Zhou. 2010. "Morality or Equality? Ideological

Framing in News Coverage of Gay Marriage Legitimization." *Social Science Journal* 45:630–45.

Parents, Families, and Friends of Lesbians and Gays (PFLAG). 2012. "Welcome to TNET." Accessed April 3, 2012. http://community.pflag.org/page.aspx?pid=380.

Piepenburg, Erik. 2012. "Keepers of the Gay Film Legacy." *New York Times,* March 16.

Price, Vincent, Lilach Nir, and Joseph N. Cappella. 2005. "Framing Public Discussion of Gay Civil Unions." *Public Opinion Quarterly* 69:179–212.

Public Religion Research Institute. 2011. "Strong Majorities Favor Rights and Legal Protections for Transgender People." November. Accessed April 5, 2012. http://publicre ligion.org/newsroom/2011/11/news-release-strong-majorities-favor-rights-and-le gal-protections-for-transgender-people/.

Rimmerman, Craig A. 2008. *The Lesbian and Gay Movements: Assimilation or Liberation?* Boulder: Westview Press.

Savage, David G. 1999. "High Court to Hear Conflict over Student Fees." *Denver Post,* March 30.

Schiappa, Edward, Peter B. Gregg, and Dean E. Hewes. 2005. "The Parasocial Contact Hypothesis." *Communication Monographs* 72:92–115.

Schram, Sanford, and Joe Soss. 2001. "Success Stories: Welfare Reform, Policy Discourse, and the Politics of Research." *Annals of the American Academy of Political and Social Science* 557:49–65.

Simon, Stephanie. 2003. "Transgender Chaperon Ignites School Dispute." *Los Angeles Times,* January 5.

Snow, David A., and Robert D. Benford. 1988. "Ideology, Frame Resonance, and Participant Mobilization." *International Social Movement Research* 1:197–218.

Snow, David A., E. Burke Rochford Jr., Steven K. Worden, and Robert D. Benford. 1986. "Frame Alignment Processes, Micromobilization, and Movement Participation." *American Sociological Review* 51:464–81.

Spade, Dean, and Paisley Currah. 2008. "The State We're In: Locations of Coercion and Resistance in Trans Policy, Part II." *Sexuality Research & Social Policy* 5:1–4.

Sylvia Rivera Law Project. 2012. "About: Mission." Accessed April 3, 2012. http://srlp.org/about.

Tadlock, Barry L., C. Ann Gordon, and Elizabeth Popp. 2007. "Framing the Issue of Same-Sex Marriage: Traditional Values versus Equal Rights." In *The Politics of Same-Sex Marriage,* ed. Craig A. Rimmerman and Clyde Wilcox, 193–214. Chicago: University of Chicago Press.

Tversky, Amos, and Daniel Kahneman. 1981. "The Framing of Decisions and the Psychology of Choice." *Science* 211:453–58.

Tversky, Amos, and Daniel Kahneman. 1986. "Rational Choice and the Framing of Decisions." *Journal of Business* 59:S251–S278.

Vaid, Urvashi. 1995. *Virtual Equality: The Mainstreaming of Gay and Lesbian Liberation.* New York City: Anchor Books.

Wald, K. D., J. W. Button, and B. A. Rienzo. 1996. "The Politics of Gay Rights in American Communities: Explaining Antidiscrimination Ordinances and Policies." *American Journal of Political Science* 40:1152–78.

Zaller, John. 1991. *The Nature and Origin of Mass Opinion.* New York: Cambridge University Press.

Jacob R. Longaker and Donald P. Haider-Markel

2 | Transgender Policy in Latin American Countries

An Overview and Comparative Perspective on Framing

Although gays and lesbians have achieved important milestones toward equality in the Western Hemisphere, transgender individuals continue to face equality barriers as citizens in many countries. Perhaps in no moment is this more salient than at the presentation of government-issued identification documents in public spaces—there may not be a match between officially recorded sex and a person's gendered name. Thus, the capacity for transgender persons to modify their legal name in accordance with their gender identity is an important step forward in recognizing the equal rights and dignity of these individuals.

In Latin America, five countries currently guarantee the right to change one's name through national policy. To understand the politics behind this issue, this chapter examines national policy proposals in Brazil, Argentina, and Chile that would grant trans persons the right to change their names on official government documents. Specifically, three questions are posed related to policy formulation and adoption: (1) what requirements are set forth by these proposals? (2) how do policymakers frame these proposals? (3) how does the rhetoric in the proposals reflect social constructions of trans persons? We content analyze fourteen national policy proposals to answer these questions.

First, we find that the requirements set forth by the proposals have softened over time. Second, proposals generally frame the issue of name changes for trans persons using legal, equality, and discrimination frames. Pedagogical and international frames are present to a lesser extent. What we call a pedagogical frame is linked to an increasing understanding and awareness of gender diversity and gender identity issues (Corrales and

Pecheny 2010, 10)—an educative aspect. What we refer to as an international frame is suggestive of an informative process based on the policies of other jurisdictions. Our analysis suggests that there is evidence of regional diffusion of policy innovations on trans issues. Third, the increasing trend in the use of the phrase "gender identity" is related to rhetorical changes in the language employed in the proposals.

We begin with a review of the existing literature on transgender public policy, targeting theory, and issue frames. Next, we provide a detailed discussion of the qualitative methodology employed in this research and then discuss the main findings of the empirical work. We find that policy proposals generally frame the issue of name changes for transgender individuals using legal, equality, and discrimination frames. Pedagogical and international frames are present to a lesser extent, with the former being tightly linked to an increasing recognition of the concept of gender identity. The presence of the international frame suggests evidence for the regional diffusion of policy formulations. In general, the requirements set forth by proposals have softened over time. Finally, we conclude with an acknowledgment of the limitations of this study and suggestions for future research.

Trans Rights and Latin America

Latin America is a dynamic area of study for transgender policy in a comparative perspective. As we explain below, an examination of Latin American countries allows for consideration of some of the social and political complications for achieving transgender rights that are not present in the European or North American contexts. Countries in the region provide examples of the process of securing public policies for transgender individuals in developing democracies. Many of these states contend with concurrent goals of achieving economic prosperity and social equality. The rise of leftist governments in the regions through the 1990s opened potential pathways for many previously marginalized groups, such as those comprising the LGBT community, to seek recognition by the state (Escobar and Alvarez 1992). The extent to which these demands have been adequately attended by state apparatuses is a question worthy of scholarly attention because of the normative implications of citizenship in democratic governance.

Several states in the region are increasingly prominent on the international stage, especially in the area of human rights. Notably, Brazil hosted the first World Social Forum in 2001, and the 25th International Lesbian, Gay, Bisexual, Trans, and Intersex Association (ILGA) meeting in 2010. Lesbian, gay, bisexual, and transgender rights groups have been notable in their participation in international advocacy networks, suggesting the potential for the coordination of transnational advocacy for policy change. This offers a unique opportunity to observe the potential diffusion of transgender policy in Latin America.

Finally, a look to Latin America contextualizes the experiences of transgender individuals in an area of the world with a distinct political culture of *machismo* (Borrillo 2010). This tradition negatively affects gains in gender equality for women and LGBT identified people. Notably, the United Nations Gender Equality Index ranks Chile 44, Argentina 45, and Brazil 84 (Gender Equality Index 2011). While the index is primarily concerned with the economic and political equality of women, Latin American scholars argue that lingering systems of patriarchy are at the root of homophobia (Borrillo 2010; Venturi 2011). Moreover, acceptance of homosexuality is generally low in the region, though longitudinal data suggest it has been increasing in the last decade. According to the 2009 Latinobarometer (a regularly administered public opinion poll in the region), the percentage of respondents indicating that homosexuality is never justifiable numbered 24.8 percent in Brazil, 21.2 percent in Argentina, and 11.9 percent in Chile.[1] These numbers indicate significant changes in attitudes since 2002, when respondents for the same question numbered 61.7 percent in Brazil, 47.3 percent in Argentina, and 43.4 percent in Chile.[2] In 2009, those indicating that homosexuality is always justifiable were 11.4 percent in Brazil, 26.6 percent in Argentina, and 10.9 percent in Chile.[3] Although these measures do not directly speak to the political acceptance of transgender individuals, we can reasonably infer that indicators of gender equality and acceptance of homosexuality serve as rough proxies to illustrate the general state of affairs for trans persons.

A Primer on Transgender Studies and Language in Latin America

Research in transgender studies primarily focuses on normative accounts of gender and sexuality informed by queer theory (Currah, Juang, and Minter 2006). Scholars emphasize that sex and gender are socially constructed through the continual repetition (or reiteration) of socially prescribed gender roles, contingent upon the dominant narratives of each specific culture (Butler 1990, 2004). The normalization of gender roles depends upon the reproduction of these performances by members of society. The adoption of gender as part of one's identity (gender identity) is therefore not predetermined by one's biological sex. To roughly paraphrase Butler (1990, 2004), individuals perform gender through dress, behavior, and so forth, which also means that the norms of gendered performance can be challenged (for individual, social, or political purposes) by individuals who choose to violate the norms. In this process, trans individuals can begin to shift social understandings of gender norms.

A few notes on regional terminology should be made. In Latin America, transsexuals are generally considered to be those individuals who have completed sex reassignment surgery (Benedetti 2005; Bento 2006). These individuals are frequently described as feeling entrapped within a body that does not conform to their gender identity. The term *travesti* refers to individuals who are biologically male and self-identify spiritually with the feminine (Kulick 1997a, 1997b).[4] As such, the *travesti* transform their bodies through the injection of silicone implants in the buttocks, chest, and thighs, replicating the curvature of a feminine body. Along with long natural hair and hormone supplements, the result is the embodiment of the feminine by a biologically masculine subject who recognizes their masculine and feminine qualities at all times. Many authors consider the *travesti* to epitomize transgression of sexuality in Brazilian society (Benedetti 2005; Bento 2006; Costa 2008). Finally, the terminology transgender is typically reserved for a broader understanding of any gender identity that transgresses the traditional binaries of heterosexuality. Although the term subsumes these former identities in the U.S. context, movements often refer to themselves as LGBTTT (lesbian, gay, bisexual, transgender, *travesti*, and transsexuals). Throughout this chapter, we opt to employ the generic prefix trans to avoid privileging any particular term.

The Literature on LGB and Trans Public Policy

Theoretical literature in trans studies unravels the normative assumptions of gender and sexuality. However, empirical study on the treatment of trans persons in public policy is lacking. Even work on lesbian, gay, bisexual, and transgender (LGBT) public policy prioritizes studies of gay and lesbian issues at the expense of transgender issues (e.g., Haider-Markel 2010). Many scholars carelessly employ the term LGBT, assuming that the interests of the movement are uniform, in spite of the fact that their work does not explicitly address trans persons (Minter 2006). To fill this gap, research in public policy must address those issues that are of interest to the transgender community: nondiscrimination policies, the change of legal names, and access to public health care, among others (Taylor 2007).

As is clear from other chapters in this volume (see chapters 5–9), a primary focus of scholarly work on transgender public policy is gender-identity-inclusive nondiscrimination policy. The adoption of these policies is more likely in communities that are racially diverse, highly educated, and politically liberal (Colvin 2008). However, improvements need to be made to ensure proper implementation and enforcement at the municipal level (Colvin 2007). Trans activists actively target communities that have previously been sympathetic to gay and lesbian equality issues (Colvin 2008; also see chapters 6–9 in this volume). However, event history analysis shows that states that previously adopted nondiscrimination policies that only included sexual orientation are no more likely to later include gender identity protections (Taylor et. al. 2012), nor are states with same-sex partnership or hate crime laws (Taylor and Lewis 2012). On the other hand, when proposed together, policies that include both sexual orientation and gender identity are more likely to succeed, especially in the 2000s (Taylor and Lewis 2012). Finally, the adoption of gender-identity-inclusive nondiscrimination policy is strongly influenced by regional and neighboring state adoption (diffusion effects), while sexual orientation nondiscrimination policy is not (Taylor et. al. 2012).

One explanation for the divergent results in adoption of sexual orientation and gender-identity-inclusive nondiscrimination policies focuses on the role of interest groups. Although empirical studies demonstrate the mobilization capacity of trans interest groups as independent entities (Nownes 2010), they are often subsumed under the broader umbrella of the LGBT movement. However, as part of an LGBT advocacy coalition, trans interests are usually treated as secondary in the hierarchy of movement goals (Taylor and Lewis 2012). As such, trans rights are relegated to minor status, subject to bargaining in moments of prolonged conflict, as the LG movement pursues its primary goals related to equal rights (see chapter 5 in this volume). Thus, it is generally true that gender-identity-inclusive nondiscrimination policy does not precede sexual orientation nondiscrimination policy.

In Latin American countries, the pattern is similar—sexual orientation protections have been adopted more widely than protections for trans people, and the concerns of trans activists have been secondary to the concerns of lesbian and gay activists (Corrales and Pecheny 2010). Indeed, we could not identify any Latin American or Spanish countries where progressive policies for trans people were adopted prior to progressive policies on sexual orientation. For example, Colombia and Spain adopted nondiscrimination policies for sexual orientation as early as 1995, but neither country has protections for trans people (Paoli Itaborahy 2012). In Argentina, activists secured rights to same-sex marriage in 2010 and returned to pursue gender identity policy in 2012 (Barrionuevo 2010; Schmall 2012).

Nevertheless, in some Latin American countries, policies were adopted that provide protections for the LBGT community as a whole. For example, Uruguay adopted broad LGBT protections in 2003 (effective 2004) and Chile provided LGBT protections in 2012. Both of these countries did this through the legislative process (Paoli Itaborahy 2012). In El Salvador, inclusive LGBT protections were adopted in 2010 by presidential decree (Paoli Itaborahy 2012). Bolivia (2009) and Ecuador (2008) adopted inclusive LGBT protections by constitutional referenda (Paoli Itaborahy 2012).

Transgender Policy in Latin American Countries

To complement this empirical work, we survey the general state of transgender public policy in 21 Latin American democracies.[5] For each country, we identify the existence (or absence) of national policy regulating the following issue areas: (1) name change on official documents, (2) sex marker change on official documents, (3) prohibition of discrimination on sexual orientation, (4) prohibition of discrimination on gender identity, and (5) state financial support for sex reassignment surgery through national health care plans. Data was collected through examination of national legislation, national policy programs, interest group publications, and through several international nongovernmental organizations. The source material generally covers the period 1995 to 2012, but some material was older.[6] Findings were corroborated through e-mail consultation with national activist groups when available.[7] The results from this analysis are presented in table 2.1.

In total, eleven countries currently have at least one national policy in the five issue areas addressed by this study. Overall, laws prohibiting discrimination based on sexual orientation exist in seven Latin American countries; although sexual orientation policies may not directly pertain to trans persons, work in the United States indicates that sexual orientation protections usually precede gender identity protections, so their adoption in Latin American countries may foreshadow the adoption of trans protections. However, given the legal protections for gender in some Latin American counties, it is sometimes possible to obtain some legal protections for trans people in the courts on a case-by-case basis without a general policy being adopted. In our examination, we saw few trans-related policies adopted concurrently with LGB policies or protections. However, in Uruguay an antidiscrimination law that protects both sexual orientation and gender identity took effect in 2004 (Lavers 2012c).[8] Interestingly, some Latin American countries have also seen trans candidates achieve electoral success before lesbian or gay candidates; in Chile the first openly

TABLE 2.1. Transgender Public Policy in Latin America

Country	Documents: Name	Documents: Sex	Discrimination: Sexual Orientation	Discrimination: Gender Identity	Health: Sex Reassignment Surgery	Index
Argentina	yes	yes	no	no	yes	3
Bolivia	no	no	yes C	yes C	no	2
Brazil	no	no	no	no[a]	yes	1
Chile	no	no	yes	yes	no	2
Colombia	no	no	yes	no	yes	2
Costa Rica	no	no	no	no	?	0
Cuba	no	yes	no	no	yes D	2
Dom. Rep.	no	no	no M	no M	no	0
Ecuador	yes	no	yes C	yes C	no	3
El Salvador	no	no	yes D	yes D	no	2
Guatemala	no	no	no	no	no	0
Honduras	no	no	no	no	no	0
Mexico	no	no	no	no	no	0
Nicaragua	no	no	no	no	no	0
Panama	yes	yes	no	no	no	2
Paraguay	no	no	no	no	no	0
Peru	no	no	no	no	no	0
Puerto Rico	no	no	yes	yes	no	0
Spain	yes	yes	yes	yes	yes	5
Uruguay	yes	yes	yes	yes	Maybe	4
Venezuela	no	no	no	no	no	0
Total	5	5	7	6	5	

Note: Developed by the authors based on governmental records. A "yes" indicates the existence of a national policy regulating the following issue areas: Does national policy allow for name change on official documents? Does national policy allow for sex change on official documents? Does national policy prohibit discrimination based on sexual orientation? Does national policy prohibit discrimination based on gender identity? Does national policy regulate and provide for sex reassignment surgery? The total number of policies per country is listed in the index column.

C = Constitutional; D = Presidential Decree; M = Minors.

[a]This is prohibited in a domestic violence law, but it only pertains to women.

ian candidate was elected in 2012, but this occurred with the ..on of a trans candidate and the reelection of another trans candidate that had been elected in the previous election cycle (Beyer 2012). Nevertheless, there is evidence that trans-related policies might be more likely to follow the adoption of policies related to sexual orientation. Another six countries have policies prohibiting discrimination based on gender identity. It is notable that protections for gender identity do not exist independent of protections for sexual orientation. In Colombia, the penal code was modified in 2011 to prohibit discrimination based on race, nationality, sex, or sexual orientation, but not gender identity. In Bolivia and Ecuador, protections for both discrimination on sexual orientation and gender identity is constitutionally guaranteed (ILGA indicates that Colombia offers constitutional protections for sexual orientation, but we were not able to verify this claim). Similar protections were passed by executive decree in El Salvador. The Dominican Republic prohibits discrimination based on sexual orientation and gender identity, but the law only pertains to minors,

National policy legalizes name changes on official documents in six Latin American countries. Of these, amended sex markers appear on legal documents in all of these countries except Ecuador. Currently, Ecuadorian citizens are appealing for allowing these sex marker changes on official documents under the grounds that it violates constitutional protections of discrimination based on gender identity; currently such changes on official documents are allowed only on a case-by-case basis by the judiciary (Jones 2013). Finally, state regulation and provision of sex reassignment surgery is available in five countries: Argentina, Brazil, Colombia, Cuba, and Spain. These countries offer access to sex reassignment surgery through the public health system.

In terms of regional trends, we note that the majority of trans-inclusive policy exists in South American democracies rather than in Central America. In part, this might be driven by the stronger influence of Spain in South America. Spain has been progressive on trans-inclusive public policy, and there is some indication that these policies have diffused to South America more readily (Platero 2009, 2011).[9] Argentina, Chile, Uruguay, and Ecuador follow closely with over three policies each. In Central America, we note the general absence of trans-inclusive public policy. Only Panama and El Salvador currently possess national policy in any of the five areas.

A few important caveats to this survey must be noted. First, we collected data only on national-level policies regulating each issue area. This was done to facilitate cross-national comparisons of policy, but it ultimately overlooks advances made at state and local levels of government. For example, in Argentina and Brazil, some states have policies that prohibit discrimination based on sexual orientation and gender identity (de la Dehesa 2010; Mello, Brito, and Moraj 2012; Paoli Itaborahy 2012). Second, in our analysis of discrimination, we collected data only on comprehensive national-level policy prohibiting trans-based discrimination in employment, housing, and public accommodations. Once again, this strict requirement does not capture instances where discrimination is prohibited in different issue areas (see Taylor et al. 2012).[10] Finally, totals for policies allowing for name and sex marker change on official documentation only include countries with nationally adopted policies. In several instances, such as Peru, Colombia, Ecuador, and Puerto Rico, trans persons have successfully secured these changes on documentation through individual judicial rulings (ACLU of Puerto Rico 2012; Marcos and Cordero 2009; Salinas and Barrera 2011). However, judicial systems in Latin American democracies operate on the system of civil law, which generally does not include the principle of stare decisis found in common law systems (Stepan 2000). Thus, favorable court rulings do not establish policy per se, and rulings must be issued on a case-by-case basis. For a national policy to be established the legislative branch must reform the civil code to reflect these rulings or an executive decree or order must be issued.

The Process of Policy Adoption: Issue Framing on Sex Identification and Official Documents

Currently, there is limited scholarly work on public policy allowing for trans persons to change legal names and sex markers on official documents (but see chapter 10 in this volume and Taylor, Tadlock, and Poggione 2014). The ability to do so represents a significant advancement in the reduction of discrimination faced by these individuals on a daily basis. To begin work in this area, we start with the policy formulation stage. Our analysis is informed by the social construction theory of policy design. We investigate how policy proposals frame the issue of legal name changes for trans persons, what requirements they stipulate, and what rhetoric they employ.

Social Construction, Issue Framing, and Policy Design

Social construction theory grew out of a desire to understand and explain one of the more pernicious problems of public policy: given democratic commitment to political and legal equality, why is it that the design of public policy disproportionately favors some groups and disfavors others (Ingram, Schneider, and DeLeon 2007)? The parsimonious explanation to this inconsistency is that target groups are defined in ways that portray them in either a positive or negative manner and as politically weak or powerful. Policy design allocates benefits and burdens according to the level of power and construction of target groups: "policymakers typically socially construct target populations in positive and negative terms and distribute benefits and burdens so as to reflect and perpetuate these constructions" (Ingram, Schneider, and deLeon 2007, 93). A typology of target groups based upon positive/negative social constructions and high/low designations of political power guides the expectations of the theory (Schneider and Ingram 1997; Ingram, Schneider, and deLeon 2007). The typology yields four classifications of target groups, as advantaged (high power, positive construction), contender (high power, negative construction), dependents (low power, positive construction), or deviant (low power, negative construction). These classifications are seen as fluid with "various groups having contested social constructions, with different actors perceiving their attributes differently" (Ingram, Schneider, and deLeon 2007, 103).

Social construction theory, therefore, suggests that "policy design elements, including tools, rules, rationales, and delivery structures, differ according to the social construction and power of target groups" (Ingram, Schneider, and deLeon 2007, 104).[11] Here, we focus on the design of rules and rationales in policy proposals that would grant trans persons the ability to change their name on official documentation.

In terms of rules, policy design often contains specific language identifying target groups that qualify for benefits or burdens. Additionally, policy stipulates administrative procedures for assessing individual claims to receive treatment as a member of the target group. In work on policy design of veterans' programs, Suzanne Mettler (2005) conceptualizes these ideas as the *scope of eligibility* and *procedures for determining eligibility*, respectively. These categories indicate whether a policy is inclusive and accessible, or exclusive and discriminatory. Due to transgender individuals' negative social construction, we hypothesize that policy design will be exclusive and discriminatory. Specifically, we hypothesize that the scope of eligibility for these policies will be fairly limited, carefully specifying which individuals qualify for name changes. Similarly, we hypothesize that procedures for determining eligibility will be burdensome, most likely involving strict medical examinations.

In terms of rationales, rhetoric that justifies the design of public policy is strongly influenced by the social constructions of target groups (Donovan 2001). While historically constructed as deviants, LGBT-identified people increasingly represent emergent contenders with "power . . . in their legal, ethical and moral claims for equality and justice" (Schneider and Ingram 1997, 119). Thus, policy benefits are justified in reference to democratic norms such as equal rights, but rationalized in abstract terms so as to avoid direct praise of the target group (Schneider and Ingram 1997, 133). Indeed, politicians and policy entrepreneurs seek to limit the traceability of their actions when conferring benefits to negatively constructed target groups (Donovan 2001). Thus, we hypothesize that rationales offered in favor of the adoption of policy that allows trans persons to change their name to be abstract and detached from direct praise of the target group; conversely, rationales offered in opposition to the adoption of such legislation should reflect negative biases against these groups. Indeed, opponents often argue that the claims of emergent contenders threaten traditional values while conferring undeserved, special group benefits to societal deviants

For a closer understanding of these arguments, we turn to the vast literature on framing theory related to gay and lesbian public policy. Framing theory offers a literature that is rich with empirical studies that complement the expectations of social construction theory. Literature on issue frames (see chapter 1 by Barry Tadlock for additional discussion of frames) and transgender policy does not exist, so we turn to work on gay and lesbian policy issues for guidance. A considerable body of empirical work documents the frames employed in same-sex marriage debates (e.g., Brewer 2008). Since this issue is generally considered representative of the rhetoric faced by the LGBT community, we use this literature to guide our expectations of framing for transgender-specific issues.

Issue frames

Issue framing refers to active redefinition of an issue in terms that favor one particular viewpoint (Baumgartner, De Boef, and Boydstun 2008; Chong and Druckman 2007; Druckman 2001). Frames combine a series of arguments into one cohesive message and guide attention to specific aspects of the broader issue (Haider-Markel and Joslyn 2001). Typically, an issue frame attempts to define a topic in a manner that reduces the most threatening aspects, while simultaneously emphasizing appealing characteristics (Mucciaroni 2008). Frames that successfully elicit favorable responses from the public, media, or elites, or a combination of these, can provide important support to interest groups pressing a specific issue (Tadlock, Gordon, and Popp 2007). Those that become dominant have the potential to set the terms of public discourse, control the language of debate, and shape political thinking about issues (Schattschneider 1960; Tadlock, Gordon, and Popp 2007). Complex issues may become simplified and readily available through the use of value-choice frames that activate personal normative values or morals (Mooney 2000; Schneider and Ingram 1990; Stone 1989; Tadlock, Gordon, and Popp 2007).

Value-choice frames are prevalent in empirical work on LGBT public policy, especially on the issue of same-sex marriage. In general, scholars describe the debate as a contest between an equal rights frame and a traditional values frame (Cahill 2007; DeLaet and Caufield 2008; Goldberg-Hiller 2002; Rom 2007; Tadlock, Gordon, and Popp 2007). The equal rights frame used by supporters of same-sex marriage "encompasses a broad range of discussion about rights, discrimination, fairness, and specific benefits that are afforded to married couples" (Tadlock, Gordon, and Popp 2007, 200). Similarly, Mark Rom finds that supporters of same-sex marriage "emphasize certain themes . . . civil rights, citizenship, equality, and fair treatment" (Rom 2007, 21). The traditional rights frame used by opponents of same-sex marriage includes "arguments featuring religious and biblical elements, threats to the family structure, and threats to our traditionally held morals" (Tadlock, Gordon and Popp 2007, 201). Opponents argue that same-sex marriage is a slippery slope to the demise of the nuclear family, the loss of innocence of children, the permissiveness of marginalized sexualities, and a threat to the well-being of future generations of society (Cahill 2007; Rom 2007).

The framing literature provides several key hypotheses for our investigation of frames used in trans public policy. Consistent with social construction theory, we hypothesize that policy proposals to allow trans persons to change legal names will be framed in terms of equal rights. Conversely, we hypothesize that policy proposals to prohibit trans persons to change legal names will be framed in terms of traditional values. Our view is that the target populations of these policies represent challenges to conventional norms of gender and sexuality, raising the specter of a threat to traditional values.

Methods

To test these hypotheses, we selected a multiple qualitative case study approach. Specifically, policy design was analyzed for fourteen policy proposals in Brazil, Argentina, and Chile. Thus the data set includes proposals from: Brazil, 1995–2012; Argentina, 2007–2012; and Chile, 2008–2012 (the start date being the first relevant proposal in each country). The following section details the methodologies used in this study.

Case studies provide a nuanced treatment of complicated political processes, substantiating explanations for empirical phenomena with heavily descriptive accounts of causal mechanisms and contextual factors (Miles and Huberman 1994; Wiener and Koontz 2010; Yin 2003). In public policy, case studies are especially useful in the development of knowledge and theory in underresearched issue areas (Rochefort and Cobb 1994; Schlager 2007). Case studies should be selected based upon one of three criteria: comparing similar cases, comparing different cases, or illuminating unique cases (King, Keohane, and Verba 1994; Lijphart 1971; Yin 2003). This research employs a different cases design, using three unique experiences from Brazil, Argentina, and Chile with substantial variation in policy proposals for transgender individuals to change their name.

Content analysis is an appropriate method by which one can analyze texts such as governmental documents, public policies, and legislative proposals (Weber 1990). This study analyzes fourteen national legislative proposals related to transgender individuals and legal names in Brazil, Argentina, and Chile. We identified proposals using keyword searches on legislative databases and interest group websites for each country. These keyword searches included the terms "gender identity" and "name change."[12]

In total, five proposals have been introduced in the Brazilian Chamber of Deputies since 1995.[13] Six proposals have been introduced in the Argentine Chamber of Deputies since 2007. The most recent proposal, Policy A6, became law in 2012. Two proposals have been introduced in the Chilean Chamber of Deputies since 2008. For purposes of discussion, each policy proposal used in this research is assigned a country letter and number by order of introduction (for example, Policy B1 refers to the first proposal introduced in Brazil). Table 2.2 presents the descriptive statistics of the policy proposals.

Legislative proposals in Brazil, Argentina, and Chile contain two parts. Part one defines the scope of the proposal and subsequent modifications to current law in short articles that resemble legal prose. This allowed for an examination of rules and requirements, providing data on the scope of eligibility and procedures of eligibility. Part two provides justification of the proposal written by the sponsor(s) of the law. The explanatory quality of the second part facilitated an examination of frames and rhetoric employed in justification of the policy.

A systematic and standardized coding schema for each primary research question was developed to ensure for the accuracy of results (Weber 1990, 17). All three coding schema were created inductively through the analysis of legislative proposals,[14] allowing for emergent categories to be included in this study. Analysis is weighted to control for variation in proposal length.

Scope of eligibility is measured as the target group identified in the policy proposal: *travestis,* transgenders, and transsexuals. Procedures for eligibility are constructed as a dichotomous variable (yes/no) referring to the presence of three requirements: (1) judicial determination, (2) medical examinations, (3) medical surgery. Effectively, each of these requirements restricts the conditions under which trans persons can legally change their name.

Policy frames are categorized in thematic terms. Consistent with framing LGBT policies, we expect to witness the emergence of an equality and traditional rights frame. Each paragraph in the justification section of the proposal was coded exclusively for one distinct theme. Consistent with

TABLE 2.2. National Policy Proposals Related to Trans Persons and Name Change

Country	Proposal	Year	Citation
Argentina	A1	2007	5259-D
Argentina	A2	2009	1736-D
Argentina	A3	2010	7243-D
Argentina	A4	2010	7644-D
Argentina	A5	2010	8126-D
Argentina	A6	2011	1879-D
Brazil	B1	1995	70
Brazil	B2	1997	3727
Brazil	B3	2005	5872
Brazil	B4	2006	6655
Brazil	B5	2008	2976
Brazil	B6	2011	1281
Chile	C1	2008	6913-07
Chile	C2	2010	5679-18

Note: Developed by the authors; this table lists the policy proposals under investigation in this study. The proposals are referenced throughout the text using the shorthand A1, A2, A3, etc. Complete citations for each proposal are provided in the bibliography.

framing theory, these themes represent broad categories, made up of arguments with a high degree of internal covariance and consistency.[15] The coding criteria for frames are presented below:

LEGAL: need for public policy, legislative action, jurisprudence

SCIENCE: medicine, science as progress, science as authority, surgical processes

INTERNATIONAL: appeal to international law, mention of international examples

PEDAGOGY: explanation of gender, gender identity

DISCRIMINATION: discrimination faced by trans persons, specific examples

EQUALITY: rights, equality, justice

MORALITY: moral values, religious values, natural and essentialist arguments

Finally, the rhetoric of the policy proposal measures the overall tone of the policy, capturing the expectations of social construction theory. Additionally, these codes reflect the epistemological assumptions of feminist empiricism, paying special attention to three factors: what language is being employed, what language is missing, and scope of eligibility. Specifically, we identify whether the text speaks in terms of sex or gender identity, transsexualism or transsexuality. These distinctions reflect important choices in policy design on behalf of the policy authors.

Analysis, Policy Design

The results of the content analysis for scope of eligibility are presented in table 2.3 and the procedural requirements are presented in table 2.4. In the Brazilian case, several trends and inconsistencies are apparent. In terms of scope of eligibility, all Brazilian proposals focus on transsexuals. The only exception is Proposal B5 (2008), which targets *travestis* and, notably, employs gender identity language. However, even in this instance, the terminology transgender (arguably more comprehensive and inclusive) is not used. For procedural requirements, all Brazilian legislative proposals, except Proposal B6 (2011), require judicial approval before authorizing a name change. Three require medical approval, usually in the form of complete and thorough diagnostics to confirm transsexuality. Although none of the proposals were explicit, these examinations most likely follow the diagnostic procedures set forth in the DSM-IV for the classification of gender identity disorder.[16] Furthermore, two proposals require sex reassignment surgery before the individual may request a legalized name change.

The requirements set forth by the Argentine policy proposals are less challenging than those of their Brazilian counterparts. In terms of scope of eligibility, five proposals target all three categories of *travesti*, transsexual, and transgender individuals. Policy A3 does not mention any target group and employs neutral language in the proposal. Policies A1 and A2 require judicial approval for the completion of a name change. The majority of the policies only required the submission of a form at the local registrar. This is a largely administrative task that was not included as a category for this study, as any policy would require this as a baseline. Thus, it was not considered to be a requirement above and beyond normal expectations. Interestingly, no policy in Argentina *requires* sex reassignment surgery, as seen in Brazil. In one instance, Policy A3, complainants must provide testimony from acquaintances to verify identity. However, this is waived in lieu of sex reassignment surgery or possession of a medical diagnosis of "gender identity disorder." The most recent bill, Policy A6, explicitly rejects any procedures for eligibility aside from basic administrative tasks in order to reduce any potential discrimination faced by trans persons seeking the name change. Policy A6 became law in 2012.

TABLE 2.3. Scope of Eligibility

Proposal	*Travesti*	Transexual	Transgender
A1	yes	yes	yes
A2	yes	yes	yes
A3	no	no	no
A4	yes	yes	yes
A5	yes	yes	yes
A6	yes	yes	yes
B1	no	yes	no
B2	no	yes	no
B3	no	yes	no
B4	no	yes	no
B5	yes	no	no
B6	no	yes	no
C1	no	yes	yes
C2	no	no	no

Note: Developed by the authors; this table provides information on the scope of eligibility established by the policy proposals in this study. Target groups are identified as *travesti*, transsexual, or transgender.

The requirements set forth by the Chilean proposals are similar to Policy A3 in Argentina. These do not require judicial approval, but the language employed indicates some necessity to complete either a medical diagnosis or sex reassignment surgery. Specifically, in Policy C1 the complainant must either be in the process of sex reassignment or provide testimony, confirmed by doctors, that they have lived for two years as the opposite gender. The language employed in Policy C2 largely reflects these assumptions, but it does not contain much detail. The final process for changing documents and the like is considered administrative.

Issue Frames

In the aggregate, attention is evenly divided between three frames: legal (23.5%), equality (19.3%), and discrimination (20.7%). The international frame appears in 12.5 percent of cases, and the pedagogical frame appears in 10 percent of cases. Both the morality and science frames appear less frequently in more recent proposals. Together, they only account for about 6 percent of the paragraphs. The distribution of the frames is presented in

TABLE 2.4. Procedures for Eligibility

Proposal	Judicial Approval	Medical Approval	Sex Reassignment Surgery
A1	yes	no	no
A2	yes	no	no
A3	no	yes or	yes or
A4	no	no	no
A5	no	no	no
A6	no	no	no
B1	yes	yes	yes
B2	yes	—	yes
B3	yes	no	no
B4	yes	yes	no
B5	yes	no	no
B6	no	yes	yes
C1	no	yes or	yes or
C2	no	yes or	yes or

Note: Developed by the authors; this table provides information on the procedures for eligibility established by the policy proposals in this study. Judicial approval requires appearance before a judge; medical approval requires a full medical examination for evidence of gender identity disorder; medical operations require sex reassignment surgery. All requirements are marked as yes/no; "—" indicates lack of clarity; "yes or" indicates that one of the two is necessary.

table 2.5. The analysis below disaggregates these numbers to consider country-by-country variation in framing.

In Brazil, the legal frame occurs with the highest frequency. Twelve unique paragraphs are dedicated to addressing the gap in current legislation in regard to trans rights and legal names. Additionally, it appears with relative consistency across most legislation favoring the extension of this right. The exception is Policy B3 of 2005, which sought to prohibit the ability of trans persons to petition a judge for a name change. This is the only instance of a backlash policy proposal found in this study, though more may exist. The science frame appears in nearly one-third of the paragraphs in Policy B1 of 1995. The language employed in Policy B1 appeals to science as an authority in establishing the need of trans persons to both undergo surgery (and decriminalize such surgeries) and receive a legal name change. Three paragraphs cite the opinions of doctors and professors to establish the correct procedure for dealing with the situation:

> Doctor Roberto Farina, a well-known specialist in the area, analyzing a specific case, affirmed: "the correct [way of treating transsexuals] would be through psychiatry, psychoanalysis, or psychotherapy, changing the mind to make it consistent with the physical attri-

TABLE 2.5. Frames

Proposal	Legal	Science	International	Pedagogy	Discrimination	Equality	Morality	Total
A1	24	2	17	5	24	29	0	(42)
A2	26	3	16	5	26	24	0	(38)
A3	47	0	12	18	6	18	0	(17)
A4	25	0	14	14	27	20	0	(44)
A5	14	0	16	30	24	16	0	(37)
A6	22	0	13	9	29	22	0	(45)
B1	25	50	17	8	0	0	0	(12)
B2	75	25	0	0	0	0	0	(4)
B3	0	0	0	0	0	0	100	(9)
B4	30	0	0	50	10	10	0	(10)
B5	25	0	0	0	38	38	0	(8)
B6	57	14	0	0	0	29	0	(7)
C1	70	0	8	0	0	23	0	(13)
C2	30	0	10	27	3	30	0	(30)
Total	22	4	14	14	23	21	4	(250)

Note: Developed by the authors; this table indicates the percentage of frames used by the policy proposals in this study. Frames are coded as mutually exclusive. The percentage of frames per category is provided in the total row; the raw frequency of frames per policy is provided in the total column.

butes that are masculine. Now, since such treatment [technical psychotherapy] fails systematically in these cases, we have no other solution but to follow the opposite path, adapting the body to the feminine mind' . . ." (Policy B3)

This trend quickly disappears in the subsequent years. Only Policy B2 includes a single mention of the value and importance of medical science in the debate. More recently, Policy B5 (2008) and Policy B6 (2011) dedicate more space to addressing the importance of equal rights, social justice, and the degree of discrimination faced by trans persons. The following passage illustrates this frame: "Respecting the identity of *travestis* is an evolutionary step in the construction of a society that is more just and egalitarian" (Policy B5).

Finally, Policy B3 (2005), a backlash proposal, is framed in moral terms, similar to the pattern for LGBT policy outlined in the literature. The passages use language that evokes the importance of religion, such as "the transsexual, by removing the sexual characteristics which nature beheld him, casts himself in rebellion to God" (Policy B3). The arguments focused primarily on the societal implications of a name change, using words such as "essential" and "natural" alongside verbs such as "to birth." For example, the sponsor claims that "the name is a right to moral integrity composing one of the distinctive signs of the human being . . . it is born out of the necessity to distinguish individuals." (Policy B3).

The policy proposals for Argentina are notably longer than the others. The trends in the Argentine proposals drive the aggregate interpretation that the legal, discrimination, and equality frames are used most. Indeed, a closer look at these three categories for the six Argentine proposals reveals remarkable consistency in the distribution of their use. Almost a quarter of the paragraphs for each policy proposal are dedicated to each of these three frames.

The discrimination frame merits more attention in the Argentine case. Compared to the Brazilian experience, where discrimination was cited in only one of the five proposals, Argentine proposals focus on the discrimination faced by trans persons. These passages provide statistics from interest groups about the precarious health situation of transgender individuals. For example, Policy A4 writes:

To illustrate this situation, we cite some results of an investigation about the situation of *travestis,* transsexuals, and transgenders in the City of Buenos Aires, Mar del Plata and in localities of Concur-

bano Bonaerense, conducted under the coordination of the Association of the Struggle for the Identity of *Travestis* and Transsexuals—
ALITT—in the course of the year 2005. During the fieldwork, 420
names were revealed of friends who had passed away, with HIV/
AIDS as the principal cause of death (62%)." (Policy A4)

The pedagogy frame also appears with higher frequency in the Argentine
proposals than in other cases. This frame focuses primarily on decon-
structing the biological links between sex and gender. In general, the pedagogical frame is employed at the start of the policy text, as a precursor to
explaining gender identity to a lay audience. Finally, the international
frame appears with a median frequency of six paragraphs in the Argentine
case. International norms are frequently cited, such as the Yogyakarta
Principles,[17] and European exemplars, such as the Spanish policy for
transgender identity. The most recent proposal, Policy A6, also indicates
that it was drafted as part of a binational effort with Uruguayan activists
where legislation passed in 2009. This suggests policy diffusion on behalf
of a transnational policy network, probably consisting of LGBT activists.

In Chile, the frames of Policy C2 resemble the Argentine case. Of 32
paragraphs, 9 are devoted to legal arguments and the need for public policy, 8 are devoted to explaining gender identity, and 9 are devoted to
equality. The international frames explicitly mention the UN Declaration
of Human Rights, the Organization of American States, and the European
Union. There is also reference to a meeting held at the University of Buenos Aires, Argentina, again suggesting some amount of policy diffusion in
the region. Notably, Policy C1 does not employ the pedagogical language
of the latter proposal. This suggests that the incorporation of clear definitions of gender identity is now an important mechanism in proposing
transgender public policy.

Rhetoric

The results of the content analysis for rhetoric are presented above in table
2.6. Several results merit discussion. In Brazil, only Policy B5 (2008) uses
the term "gender identity"; all other proposals referred simply to sex
changes and biological notions of sex. Additionally, the terminology
transsexualism uses the suffix -ism to denote an illness. This appears in
Policy B1 (1995) and Policy B3 (2005). Proposal B1 (1995) also refers to
homosexualism, widely abandoned after homosexuality was removed
from the DSM-III list of mental illnesses in Brazil in 1985 (Mott 2011).

Transsexuality (suffix -ality), indicating a state of being, is used in Policy B2 of 1997. The most recent proposals do not use either term.

The rhetoric used in the Argentine policy proposals is notably more inclusive. In terms of target groups, five of the six proposals explicitly identify all three categories, *travesti*, transsexual, and transgender individuals. Policy A3 does not mention any target group and employs neutral language in the proposal. The policies generally employ the term transsexuality. Finally, the proposals differ from the Brazilian experience in their focus on gender identity and gender expression, rather than simply on biological sex. This also reflects the use of the pedagogical frame to establish the difference between gender identity and biological sex. Policy A6, which became law in 2012, does not explicitly mention the target groups in the articles of the proposal. The absence of the target groups in the legal portion of the proposal may reflect a strategy to reduce attention to the target groups of the law.

The Chilean proposals also use gender identity language. Both Chilean proposals, Policy C1 and Policy C2, employ the term transsexuality to denote a state of being. Policy C1 targets transsexuals, while Policy C2 includes transgenders as well. Consistent with the Argentine experience, the

TABLE 2.6. Rhetoric

Proposal	Sex	Gender Identity	Gender Expression	Transsexualism	Transsexuality
A1	yes	yes	no	no	yes
A2	yes	yes	no	no	yes
A3	yes	yes	no	no	no
A4	yes	yes	yes	no	yes
A5	yes	yes	yes	no	yes
A6	yes	yes	yes	no	yes
B1	yes	no	no	yes	no
B2	yes	no	no	no	yes
B3	yes	no	no	yes	no
B4	yes	yes	no	no	yes
B5	yes	yes	no	no	no
B6	yes	no	no	no	no
C1	yes	yes	no	no	yes
C2	yes	yes	no	no	yes

Note: Developed by the authors; this table provides information on the rhetoric used by the policy proposals in this study. Policies are coded for referencing biological sex, gender identity, and/or gender expression. Policies are coded for using the terminology *transsexualism* and/or *transsexuality*.

use of the term transgender is accompanied by the presence of pedagogical frames that explain gender identity.

Discussion

Our research sought to answer three questions related to legislative proposals guaranteeing the right to legal name changes for transgender individuals in Brazil, Argentina, and Chile: How does policy design determine scope of eligibility and procedures for eligibility? How are the arguments framed in thematic terms? How does the rhetoric reflect social constructions of trans persons? We hypothesized that (1) policy design would create exclusive and discriminatory policies through the establishment of a limited scope of eligibility and burdensome procedures for eligibility; (2) favorable arguments for these policies would be framed in terms of equal rights; and (3) rhetoric would reinforce negative constructions of trans persons and distance policymakers from this social group. We discuss important findings from our research below.

No fewer than fourteen unique legislative proposals allowing for name change in the case of transgender individuals have been introduced in these three countries. In Brazil, the proposals display remarkable inconsistency in their establishment of requirements, thematic focuses, and use of rhetoric. It is perhaps for this very reason that no proposal has been adopted, given their individual shortcomings and a failure to create a cohesive argument grounded in egalitarian principles. These findings support Hypothesis 1 and 3, yet contradict our Hypothesis 2 related to framing.

For instance, Policy B1 (1995) requires judicial and medical approval, as well as a medical operation before a transsexual can petition for a legal name change. If granted, a special notation would be kept on their records indicating transsexual status. With the use of language such as transsexualism and arguments framed in scientific terms, it is not surprising that the motion failed to receive support. Subsequent proposals relinquish the stipulation that transsexual status be recorded on an individual's official documentation yet display inconsistency in procedures for eligibility. Of the three requirements identified by the content analysis, Proposal B5 (2008) and Proposal B6 (2011) reverse their stances in relation to the judicial and medical aspects. Proposal B5 does not require medical approval or a medical operation for a *travesti* to seek a name change, only a judicial ruling. This is perhaps because the *travesti* is understood in terms of gender identity, as an individual who identifies psychologically with the opposite sex (usually male to female), and pursues some, though not complete, alterations of corporeal features through injections of silicone and consumption of hormones. Proposal B6 even makes explicit that judicial oversight is an unnecessary burden for individuals to obtain a name change. Ironically, the sponsor of this legislation did not consider medical diagnostics and a medical operation to be problematic. This could be emblematic of a deeper division within the trans community as to the adequacy and appropriateness of medical surgery and the concomitant pathologization of transsexuality by the medical community (a topic further explored by Ryan Combs in chapter 9). Ultimately, both requirements are burdensome to the individual. It is notable that all Brazilian proposals recognize the need for clear legislative guidelines to allow for trans persons to pursue name changes. Earlier arguments were framed by their attention to bridging the gap between law and medical technology. In other words, with new technology and the ability to undergo sex reassignment surgery, the legal code must be updated to address these new possibilities. More recent proposals emphasize the need for legislation through appeals to equal rights and a focus on the discrimination faced by transgender individuals.

The results for the Brazilian case reveal a policy environment that has thus far failed to create a satisfactory proposal that could be turned into law. Given the evidence at hand, the reasons for these failures are speculative. It is apparent, however, that all proposals submitted impose some requirement subjecting transsexuals to evaluation by a third party, a party that ostensibly possesses the authority to decide whether or not the individual is in fact a "genuine" transsexual. It seems that this would fail to receive support by even the transgender community.

To establish support for this conclusion, we can turn to proposals in Argentina. These proposals frequently contain language that cites national transgender interest groups (or LGBT groups). The Argentine proposals incorporate inclusive language through the use of gender identity, supported through pedagogical frames that deconstruct traditional binaries of gender. From a normative standpoint, this approach is preferable in that it allows for all individuals who self-identify as trans to seek a name change.

The Argentine proposals also attempt to make the process more accessible by eliminating burdensome requirements in the procedures for eligibility. This finding is contrary to our hypothesis that policy design would be more burdensome for a negatively constructed target group. The three most recent proposals, Policies A4, A5, and A6, do not require sex reassignment surgery, medical evaluations, or judicial approvals. They only require a simple administrative action on behalf of the complainant. As such, the recent passage of policy A6 into law has been met with acclaim by activists (Schmall 2012).

Finally, our general findings contradict our hypothesis regarding the framing of these policies. Rather than following the experience of gay and lesbian policy proposals, frames for policy allowing trans individuals to change social names do not focus on an equality frame. Rather, as indicated by table 2.5, only 21 percent of all frames in these proposals are equality based. Instead, we observe an equal presence of frames that highlight discrimination faced by trans individuals and the need to pass national legislation to address a pressing issue. To a lesser extent, we also see the presence of pedagogical and international frames, the first of which seeks to educate policymakers on questions of sexuality, and the second of which highlights advances made by other democracies, notably Spain.

Conclusion

This chapter provides an empirical examination of Latin American policies addressing transgender rights and a systematic content analysis of policy design for fourteen policy proposals relating to name changes for trans persons. The proposals are drawn from national legislatures in Brazil, Argentina, and Chile. The sample represents considerable variation in success, with one country adopting a policy (Argentina), and two countries exhibiting policy failure (Brazil and Chile).

The results from this study contribute to a broader understanding of the politics of transgender policy. This work fills an existing gap in the policy literature for transgender rights. In addition to providing descriptive statistics on transgender policy in five issue areas, we explore policy formulation and issue framing in one issue area—the legal right to name changes—in three Latin American countries. Due to the small-n nature of the second part of this study, the results are not generalizable without some caution. Even so, they provide an excellent starting point when considering how transgender policies are designed, in terms of scope of eligibility, procedures for eligibility, issue frames, and rhetoric in general.

Future work should build on the results of this study by incorporating more countries and policy proposals into the analysis. A comprehensive overview of the Latin American experience will allow more concrete evidence of whether or not policy diffusion exists in the region. The results of this study suggest that transnational interest groups are actively involved in constructing policy, at least in the case of Argentina and Chile. In recent proposals, the presence of more inclusive language and less exclusive requirements suggests evidence of policy learning by activists. Aside from broadening the scope of this study, future work would benefit from in-depth interviews with national interest groups to confirm some of the speculation raised above, such as policy diffusion and policy learning. Finally, this study would benefit from consideration of the political institutions within each country, addressing factors such as the ideological composition of the legislatures. Although significant gaps exist in the rights of trans persons, recent trends leave the authors optimistic for future gains in Latin America. The presence of frames employing the language of equal rights, the relative absence of morality frames, and the insertion of pedagogical language suggests that debates over the rights of trans persons occur within a deliberative space amenable to democratic principles. And the recent example of Argentine activists in passing comprehensive gender identity legislation may serve as a model for future policy initiatives by neighboring states. Scholars should remain attentive to the policy successes of this dynamic region.

NOTES

1. Data are available through http://www.latinobarometro.org/latino/LATDatos.jsp.

2. Data are available through http://www.latinobarometro.org/latino/LATDatos.jsp.

3. Data are available through http://www.latinobarometro.org/latino/LATDatos.jsp.

4. *Travesti* is sometimes translated incorrectly as transvestite. For a discussion of *travesti* as a form of gender identity, see Kulick 1997a and 1997b.

5. Although we did not systematically track LGBT officials in Latin America, we do note that Cuba elected its first transgender public official in November 2012. Adela Hernandez was elected as a delegate to the city government of Caibarien in the province of Villa Clara, which also makes her eligible to be selected as a representative to parliament (Associated Press 2012). In 1993, Kátia Tapety was the first *travesti* public official to be elected in Brazil and became the subject of a documentary film in 2012 (Tavares 2012).

6. Subnational governments in some Latin American countries might have policies not captured in our analysis. For example, although Brazil does not allow for same-sex marriages (even though same-sex civil unions have been legal since 2011), the state of Sao Paulo has allowed for same-sex marriages via a court order effective February 2013 (Lavers 2012a).

For comparative purposes, our interest is in national-level policy. Subnational governments in some Latin American countries likely have policies not captured in our analysis. For example, Rosario, Argentina, and nearly half of Brazilian states prohibit discrimination based on sexual orientation in employment (de la Dehesa 2010; Paoli Itaborahy 2012). Mello, Brito, and Maroj (2012) explain that the piecemeal nature of policy in Brazil is the result of activist engagement with various governmental organs while the national legislature refuses to act. Mello, Brito, and Maroj (2012) recognizes that challenge that this poses to policy analysts.

7. We also corroborated our index with the LGBT Rights and Representation Initiative at the University of North Carolina, Chapel Hill (http://globalstudies.unc.edu/lgbt-representation-and-rights-research-initiative/lgbt-representation-and-rights-research-initiative/). We encountered a number of discrepancies in the policies surveyed in our index (for example, see policy in Brazil). After more extensive cross-checking, we are confident in the accuracy our results.

8. We did not include the Caribbean island group in our analysis. Some of the islands still have laws criminalizing homosexual sodomy and they have seen little progress on LGBT rights. However, the former Dutch colonies in the area have begun to slowly adopt same-sex marriage laws since the Netherlands legalized same-sex marriage in 2001. In December 2012 the Dutch island of Saba became the first jurisdiction in the Caribbean to allow same-sex couples to legally marry (Lavers 2012b).

9. Several policies included in this study cite Spanish legislation. For a discussion of the Spanish case, see Platero (2009, 2011).

10. In short, our analysis could have missed instances where the national government had trans protections in one area, such as housing, but not in employment and public accommodations.

11. The tools available to public policymakers depend upon how they socially construct target groups and the behavioral assumptions underlying these beliefs. Schneider and Ingram (1990) explore five categories of such tools: authority, incentives, capacity-building, symbolic, and learning. For example, the choice of an incentive tool to achieve policy goals reflects a utilitarian, rational actor view of target groups, whereby material benefits coerce behavioral changes given sufficient information and resources. In contrast, the use of a capacity-building tool reflects a view of human nature that assumes bounded rationality: incentives and motivation exist, but information and/or resources are lacking. More provocatively, Schneider and Ingram posit that the historical trend of policy tools could serve as a useful heuristic for identifying these dominant social constructions and assumptions of human behavior (523). Thus, a change in policy tools could be an indication of a more fundamental shift in the social constructions surrounding the target group. Theoretically, a shift from the use of coercive, punitive tools (such as incentives/sanctions) to capacity-building tools may suggest the transition of a target group from deviant to contender (or emergent contender).

12. Searches were conducted in the original language for gender identity (Spanish, *identidad de género*; Portuguese, *identidade de gênero*) and name change (Spanish, *cambio de nombre*; terminology not employed in Brazil).

13. The Chamber of Deputies is generally the name given to the lower house of Latin American legislatures.

14. The coding was based on the original language. The translation to English is for the categories employed.

15. In two instances, a paragraph contained multiple potential frames. This discrep-

ancy was annotated, yet not deemed important enough to merit a nonmutually exclusive coding technique.

16. The Diagnostic and Statistical Manual for the Diagnosis of Mental Disorders (DSM-IV-TR) was published by the American Psychiatric Association in 2000. The DSM-V reclassified gender identity disorder to gender dysphoria.

17. These are a set of international principles regarding universal human rights that outline protections for sexual orientation and gender identity.

REFERENCES

ACLU of Puerto Rico. 2012. "Lesbian, Gay, Bisexual and Transgender Rights." *ACLU*, January 19. http://www.aclu-pr.org/EN/WhatWeDo/LGBTRights/LGBT.htm.

Associated Press. 2012. "Cuban Transsexual Elected to Public Office." *Guardian*, November 18.

Barrionuevo, Alexei. 2010. "Argentina Approves Gay Marriage, in a First for Region." *New York Times*, July 15.

Baumgartner, Frank R., Suzanna L. De Boef, and Amber E. Boydstun. 2008. *The Decline of the Death Penalty and the Discovery of Innocence*. Cambridge: Cambridge University Press.

Benedetti, Marcos Renato. 2005. *Toda Feita: O Corpo e o Gênero das Travestis*. Rio de Janeiro: Editora Garamond.

Bento, Berenice. 2006. *A Reinvenção do Corpo: Sexualidade e Gênero na Experiência Transexual*. Rio de Janeiro: Editora Garamond.

Beyer, Dana. 2012. "Why the Silence over Trans Victories?" *Washington Blade*, December 12.

Borrillo, Danilo. 2010. *Homofobia: Historia e Critica de um Preconceito*. Sao Paulo: Autentica.

Brewer, Paul R. 2008. *Value War: Public Opinion and the Politics of Gay Rights*. Lanham, MD: Rowman and Littlefield.

Butler, Judith. 1990. *Gender Trouble: Feminism and the Subversion of Identity*. New York: Routledge.

Butler, Judith. 2004. *Undoing Gender*. New York: Routledge.

Cahill, Sean. 2007. "The Anti-Gay Marriage Movement." In *The Politics of Same-Sex Marriage*, ed. Craig A. Rimmerman and Clyde Wilcox. Chicago: University of Chicago Press.

Chong, Dennis, and James N. Druckman. 2007. "Framing Theory." *Annual Review of Political Science* 10:103–26.

Colvin, Roddrick. 2007. "The Rise of Transgender-Inclusive Laws: How Well Are Municipalities Implementing Supportive Nondiscrimination Public Employment Policies?" *Review of Public Personnel Administration* 27:336–60.

Colvin, Roddrick. 2008. "Innovations in Non-discrimination Laws: Exploratory Research on Transgender-Inclusive Cities." *Journal of Public Management & Social Policy* 24 (4): 19–34.

Corrales, Javier, and Mario Pecheny. 2010. *The Politics of Sexuality in Latin America: A Reader on Lesbian, Gay, Bisexual, and Transgender Rights*. Pittsburgh: University of Pittsburgh Press.

Costa, Hóracio et. al. 2008. *Retratos do Brasil Homossexual: Fronteiras, Subjetividades, e Desejos*. Sao Paulo: Editora USP.

Currah, Paisley, Richard Juang, and Shannon Minter, eds. 2006. *Transgender Rights*. Minneapolis: University of Minnesota Press.

de la Dehesa, Rafael. 2010. *Queering the Public Sphere in Mexico and Brazil: Sexual Rights Movements in Emerging Democracies*. Durham: Duke University Press.

DeLaet, Debra L., and Rachel Paine Caufield. 2008. "Gay Marriage as a Religious Right: Reframing the Legal Debate over Gay Marriage in the United States." *Polity* 40 (3): 297–320.

Donovan, Mark C. 2001. *Taking Aim: Target Populations and the Wars on AIDS and Drugs*. Washington, DC: Georgetown University Press.

Druckman, James N. 2001. "On the Limits of Framing Effects: Who Can Frame?" *Journal of Politics* 63 (4): 1041–66.

Escobar, Arturo, and Sonia Alvarez. 1992. *The Making of Social Movements in Latin America*. Boulder: Westview Press.

Gender Equality Index. 2011. *International Human Development Indicators*. http://hdrstats.undp.org/en/indicators/68606.html. Accessed May 5, 2012.

Goldberg-Hiller, Jonathan. 2002. *The Limits to Union: Same-Sex Marriage and the Politics of Civil Rights*. Ann Arbor: University of Michigan Press.

Haider-Markel, Donald P. 2010. *Out and Running: Gay and Lesbian Candidates, Elections, and Policy Representation*. Washington, DC: Georgetown University Press.

Haider-Markel, Donald P., and Mark R. Joslyn. 2001. "Gun Policy, Opinion, Tragedy, and Blame Attribution: The Conditional Influence of Issue Frames." *Journal of Politics* 63 (2): 520–43.

Ingram, Helen, Anne L. Schneider, and Peter deLeon. 2007. "Social Construction and Policy Design." In *Theories of the Policy Process*, ed. Paul A. Sabatier, 93–128. Boulder: Westview.

Jones, Rochelle. 2013. "Transgender Rights in Ecuador: A Legal, Spatial, Political, and Cultural Acquittal." *awid*, January 4. http://www.awid.org/News-Analysis/Friday-Files/Transgender-Rights-In-Ecuador-A-Legal-Spatial-Political-And-Cultural-Acquittal.

King, Gary, Robert D. Keohane, and Sidney Verba. 1994. *Designing Social Inquiry*. Princeton: Princeton University Press.

Kulick, Don. 1997a. "A Man in the House: The Boyfriends of Brazilian *Travesti* Prostitutes." *Social Text* 52–53, 15 (3–4): 135–62.

Kulick, Don. 1997b. "The Gender of Brazilian Transgendered Prostitutes." *American Anthropologist* 99 (3): 574–85.

Lavers, Michael K. 2012a. "Brazil's Most Populous State to Allow Same-Sex Marriage." *Washington Blade*, December 21.

Lavers, Michael K. 2012b. "Saba Becomes First Caribbean Island to Legalize Same-Sex Marriage." *Washington Blade*, December 19.

Lavers, Michael K. 2012c. "Uruguay Lawmakers Approve Same-Sex Marriage Bill." *Washington Blade*, December 12.

Lijphart, Arend. 1971. "Comparative Politics and the Comparative Method." *American Political Science Review* 65 (3): 682–93.

Marcos, Natalia, and Tatiana Cordero. 2009. "Situation of Lesbian and Trans Women in

Ecuador." Shadow report, International Covenant on Civil and Political Rights. Quito, Ecuador: Taller de Comunicación Mujer/Global Rights/IGLHRC.

Mello, Luiz, Walderes Brito, and Daniela Maroj. 2012. "Políticas públicas para a população LGBT no Brasil: Notas sobre alcances e possibilidades." *cadernos pagu* 39 (July–December): 403–29.

Mettler, Suzanne. 2005. "Policy Feedback Effects for Collective Action: Lessons from Veterans' Programs." In *Routing the Opposition: Social Movements, Public Policy, and Democracy,* ed. David S. Meyer, Valerie Jenness, and Helen Ingram. Minneapolis: University of Minnesota Press.

Miles, Matthew B., and A. Michael Huberman. 1994. *Qualitative Data Analysis: An Expanded Sourcebook.* 2nd ed. London: Sage Publications.

Minter, Shannon Price. 2006. "Do Transsexuals Dream of Gay Rights?" In *Transgender Rights,* ed. Paisley Currah, Richard Juang, and Shannon Price Minter. Minneapolis: University of Minnesota Press.

Mooney, Christopher Z. 2000. "The Decline of Federalism and the Rise of Morality-Policy Conflict in the United States." *Publius* (Winter–Spring): 171–88.

Mott, Luiz. 2011. *Boletim do Grupo Gay da Bahia: 1981–2005.* Salvador: Editora Grupo Gay da Bahia.

Mucciaroni, G. 2008. *Same Sex, Different Politics: Success and Failure in the Struggles over Gay Rights.* Chicago: University of Chicago Press.

Nownes, Anthony J. 2010. "Density Dependent Dynamics in the Population of Transgender Interest Groups in the United States, 1964–2005." *Social Science Quarterly* 91 (3): 689–703.

Paoli Itaborahy, Lucas. 2012. *State Sponsored Homophobia: A World Survey of Laws Criminalising Same-Sex Sexual Acts between Consenting Adults.* Brussels: International Lesbian, Gay, Bisexual, Trans and Intersex Association. Accessed January 21, 2013. http://old.ilga.org/Statehomophobia/ILGA_State_Sponsored_Homophobia_2012.pdf.

Platero, Raquel. 2009. "Discriminación por orientación sexual e identidad de género." In *Estudios interdisciplinares sobre igualdad,* ed. Enrique Álvarez, Ángela Figueruelo, and Laura Nuño, 169–82. Madrid: Iustel.

Platero, Raquel. 2011. "The Narratives of Transgender Rights Mobilization in Spain." *Sexualities* 14:597–614.

Projeto de Lei 1281. 2011. Accessed February 9, 2012. http://www.camara.gov.br/proposicoesWeb/fichadetramitacao?idProposicao=501425.

Projeto de Lei 6655. 2006. Accessed June 16, 2013. http://www.senado.gov.br/atividade/materia/getPDF.asp?t=51002&tp=1.

Projeto de Lei n. 70. 1995. Accessed February 9, 2012. http://www.camara.gov.br/proposicoesWeb/fichadetramitacao?idProposicao=15009.

Projeto de Lei n. 2976. 2008. Accessed February 9, 2012. http://www.camara.gov.br/proposicoesWeb/fichadetramitacao?idProposicao=386164.

Projeto de Lei n. 3727. 1997. Accessed February 9, 2012. http://www.camara.gov.br/proposicoesWeb/fichadetramitacao?idProposicao=20118.

Projeto de Lei n. 5872. 2005. Accessed February 9, 2012. http://www.camara.gov.br/proposicoesWeb/fichadetramitacao?idProposicao=299666.

Projeto de Lei n. 6.655-B. 2006. Accessed April 29, 2012. http://www.camara.gov.br/proposicoesWeb/fichadetramitacao?idProposicao=315120.

Proyecto de Ley n. 1736-D. 2009. Ley de identidad de género. Accessed April 29, 2012. http://www.diputados.gov.ar/proyectos/proyecto.jsp?id=104839.

Proyecto de Ley n. 18.620. 2009. Derecho a la identidad de género y al cambio de nombre y sexo en documentos identificatorios. Accessed April 29, 2012. http://www.par lamento.gub.uy/leyes/AccesoTextoLey.asp?Ley=18620&Anchor=.

Proyecto de Ley n. 1879-D. 2011. Ley de identidad de género. Accessed April 29, 2012. http://www1.hcdn.gov.ar/proyxml/expediente.asp?fundamentos=si&numexp=1879-D-2011.

Proyecto de Ley n. 5259-D. 2007. Ley de identidad de género. Accessed April 29, 2012. http://www.diputados.gov.ar/proyectos/proyecto.jsp?id=91135.

Proyecto de Ley n. 5679-18. 2008. Modifica la ley N° 4.808, sobre Registro Civil e Identificación, permitiendo el cambio de sexo de las personas con disforia de sexo. Accessed April 30, 2012. http://www.senado.cl/appsenado/templates/tramitacion/in dex.php?boletin_ini=5679–18.

Proyecto de Ley n. 6.913-07. 2007. Relativo a la identidad sexual o de género. Accessed April 30, 2012. http://www.senado.cl/appsenado/templates/tramitacion/index. php?boletin_ini=6913–07.

Proyecto de Ley n. 7243-D. 2010. Ley de identidad de género. Accessed May 1, 2012. http://www.diputados.gov.ar/proyectos/proyecto.jsp?id=120220.

Proyecto de Ley n. 7643-D. 2010. Ley de atención sanitaria para la reasignación del sexo. Accessed April 29, 2012. http://www1.hcdn.gov.ar/proyxml/expediente. asp?fundamentos=si&numexp=7643-D-2010.

Proyecto de Ley n. 7644-D. 2010. Ley de reconocimiento y respeto a la identidad de género. Accessed May 1, 2012. http://www.diputados.gov.ar/proyectos/proyecto. jsp?id=120555.

Proyecto de Ley n. 8126-D. 2010. Regimen para el reconocimento y respeto a la identidad de género. Accessed May 1, 2012. http://www.diputados.gov.ar/proyectos/ proyecto.jsp?id=121011.

Proyecto de Ley. 26.743. 2012. Identidad de género. May 9. http://www.infoleg.gov.ar/ infolegInternet/anexos/195000-199999/197860/norma.htm.

Rochefort, David A., and Roger W. Cobb. 1994. The Politics of Problem Definition: Shaping the Policy Agenda. Lawrence: University Press of Kansas.

Rom, Mark Carl. 2007. "Introduction: The Politics of Same-Sex Marriage." In The Politics of Same-Sex Marriage, ed. Craig A. Rimmerman and Clyde Wilcox. Chicago: University of Chicago Press.

Salinas, Liurka Otsuka, and Soledad Arriagáda Barrera. 2011. "Informe Annual Sobre Derechos Humanos de Personas Trans, Lesbianas, Gays y Bisexuales en el Perú 2011." Lima, Peru: PROMSEX Centro de Promoción y Defensa de los Derechos Sexuales y Reproductivos and Red Peruana TLGB Red Peruana de Trans, Lesbianas, Gays y Bisexuales.

Schattschneider, E. E. 1960. The Semi-Sovereign People. New York: Holt, Reinhardt and Winston.

Schlager, Edella. 2007. "A Comparison of Frameworks, Theories, and Models of Policy Processes." In Theories of the Policy Process, ed. Paul A. Sabatier. Boulder: Westview Press.

Schmall, Emily. 2012. "Transgender Advocates Hail Law Easing Rules in Argentina." New York Times, May 24.

Schneider, Anne, and Helen Ingram. 1990. "Behavioral Assumptions of Policy Tools." *Journal of Politics* 52:510–29.

Schneider, Anne, and Helen Ingram. 1997. *Policy Design for Democracy.* Lawrence: University Press of Kansas.

Stepan, Alfred. 2000. "Brazil's Decentralized Federalism: Bringing Governments Closer to the Citizens?" *Daedalus* 129 (2): 145–69.

Stone, Deborah A. 1989. "Causal Stories and the Formation of Policy Agendas." *Political Science Quarterly* 104 (2): 281–300.

Tadlock, Barry L., C. Ann Gordon, and Elizabeth Popp. 2007. "Framing the Issue of Same-Sex Marriage: Traditional Values versus Equal Rights." In *The Politics of Same-Sex Marriage,* ed. Craig A. Rimmerman and Clyde Wilcox. Chicago: University of Chicago Press.

Tavares, Jamila. 2012. "Primeiro *travesti* eleito no país é tema de documentário no Festival de Brasília." *G1Globo,* September 19. http://g1.globo.com/pop-arte/cinema/noticia/2012/09/1-travesti-eleita-no-pais-e-tema-de-documentario-no-festival-de-brasilia.html.

Taylor, Jami K. 2007. "Transgender Identities and Public Policy in the United States: The Relevance for Public Administration." *Administration Society* 39:833–56.

Taylor, Jami K., and Daniel C. Lewis. 2012. "The Advocacy Coalition Framework and Transgender Inclusion in LGBT Rights Activism." Presented at the 2012 Midwest Political Science Association, April, Chicago.

Taylor, Jami K., Daniel C. Lewis, Matthew L. Jacobsmeier, and Brian DiSarro. 2012. "Content and Complexity in Policy Reinvention and Diffusion: Gay and Transgender-Inclusive Laws against Discrimination." *State Politics & Policy Quarterly* 12 (1): 75–98.

Taylor, Jami K., Barry L. Tadlock, and Sarah Poggione. 2014. "State LGBT Rights Policy Outliers: Transsexual Birth Certificate Laws." *American Review of Politics* 34 (Winter 2013–14): 245–70.

Venturi, Gustavo. 2011. *Diversidade sexual e homofobia no Brasil.* Sao Paulo: Fundaçao Perseu Abramo.

Weber, Robert P. 1990. *Basic Content Analysis.* 2nd ed. London: Sage.

Wiener, Joshua G., and Tomas M. Koontz. 2010. "Shifting Winds: Explaining Variation in State Policies to Promote Small-Scale Wind Energy." *Policy Studies Journal* 38 (4): 629–51.

Yin, Robert K. 2003. *Case Study Research: Design and Methods.* 3rd ed. Thousand Oaks, CA: Sage.

Advocacy and Interest Groups

Anthony J. Nownes

3 | Interest Groups and Transgender Politics

Opportunities and Challenges

Transgender people perhaps have better representation today than they did even 15 years ago. Research indicates that there are now over a dozen nationally active transgender advocacy groups in the United States (Nownes 2010), and there are perhaps hundreds more operating in states and localities across America. Moreover, numerous LGB groups such as the National Gay and Lesbian Task Force, GLAAD (Gay & Lesbian Alliance Against Defamation), and the Human Rights Campaign now work on behalf of transgender people. In short, transgender advocacy is alive and well in the United States.

Yet developments in transgender interest group politics over the past 20 years have not been uniformly positive. For example, although the population of transgender interest groups grew in the latter part of the last century, that growth seems to have stalled in this century. In addition, transgender rights groups now compete openly for members and support with LGB groups—groups that have wider constituencies and thus may focus less on issues of interest to transgender individuals than do standalone transgender rights groups. In this chapter, I ask: What is the current state of national transgender interest group advocacy in the United States? In addressing this question, I pay special attention to density dependence theory, a theory that purports to explain population dynamics within interest group populations. This theory is popular among sociologists, and has begun receiving attention from political scientists. It is an intriguing and convincing lens through which to view the development of transgender rights interest group representation. After addressing this question, I ask another: What challenges face transgender interest group advocates and their allies in the new century? Political science and related disciplines have long theorized about the trajectory of social movements and interest group populations. I address this question in an attempt to discover what existing theories can tell us about the possible future of transgender interest group representation in the United States.

Transgender Advocacy in the United States:
A Brief Overview

Interest group scholars define the term *interest group* quite broadly to include virtually any organization that attempts to influence government decisions. The interest group universe in the United States is incredibly large and almost unfathomably varied. Estimates suggest that there are upwards of 200,000 interest groups working to influence government decisions in the United States, and few constituencies have no representation by interest groups (Nownes 2013). Of course, not all groups and causes are represented equally before government. Virtually every reputable study shows that the interests of America's largest business institutions are vastly overrepresented before government (Baumgartner et al. 2009; Baumgartner and Leech 1998; Salisbury 1984).

Transgender interest groups are now part of the national interest group universe. So what is a transgender interest group? In an earlier study (Nownes 2010, 692–93), I defined a transgender interest group very broadly as "an interest group whose primary political purpose is to advocate on behalf of transgender men, and/or women, and/or minors." This definition excludes groups that work on transgender issues but have other concerns as well. Thus, it excludes LGBT groups such as those mentioned above, as well as broad-based civil liberties and civil rights groups such as the American Civil Liberties Union and the NAACP, as well as business firms, trade associations, labor unions, and other types of groups that might occasionally weigh in on transgender rights issues.

The Population of Transgender Interest Groups in America

In an earlier article on nationally active transgender interest groups in the United States (Nownes 2010), I found that between the years 1964–2005, 26 such groups were founded.[1] Identifying these groups was not easy. I formulated an initial list by using the *Encyclopedia of Associations* (Gale Research Company 1964–2010).[2] For each edition of this encyclopedia of groups, I turned to the index and looked up the words "transgender" and

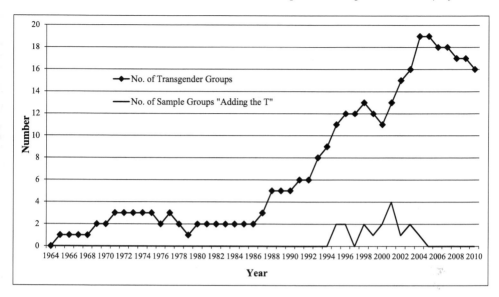

Fig. 3.1. The number of nationally active transgender rights interest groups in the United States and the number of sample LGB groups "adding the T," 1964–2010. (Data compiled by the authors.)

"transsexual." The groups listed under these headings for the period under study comprised my original master list of groups. From here, I consulted written histories of transgender politics (Califia 2003; Currah, Juang, and Minter 2006; Meyerowitz 2002) in an attempt to find the names of any additional transgender interest groups. Next, I scanned websites of interest to the transgender community (e.g., ABGender.com 2008; Delta V 2002; and Transsexual Road Map 2008), searching for the names of groups that I may have missed. From here, I used the Factiva database to locate scholarly articles and news stories that may have mentioned specific transgender groups. Finally, I e-mailed a small number of transgender activists and asked them about transgender groups in the United States. I obtained the names of a few additional groups in this way. The top series in figure 3.1 charts the evolution of the transgender interest group sector during this period. The bottom series in figure 3.1 shows the year that organizations in the sample of LGBT groups "added the T" to their mission statements (I will discuss this series subsequently). The first nationally active transgender interest group was founded in 1964. That group, the pioneering Erickson Educational Foundation, was primarily a grant-making and educational organization. As the top series in figure 3.1 shows, from 1964 to the mid-1980s the population of nationally active transgender groups remained very small. In the mid-1980s, however, the population began to grow in size. Between 1986 and 2005, the number of groups grew from only two to 19. Between 2005 and 2010, the size of population contracted a bit, as no new groups were founded and a few groups fell by the wayside.

So what explains the population trajectory that we see in the top series in figure 3.1? In other words, why did the population stay so small for so long, and then grow to the extent that it did when it did, and then level off? In addressing this question, I tested two general theories that purport to explain the dynamics of interest group populations. The first theory, the theory of political opportunity, rests upon the concept of "political opportunity structure" (or POS; see Jenkins, Jacobs, and Agnone 2003; Meyer and Minkoff 2004). The POS facing a population of groups and the activists associated with them is broadly defined as "*the institutional features or informal political alignments of a given political system*" (McAdam 1995, 224, italics in original). Essentially, POS theories posit that external political conditions determine when and which interest groups form, survive, and die. POS theorists David S. Meyer and Douglas R. Imig explain: "interest group formation and survival reflects the external political environment" (Meyer and Imig 1993, 262). When political opportunities expand, "new groups form and existing groups flourish" (262). When political opportunities wane, fewer groups form and extant groups languish. The biggest problem with POS theories is their opaque and inconsistent conceptualization of "political opportunity structure." In sum, the POS facing a population of groups may consist of anything outside the groups themselves. This difficulty with conceptualization notwithstanding, many scholars of interest groups and social movements agree that understanding where groups come from and how they develop requires that we pay close attention to contextual factors.

The second theory that I tested was density dependence theory, a general theory pulled from biology and posited by organizational ecologists to explain trajectories in populations of groups. The theory flows from two general observations about populations of groups. The first is that within an organizational population, an increase in population density (that is, the number of groups in the population) affects both (a) competition between groups, which is defined as the extent to which like groups vie for resources such as money, human capital, members, large donors, and technologies (Haider-Markel 1997); and (b) legitimation, which is defined as the degree to which an organizational form is widely seen as a socially acceptable "way to organize collectively within some realm of activity" (Ranger-Moore, Banaszak-Holl, and Hannan 1991, 38). The second observation is that legitimation and competition affect founding rates (that is, the rate at which new groups are formed).[3] Within an organizational population, "increased density initially enhances a population's (constitutive) legitimation, thereby raising its founding rate." However, persistent increases in density (again, the number of groups in the population) "eventually generate intense competition, which depresses founding rates" (Carroll and Hannan 2000, 239). Thus, the relationship between density and the founding rate within an organizational population is shaped like an inverted U.

To summarize, the theory of density dependence suggests that in a population of groups (such as transgender interest groups) the founding rate increases up to a point with population size as legitimation processes dominate. Beyond a certain point, increases in density lead to heightened competition between groups. This causes the population to decline.

I tested these theories by utilizing a statistical technique called Poisson regression (a variation of regression that accounts for truncated data) in which *Number of groups founded per year* was my dependent variable (making year the unit of analysis). I utilized two independent variables to test political opportunity theory. First, I used James Stimson's well-known *Policy mood* variable, which essentially measures public support for more government spending or activity, or both, on domestic political issues (Stimson 2008). Second, I used an original variable called *Transgender laws,* which measured the number of jurisdictions in the United States per year that had laws prohibiting discrimination on the basis of gender identity or expression. I obtained the data for this variable from the Transgender Law and Policy Institute (2007). These variables essentially tested the notion that the political opportunity structure facing transgender activists and advocates affected transgender interest group mobilization (as per Jenkins, Jacobs, and Agnone 2003; Meyer and Minkoff 2004) by testing the basic POS notion that transgender group foundings increased because the public became more liberal and more jurisdictions protected transgender people.[4] To test density dependence theory, I used two variables— *Density*, which was the number of transgender groups in existence at the start of each year, and *Density squared*. A positive coefficient on *Density* and a negative coefficient on *Density squared* would support density dependence theory. I also included a variable called *Period 2* in the model to account for other changes in the larger environment in which transgender groups operated.

My quantitative analysis (the results of which are provided in table 3.1) provided no support for political opportunity theory, as the coefficient on neither *Policy mood* nor *Transgender laws* in my model was statistically significant. In short, my results showed that increased policy liberalism and an increase in the number of jurisdictions protecting transgender people from discrimination did *not* drive transgender interest group population growth from 1986 to 2005, and were not related to population contraction after 2005. My results did not suggest, in other words, that transgender interest groups proliferated when they did because the public became more liberal, or because the political and institutional features facing transgender interest groups and advocates became more favorable. Moreover, the lack of statistically significant POS variables in my models showed that it also was not the case that a conservative onslaught in the early 2000s led to recent population contraction. So what *does* explain the population trajectory portrayed in figure 3.1? My quantitative analyses provided strong support for the theory of density dependence. In my models, as table 3.1 shows, the coefficients on *Density* and *Density squared* were statistically significant and in the expected direction. Here is what that means substantively. As figure 3.1 shows, the number of groups stayed low for approximately 20 years as the pioneering young groups of the 1960s struggled to become legitimate concerns and few new groups were founded. Potential group entrepreneurs possibly did not see the "transgender interest group" as a viable and legitimate means of collective action. After 20 years, the survival and relative success of a couple of groups signaled to other transgender advocates and potential entrepreneurs that collective action via the transgender rights interest group was possible and even desirable. One group after another formed in the 1980s, and the concept of the "national transgender interest group" became widely accepted (or "legitimated" in the parlance of organizational scholars) among transgender activists, leaders, and donors. In short, activists and group entrepreneurs formed new transgender groups, older groups survived and thrived, and the population grew as legitimation processes dominated. However, the dynamic changed by the end of the period. Indeed, the population ceased to grow, and it appears now to be in slight decline. This is what the theory of density dependence predicts—as the population grew to a certain size (around 20 transgender groups), existing groups began to compete with one another for limited resources. Late in the period under study, competition overtook legitimation as the primary process affecting the transgender interest group population. As resources required for successful foundings were monopolized by existing groups, new groups failed to materialize (and a few extant groups went out of business). The paucity of new foundings has led to population stasis and perhaps even slight decline.

Of course, there may be alternative explanations for the population trajectory that we see in figure 3.1. It may be the case, for example, that shifts in public opinion (which I did not consider in my earlier study because public opinion data for the entire period under study do not to my knowledge exist) explain the trajectory apparent in figure 3.1. Another possibility is that rising affluence among citizens as a whole or among transgender advocates and allies, or both, specifically explain the population trajectory. Still another possibility is that attacks from feminists and conservatives in the late 1980s and 1990s led to an increase in transgender group foundings (as transgender people felt politically threatened and gathered together to protect their interests), and a relative dampening of these attacks (especially from feminists) later in the period led to stasis. We also cannot discount the possibility that the politicization of an emerging and distinct transgender identity in the 1980s and 1990s contributed to the proliferation of groups evident in figure 3.1. In the end, I cannot speak to other factors that may have affected the population trajectory we see in figure 3.1. However, my analysis strongly suggests that density dependence

TABLE 3.1. Determinants of Founding Dates of Politically Relevant, Nationally Active Transgender Interest Groups in the United States, 1964–2005: Poisson Regression Results

Dependent Variable: Number of Groups Founded per Year		
Constant	−.8044***	(.2575)
Period 2	−.4969	(.3644)
Density	3.886***	(1.278)
Density^2	−4.287***	(1.595)
Policy mood	−.2196	(.3078)
Transgender laws	.8838	(.5756)
N	41	
Log-likelihood	−35.6003	
Pseudo R^2	.1782	
Prob > χ^2	.0087	

Source: Author's data based on Nownes (2010: 698).
Note: The dependent variable is the number of groups founded in each year. Cells represent the unstandardized coefficients of a Poisson regression model. Standard errors are in parentheses. Tests for overdispersion were negative. All independent variables are lagged one year. All independent variables are orthogonalized.
***$p < .01$ (two-tailed test)

theory, which zeroes in on competition between groups as a key driver of population dynamics, provides at least part of the explanation for the trends evident in figure 3.1.

The Role of Competition

But these results and those I have published earlier ignore much of the *actual politics* of transgender interest group advocacy—that is, the real world processes by which activists and group entrepreneurs started new groups and worked to keep them afloat. Moreover, my statistical analyses failed to account for changes in public opinion on transgender issues, as well as the leadership of politicians who have championed transgender rights. In short, I acknowledge that these findings might be a small part of the explanation for the rise of transgender interest groups and the subsequent population stasis. Yet a part of the explanation they likely are.

Why are my findings important? The primary answer is that density dependence theory in general and my findings in particular draw attention to the following important point about interest group politics, a point that many scholars and activists tend to overlook and one that students of transgender politics and advocacy need to keep in mind: interest groups often are forced to compete with each other. Importantly, this competition is not what most people understand as interest group competition. Virtually everyone realizes that opposing interest groups compete with each other for policy influence. For example, Handgun Control Inc. competes with the National Rifle Association for influence on gun-related legislation, and ExxonMobil and BP compete with the Sierra Club and the National Wildlife Federation for influence over environmental legislation. However, competition also takes place among groups that are on the same side of an issue. Thus, while the Sierra Club and the National Wildlife Federation tend to be on the same side in policy battles, they are on opposing sides when it comes to attracting resources from the members and large donors that provide capital to keep them afloat.

Table 3.2 contains a list of nationally active transgender groups in the United States from 1964 to 2010 (some of which are now defunct). Some of the groups listed are/were relatively large concerns, while others are/were small and obscure. In one sense the groups all work(ed) toward the same goal—the adoption of laws and policies that benefit transgender individuals. In another sense, however, the groups are/were competing. Thus, while the Sylvia Rivera Law Project and the National Center for

TABLE 3.2. List of Politically Relevant, Nationally Active Transgender Interest Groups in the U.S., 1964–2010

Organization	Year Founded–Year Disbanded
American Educational Gender Information Service (AEGIS)	1990–1998
Erickson Educational Foundation (EEF)	1964–1977
FTMInternational	1986–
Gender Education and Advocacy (GEA)	2000–2005
Gender Education and Media (GEM)	2001–
Gender Public Advocacy Coalition (GenderPAC)	1995–2009
Harry Benjamin International Gender Dysphoria Association (HBIGDA; now The World Professional Association for Transgender Health [WPATH])	1979–
International Conference on Transgender Law and Employment Policy (ICTLEP)	1992–1997
The International Foundation for Gender Education (IFGE)	1987–
Intersex Society of North America	1993–
It's Time, America!	1994–1998
National Center for Transgender Equality (NCTE)	2003–
National Coalition of Transgender Advocacy Groups	2010–
National Transgender Advocacy Coalition (NTAC)	1999–
National Transsexual Counseling Unit (NTCU)	1968–1975
The Renaissance Transgender Association	1987–
Survivor Project	1997–2010
Sylvia Rivera Law Project	2002–
Transgender American Veterans Association (TAVA)	2003–
Transgender Community of Police and Sheriffs (TCOPS)	2001–2007
Transgender Law and Policy Institute (TLPI)	2000–2010
Transgender Legal Defense and Education Fund (TLDEF)	2003–
Transgender Nation	1992–1994
Transgendered Officers Protect and Serve (TOPS)	1995–2001
Transsexual Action Organization (TAO)	1970–1978
Transsexual Menace	1994–
Tri-Ess	1976–

Source: Author's data.

Transgender Equality may be on the same side in political battles, they are on opposing sides in the ongoing battle for resources. There is a finite amount of resources available to transgender interest groups, and a dollar that goes to the Sylvia Rivera Law Project is a dollar that does not go to the National Center for Transgender Equality. In short, competition among transgender interest groups remains a fact of life for transgender activists and leaders. To understand the past, present, and future of national transgender interest group advocacy, we need to keep this in mind.

Of course, there is strong evidence that groups within the same general population often work hard to avoid competing with each other. Haider-Markel (1997, 910–11), for example, shows that LGB groups "avoid direct competition . . . by sharing available space through adaptation into separate issue niches." An issue niche is a narrow issue space that can be likened to a specialty. Haider-Markel suggests, for example, that a group such as Gay and Lesbian Parents Coalition International (now known as Family Pride Coalition) avoids competition with other LGB groups by focusing narrowly on the concerns of LGB parents rather than gay and lesbian and bisexual people per se. Similarly, the Gay and Lesbian Victory Fund operates as a political action committee (that is, a PAC, which collects money and donates it to candidates for office) and thus avoids competition with non-PAC LGB groups that engage in activities unrelated to the electoral process. Although there is general evidence that groups seek niches to avoid competition (Browne 1990), my data suggest that this sort of adaptive behavior either has not happened among nationally focused transgender groups or it has not worked to prevent population stasis. Groups may be working to avoid competition, but figure 3.1 and my statistical results suggest that competition, which was not operant in the years of population growth in the late 1980s, the 1990s, and early 2000s, continues to affect the size of the transgender group population. Part of the reason that stasis has occurred at such a relatively low level of population density is that the carrying capacity of the national transgender rights interest group universe is probably relatively small. Compared to other prominent minority groups, there are not very many trans people in the population (more about this later). Many of these individuals are also socially and economically marginalized (Grant et al. 2011). Regardless, the following is very clear: competition matters.

Competition and "Adding the T"

In sum, transgender interest groups compete with one another for valuable resources. Yet, they also compete with LGB groups that have "added the T." In the past decade, a great deal has been written about this phenomenon of "adding the T"—that is, the occurrence of LGB (lesbian, gay, and bisexual) groups grafting on a "T" (for transgender) to their mission statements (Armstrong 2002; Devor and Matte 2004; Green 2004). By 2010, virtually every leading LGB interest group in the United States had "added the T," thus changing their missions and advertising that they now worked to advocate on behalf of transgender individuals as well as gay, lesbian, and bisexual individuals.

Why did LGB groups "add the T?" In line with my previous research (Nownes 2010), I suspected that density dependence theory was part of the answer. In the parlance of organizational theory, "adding the T" is called boundary expansion. Boundary expansion occurs when an organization attempts to attract a new, previously untapped constituency to recruit as members and donors. In this case, LGB organizations "adding the T" was an attempt to serve a new market of constituents—transgender individuals and their allies. My hypothesis was straightforward—I believed that the variable that would best explain boundary expansion among LGB groups was the size of the national transgender interest group universe (that is, transgender interest group density). I based my hypothesis on the notion that competition and legitimation are key drivers of organizational vital events (again, a key notion of density dependence theory).

To test this notion empirically, I conducted a small quantitative study of LGB groups in the United States. To do this, I picked a small quota sample of 18 nationally active LGB groups in the United States (from a list of nearly 100; see table 3.3). This quota sample reflects a cross-section of differently sized LGB groups and it includes prominent organizations like the Human Rights Campaign. Again, according to density dependence theory, the number of transgender organizations in the United States will affect both legitimation and competition. At low levels of density legitimation processes will dominate. Therefore, when the population is small, the addition of new groups to the population increases the legitimacy of the organizational form, "transgender interest group." This increased legitimation will inspire the formation of new transgender rights groups. My basic hypothesis was that increased legitimation would also encourage extant LGB organizations to expand their boundaries to serve transgender individuals. After selecting the 18 groups for my sample, I then determined if and when each group "added the T." From here, I conducted a quantitative analysis in which I sought to determine why each group in the sample "added the T" when it did. Specifically, I used Cox proportional hazards regression to analyze the life history of each sample group. Cox regression essentially allowed me to estimate the probability that a

TABLE 3.3. A Sample of Nationally Active LGB Groups in the United States and When They "Added the T"

Organization	Year Founded	Year the Group "Added the T"
1. Affirmation: Gay and Lesbian Mormons	1977	2003
2. Coalition of Lesbians and Gays Everywhere (COLAGE)	1990	1995
3. DignityUSA	1969	1995
4. Family Equality Council (FEC)	1979	1998
5. Gay and Lesbian Alliance Against Defamation (GLAAD)	1985	1999
6. Gay and Lesbian Advocates and Defenders (GLAD)	1978	2001
7. Gay, Lesbian, and Straight Education Network (GLSEN)	1990	2001
8. Gay and Lesbian Victory Fund (GLVF)	1991	2001
9. Human Rights Campaign (HRC)	1980	2001
10. Integrity	1974	2000
11. Lambda Legal Defense and Education Fund	1973	2002
12. Log Cabin Republicans	1978	—[a]
13. Lutherans Concerned	1974	2000
14. National Center for Lesbian Rights (NCLR)	1977	1996
15. National Gay and Lesbian Task Force (NGLTF)	1973	1996
16. Parents and Friends of Lesbians and Gays (PFLAG)	1981	1998
17. Senior Action in a Gay Environment (SAGE)	1977	2004
18. Servicemembers Legal Defense Fund	1993	2003

Source: Author's data.
[a]Log Cabin Republicans have not "added the T" as of June 2013.

sample LGB group would "add the T" in any given year. The dependent variable in my model was *Added the T,* which was coded o if the group did not "add the T" in a given year and 1 if it did. The independent variables of interest were *Transgender density,* which was a measure of the number of transgender groups in existence at the beginning of the year, and *Transgender density squared.*

My results, which are not fully shown here but are available in my 2009 manuscript (Nownes and Kelly 2009), supported density dependence theory. The coefficients on both *Transgender density* and *Transgender density squared* were significant in numerous models. This means that the likelihood of boundary expansion among LGB groups was profoundly affected by the size of the transgender interest group population. Specifically, I discovered that the effect of the number of transgender organizations in the United States on boundary expansion by LGB groups was curvilinear. That is, as the population of transgender groups increased in size, the number of LGB groups expanding their boundaries to include transgender concerns grew as well (as legitimation processes dominated). When the population of transgender groups became relatively large, however, competition pressures slowed the rate of boundary expansion by LGB organizations. In short, I found that LGB groups "added the T" just when transgender advocacy groups proliferated. To make this point graphically, I added the bottom series in figure 3.1, which shows when groups in my small sample of LGB organizations "added the T."

It is certainly worth noting that I found that the likelihood of boundary expansion was influenced by the political opportunity structure facing LGB groups. Specifically, I found that the number of LGB groups expanding their boundaries to include the interests of transgender individuals moved in the same direction as public policy liberalism and the number of laws protecting transgender people adopted in the United States. I also found that age mattered—younger organizations were less likely to change than older ones. Why this occurred is unclear but beyond the scope of this study.

Why This Matters: The Future of Transgender Advocacy

To summarize, first I provided a graphical history of the national transgender rights interest group population in the United States. I showed that the population of transgender interest groups started small (as all interest group populations do) in the 1960s, stayed small until the mid-1980s, and then grew substantially until 2005. Since 2005, the population has stabilized at a level slightly lower than its peak. Second, and based on my earlier article (Nownes 2010), I argued that this pattern of population growth and then stasis is explained partially by density dependence theory, a theory that explains interest group population dynamics by emphasizing the dual processes of legitimation and competition. Competition among transgender rights interest groups, I noted, continues to be an important determinant of population size, as such groups, despite possible *niche-seeking, continue to vie for limited resources. This competition helps to explain the recent population stasis that I demonstrate in figure 3.1—there simply are not many new resources that group founders can draw upon to create new groups. Third, I presented evidence that boundary expansion among LGB groups in the United States in recent years—that is, "adding the T"—is also partially explained by density dependence theory. That is, LGB groups "added the T" just as transgender groups proliferated and transgender advocacy became "legitimate," in effect entering a "new market" created by thriving transgender rights interest groups. Boundary expansion has slowed as competition processes have come to dominate.[5]

In general, my empirical studies show that national transgender advocacy is alive and well in the United States. Given the number of "stand alone" and fully inclusive LGBT groups, national representation of transgender interests is as extensive as it has been at any time in U.S. history. However, there is more to what I have presented here than a rosy picture of a relatively sizeable and robust population of groups that address transgender rights. A more careful look at my empirical findings reveals a number of difficulties that transgender advocates, allies, and activists face going forward—difficulties I refer to collectively as the challenges of transgender advocacy in the new century. In the rest of this chapter, I will highlight some of these challenges. In doing so I will address the following question: What does the future hold for transgender rights interest groups? I will address this question through the lens of theories of organizational development, social movement development, political participation, and public opinion.

Population Stasis

Figure 3.1 clearly shows that the national transgender rights interest group population has ceased to grow. In fact, it has contracted a bit in recent years. Thus, one of the primary challenges facing transgender advocates is interest group population stasis. It is not necessarily the case that more groups are better than fewer groups. If existing groups are growing, then the lack of new groups does not present a serious problem to supporters of transgender rights. However, all things being equal, more groups are better than fewer groups. Clearly, for example, the large size of the LGB interest group universe has contributed to some of the victories that these groups have won in the last two decades. Thus, population stasis represents a challenge to transgender advocates and allies.

Population stasis is reversible. Organizational theorists have found that population resurgence does occur. In other words, it is not the case that once a population reaches a point of stasis it inevitably contracts or stays the same size. What factors can lead to population resurgence? In general, the answer appears to be changes in environmental conditions (Carroll and Hannan 2000, 239–40). Most of the research on population resurgence focuses on business firms and comes from business schools and sociologists. Thus, it has little to say about what sorts of changes in environmental conditions may lead to a resurgence of the transgender interest group population. However, there is a small body of political science research that speaks to what sorts of changes might spur new growth in the population of these groups.

One such change is the election of more transgender people to public office. Over the years, transgender interest groups and advocates have focused a great deal of their energy on policy. This, of course, makes sense. However, population resurgence is unlikely to occur without more electoral activity by these groups. I base this conclusion on the fact that descriptive representation can spur people to political and collective action. Haider-Markel (2010, 13) notes that "Atkeson (2003) and Wolbrecht and Campbell (2007) . . . report that increased female representation is associated with increases in female political participation, especially among young women." Haider-Markel (13) also notes that Barreto (2007) shows that "the presence of Latino candidates [on the ballot] increased mobilization among Latinos" and that "Banducci, Donovan, and Karp (2004) find that increasing descriptive representation in legislature [sic] tends to increase minority group political participation." Together, these studies imply that more transgender people running for and winning elective office may increase political participation among transgender people, which may lead to population resurgence, as more transgender people and their allies form new groups.

Public data sources suggest there is only one openly transgender person serving in elected office in the United States—Stu Rasmussen, the mayor of Silverton, Oregon (Wilson 2008). Another transgender person,

Stacie Laughton, was elected to the state legislature in New Hampshire in 2012. However, she resigned before taking office when questions were raised as to whether it would be legally permissible for her to serve given a previous felony fraud conviction (Rios 2012). There may be more, and several transgender candidates have run for office in recent years. Even if that estimate is off, there is no question that transgender people largely are absent from electoral politics in the United States. Of course, even if every transgender person in the United States joined a transgender interest group, the number and size of these groups would remain small. This is the case because, compared to other minority groups, there simply are not very many transgender people in the country. The best data we have suggest that only 0.3 percent of American adults are transgender (Gates 2011). However, this does not represent an insignificant number of people, and if transgender advocates want their organizations to thrive they need to reach more of them.

For a truly expansive movement and population resurgence to take hold, however, transgender advocates must reach nontransgender allies. Is this possible? Research suggests that the answer is "yes," and that increased electoral participation and success may help. Studies in the same vein as those I mention above show not only that descriptive representation can increase participation among those being represented but also that it can recruit supporters and spur them to action. Of particular note here is the work of Zoltan Hajnal (2007). He found that increases in African American officeholders often lead to increases in support for policies that benefit African Americans among white Democratic voters. If we extrapolate these findings, it seems likely that increases in transgender officeholders will lead to increased sympathy for policies that benefit transgender people. This may lead to a new pool of supporters that could serve as donors to and members of transgender groups.

Another possible spur to transgender interest group population resurgence is an increase in public support for transgender rights. There has been little research on public opinion regarding transgender rights, and thus we know little about how much public support there is for such rights. However, it seems clear, that increased public support for transgender rights, no matter what the level of current public support, would create a more favorable climate for the formation of new transgender rights interest groups as well as the growth of extant groups. Because studies consistently show that framing can affect public opinion (Gamson and Modigliani 1989; Page and Shapiro 1992; Zaller 1992), population resurgence is partially dependent on the ability of transgender group leaders and activists to use "issue frames" successfully to gain public support. Constructing an "issue frame" means building an "interpretive schemata that simplifies and condenses the 'world out there' by selectively punctuating and encoding objects, situations, events, experiences, and sequences of action within one's present or past environment" (Snow and Benford 1992, 137). On both sides of the abortion debate, for example, groups have tried to frame the issue to their advantage—one side by framing the issue as one of choice vs. government restriction, and the other by framing the issue as one of life vs. death.

What might a successful transgender rights issue frame look like? For now, it will suffice to say that a successful frame would appeal to widely held values such as, perhaps, self-expression and personal choice. Several interest group studies, including Kollman (1998) and West and Loomis (1998), note that interest groups can alter public opinion through "outside lobbying," or directly trying to influence the public through rallies, education, and other means. Outside lobbying that bases demands for transgender rights on these widely held values may contribute to population resurgence.

Backlash

The population stasis evident in figure 3.1 is due partially to competition between groups. Yet, backlash may be playing a role as well. This is another challenge facing transgender advocates and activists. Systematic empirical evidence of a "transgender backlash" is lacking, as no one has explored the issue in depth. However, there is reason to believe that a concerted effort by conservative forces to "fight back" against the increasing demands and increased visibility of transgender individuals is well under way. Anecdotal evidence of this backlash includes the American Family Association's threatened boycott of *Dancing with the Stars* when Chaz Bono was announced as a contestant in 2011. Additionally, groups such as Focus on the Family have adopted explicit positions against "transgenderism" (Focus on the Family 2012). There is also extensive media "trolling" by conservative activists any time anything positive or neutral is written about transgender people (Park 2011). Collectively, these instances and others suggest that a backlash is in full swing. Moreover, studies of other societal groups demonstrate that backlash is a common phenomenon when long-oppressed groups demand equality and begin successfully to defend their political and social prerogatives. For example, Haider-Markel (2010, 19–21) shows that after LGB gains in the 1970s, the 1980s were a rough period for the movement, as Ronald Reagan ascended to the presidency, conservative religious groups flourished, and arch-conservatives such as Jesse Helms held unparalleled sway on "family values" issues in Congress.

Similarly, electoral and social gains by feminists in the 1960s and 1970s led to the well-known feminist backlash of the 1980s, 1990s, and 2000s (Faludi 1991; Thomas 1994). Furthermore, the gains of civil rights activists in the 1950s and 1960s led to staunch resistance by racist white policymakers, "white flight" from inner cities, demonstrations against busing, and widespread white resentment of beneficiaries of affirmative action. In short, we probably are in a period of transgender backlash, and if we are not, we can certainly expect backlash against transgender advocates as they assert themselves and win policy battles.

It seems unlikely that population resurgence will occur as long as this backlash continues. However, transgender groups and their allies are hardly helpless in the face of this backlash. To make this point, I will say a few words about research on media and homosexuality. Numerous studies show that media images have a profound impact on the way people view gay people. For example, Levina, Waldo, and Fitzgerald (2000) found in an experimental study that viewers who watch a "pro-gay" segment on television emerge with more positive attitudes toward gay people than do viewers who watch an "anti-gay" segment. Several other studies reach similar conclusions—positive portrayals of gay individuals lead to positive attitudes about gay people (see, for example, Mazur and Emmers-Sommer 2002; Riggle, Ellis, and Crawford 1996). These studies are relevant here because they show that the media can be used to blunt backlash. In the LGB group population, GLAAD (Gay & Lesbian Alliance Against Defamation) works to promote positive images of sexual minorities in the media. In the United Kingdom, there is a transgender group analogue to GLAAD called Trans Media Watch. Such a trans-focused group, as far as I can tell, is lacking in the United States. Willow Arune (2006) notes that media portrayals of transgender people tend to be sensationalistic; in fact, Arune believes that any story becomes noteworthy if it contains a transgender element. Arune notes, for example, that a run-of-the-mill child custody case would never be covered by the media, but if one of the parents is transgender, the case gets media attention. In sum, Arune concludes that media are attracted to transgender stories because they are salacious. This makes the job of transgender advocates harder, as it suggests that media will ignore stories of transgender people being and acting "normal." Yet, it is precisely stories like this—stories that highlight transgender individuals not as curiosities but as "ordinary people," as well as positive fictional media portrayals of transgender people—that may help improve public perceptions of transgender people.

The Rise of LGB and T Interest Groups

Another challenge facing transgender advocates is the rise of LGB and T groups. As I mention above, virtually every major (and minor) LGB advocacy group in the United States has "added the T." In fact, even GLAAD has added the T to its mission and it has added transgender board members (GLAAD 2012). Many activists and scholars view this as a positive development because some LGB advocacy groups have more resources, large national memberships, and much higher media and public profiles than do transgender interest groups. However, there are reasons to question whether "adding the T" is completely good for transgender groups and their allies. Over the years, and as noted in this volume's chapter on advocacy coalitions, the relationship between transgender activists and LGB groups has sometimes been a rocky one. For example, in the early and mid-1970s, New York's pioneering groups Gay Liberation Front and Gay Activists Alliance essentially booted transgender people from their ranks to appear more mainstream (Alexander and Yescavage 2004, 40). Things got even dicier in 1979 when lesbian academic Janice Raymond published *The Transsexual Empire,* in which she called transgender people reactionaries and other less charitable things. Additionally, many transgender advocates, including Pat Califia, consider the otherwise well-regarded pioneering volume *Gay American History* (Katz 1976) as transphobic because it avoids calling anyone transgender or transsexual, and virtually denies the possibility that a person might change his or her gender (Califia 2003). In more recent decades, high-profile LGB leaders including Steve Endean (who helped found the Human Rights Campaign), Elizabeth Birch (an HRC executive in the 1990s), and Representative Barney Frank have shown a willingness to sacrifice legal protection for transgender people if it leads to protection for gays and lesbians. In sum, history suggests that trusting LGB leaders to advocate on behalf of transgender people is a risky proposition. In short, there is, and traditionally has been, tension between LGB groups and activists and transgender groups and activists.

Of course, today's LGBT leaders assert that any animosity between LGB activists and groups and transgender activists and groups are relics of the past. Even if this is the case, there are good reasons to view "adding the T" as something to be somewhat cautious about for transgender groups and advocates. In her landmark book on the activities of interest groups advocating for civil rights, economic justice, and women's rights, political scientist Dara Strolovitch (2007) notes that within specific interest groups not all individuals and groups are created equal; she shows that "intersectionally disadvantaged" subgroups within interest groups receive less attention and are given lower priority by group leaders than intersectionally advantaged subgroups. For example, mainstream civil rights groups elevate the interests of well-to-do ethnic or racial minorities over those of the poor by focusing on affirmative action rather than on welfare or public housing. Similarly, labor unions tend to focus on the issue of white-collar unionization (thus elevating the interests of white male union members) rather than job discrimination against women and minorities. In short, Strolovitch's findings indicate that interest groups, especially interest groups with wide portfolios of issues, focus on issues that are of most interest to the advantaged subgroups within them.

Strolovitch's findings have implications for transgender advocates. Specifically, they suggest (but certainly do not prove) that LGBT groups, like the groups in Strolovitch's study, may focus more on issues of interest to advantaged subgroups within them—for example, affluent, white, gay men—than they do on issues pertinent to the transgender community. On a more general level, Strolovitch's research shows that groups have to focus their finite resources and energy *somewhere*. There is little reason to believe that LGBT groups will elevate transgender issues to the top of their agendas any time soon (e.g., Minter 2006).

How transgender advocates will react to this challenge is not clear. Yet there is reason to believe that many activists will work hard to avoid becoming just another letter in the alphabet. One thing is clear, however, and it is that "adding the T" is not by definition good for the fortunes of standalone transgender interest groups. Transgender group leaders obviously will continue to work with LGBT groups, but they will, in my opinion, remain wary.

Conclusion

I began this chapter with descriptions of two studies—one that I conducted on nationally active transgender interest groups and another one on LGB groups "adding the T." I conducted these studies for two reasons.

First, I wanted to contribute to our substantive knowledge of transgender interest group representation in the United States. Second, and perhaps more important for our purposes, I wanted to test general theories of interest group development against data on transgender rights interest groups. In both of the studies, I found strong support for density dependence theory. This theory has been used for decades to explain the trajectory of organizational populations, especially populations of business firms. The theory has recently gained a foothold within political science, and my results provide further support for it. Density dependence theory ascribes special significance to interest group competition—that is, competition among like groups for finite resources. This sort of competition is a fact of life for transgender interest groups, and it may be the most important factor in determining the future of transgender interest group advocacy in the United States.

My portrait of transgender advocacy in the United States shows a group population in stasis due partially to competition among transgender interest groups, and competition between transgender groups and LGB groups, over scarce resources. Population stasis and the rise of LGBT groups are core challenges facing transgender advocates, activists, and allies. In the second half of this chapter, I described what research from political science and sociology has taught us about how we might expect transgender advocates to respond to these challenges, and what we might expect for transgender interest group representation in future years. Research suggests that population stasis is not irreversible. Indeed, scholarship on LGB and ethnic minority representation suggests that this stasis may be reversed if transgender advocates become more involved in electoral politics and frame their issue preferences in ways that recruit nontransgender people to the cause.

Other challenges facing the transgender interest group system include backlash and the rise of multi-issue LGBT groups. Research on public opinion suggests that backlash could be blunted by positive media representations of transgender people. With respect to the rise of LGBT groups, there is no question that it has brought some much-needed resources, energy, and attention to the fight for transgender rights. However, recent work by Dara Strolovitch should serve as a cautionary tale; in large, multi-issue groups, somebody takes the proverbial backseat. History suggests that for LGBT groups, it may be transgender rights that are lowest on the priority list for LGBT groups. For this reason, I suggest that transgender advocates make certain that there are always enough stand-alone transgender rights interest groups to fight policy battles.

One question that I have not addressed here is how my findings relate to issues of identity politics. The proliferation of transgender interest groups in the 1980s and 1990s may well have been spurred by the emergence of a distinct transgender identity. It may well be the case, though I cannot say for certain, that just as the earliest LGB activists had to "go public" with their sexual orientation to get LGB issues on the political agenda in the 1950s and 1960s, transgender advocates had to "come out" as transgender in the 1980s and 1990s to gain political traction. This explanation for transgender interest group proliferation certainly is plausible. If identity politics did indeed play a significant role in the growth of the transgender interest group sector, we can expect ongoing battles between those transgender activists working to ensure the acceptance of transgender people in mainstream culture and politics and those who wish to maintain an "arm's distance" from the mainstream. This intermovement struggle may represent yet another challenge to the future of transgender advocacy in the United States.

In the end, this chapter demonstrates that the study of transgender politics is not just for scholars and students with a substantive interest in the topic. Theories from political science and related disciplines can help us explain both why the transgender interest group population developed the way that it did and what we might expect from transgender rights interest group representation in the future.

NOTES

1. My discussion here closely tracks that in Nownes (2010, 694–96).

2. The *Encyclopedia* is an annual volume (but it has not always been annual) that compiles basic information on thousands of organizations including founding year, membership size, staff size, and mission (however, in some cases some of this information is missing).

3. Increases in density affect mortality rates as well. For clarity and brevity purposes, I focus only on founding rates in this chapter.

4. The consideration of *transgender laws* in my models raises some questions about causality and endogeneity. One of those questions is this: Without transgender interest groups, where would laws protecting trans people come from? There are several possible answers to this question. For example, it is possible (and probably likely) that transgender people are/were represented by other types of interest groups—broad-based civil liberties and civil rights groups, for example. Second, it is possible that government *decision-makers, because of their own personal beliefs and ideological leanings, acted on behalf of transgender people. In short, I believe that the hypothesis that more transgender laws stimulate more transgender groups (as opposed to a hypothesis that more transgender groups stimulate more transgender laws) is a reasonable one in light of POS theories.

5. I do not wish here to imply that LGB groups "added the T" due to some crass political calculation. Neither do I wish to imply that LGB groups are not sincere in their desire to represent the interests of transgender people. I am simply pointing out that many LGB groups "added the T" when they did partially because the organizational form "transgender rights" had become legitimate. There were undoubtedly a large number of variables that affected the decisions of LGB groups to "add the T." The legitimation of the "transgender interest group" organizational form was just one of them.

REFERENCES

ABGender.com. 2008. "Here You Will Find . . . Transgender & Crossdressing Organizations." Retrieved July 10, 2009, from http://www.abgender.com/tg-orgs.htm.

Alexander, Jonathan, and Karen Yescavage, eds. 2003. *Bisexuality and Transgenderism: InterSEXions of the Others.* Binghamton, NY: Harrington Park Press.

Armstrong, Elizabeth A. 2002. *Forging Gay Identities: Organizing Sexuality in San Francisco, 1950-1994.* Chicago: University of Chicago Press.

Arune, Willow. 2006. "Transgender Images in the Media." In *News and Sexuality: Media Portraits of Diversity,* ed. Laura Castañeda and Shannon B. Campbell, 111–33. Thousand Oaks, CA: Sage Publications

Atkeson, Lonna Rae. 2003. "Not All Cues Are Created Equal: The Conditional Impact of Female Candidates on Political Engagement." *Journal of Politics* 65 (4): 1040–61.

Banducci, Susan A., Todd Donovan, and Jeffrey A. Karp. 2004. "Minority Representation, Empowerment, and Participation." *Journal of Politics* 66 (2): 534–56.

Barreto, Matt A. 2007. "¡Sí Se Puede! Latino Candidates and the Mobilization of Latino Voters." *American Political Science Review* 101 (3): 425–41.

Baumgartner, Frank R., Jeffrey M. Berry, Marie Hojnacki, David C. Kimball, and Beth L. Leech. 2009. *Lobbying and Policy Change: Who Wins, Who Loses, and Why.* Chicago: University of Chicago Press.

Baumgartner, Frank R., and Beth L. Leech. 1998. *Basic Interests: The Importance of Groups in Politics and in Political Science.* Princeton: Princeton University Press.

Browne, William P. 1990. "Organized Interests and Their Issue Niches: A Search for Pluralism in a Policy Doman." *Journal of Politics* 52 (2): 477–509.

Califia, Patrick. 2003. *Sex Changes: The Politics of Transgenderism.* 2nd ed. San Francisco: Cleis Press.

Carroll, Glenn R., and Michael T. Hannan. 2000. *The Demography of Corporations and Industries.* Princeton: Princeton University Press.

Currah, Paisley, Richard M. Juang, and Shannon Price Minter, eds. 2006. *Transgender Rights.* Minneapolis: University of Minnesota Press.

Delta V. 2002. *U.S. National Transgender Organizations.* Retrieved July 10, 2009, from http://dv-8.com/resources/us/national/transgender.html.

Devor, Aaron H., and Nicholas Matte. 2004. "One Inc. and Reed Erickson: The Uneasy Collaboration of Gay and Trans Activism, 1964–2003." *GLQ: A Journal of Lesbian and Gay Studies* 10 (2): 179–209.

Faludi, Susan. 1991. *Backlash: The Undeclared War against American Women.* New York: Crown.

Focus on the Family. 2012. "Our Position: Trangenderism." Retrieved December 4, 2012, from http://www.focusonthefamily.com/socialissues/social-issues/transgenderism/our-position.aspx.

Gale Research Company. 1964–2012. *Encyclopedia of Associations: National Organizations of the U.S.* Detroit: Gale Research.

Gamson, William A., and Andre Modigliani. 1989. "Media Discourse and Public Opinion on Nuclear Power: A Constructionist Approach." *American Journal of Sociology* 95 (1): 1–37.

Gates, Gary J. 2011. "How Many People Are Lesbian, Gay, Bisexual, and Transgender?" Retrieved December 4, 2012, from http://williamsinstitute.law.ucla.edu/wp-content/uploads/Gates-How-Many-People-LGBT-Apr-2011.pdf.

GLAAD. 2012. "GLAAD's Board of Directors." Retrieved December 4, 2012, from http://www.glaad.org/about/board.

Grant, Jaime, Lisa A. Mottet, Justin Tanis, with Jack Harrison, Jody L. Herman, and Mara Keisling. 2011. *Injustice at Every Turn: A Report of the National Transgender Survey.* Retrieved December 4, 2012, from http://www.thetaskforce.org/downloads/reports/reports/ntds_full.pdf.

Green, Jamison. 2004. *Becoming a Visible Man.* Nashville: Vanderbilt University Press.

Haider-Markel, Donald P. 1997. "Interest Group Survival: Shared Interests versus Competition for Resources." *Journal of Politics* 59 (3): 903–12.

Haider-Markel, Donald P. 2010. *Out and Running: Gay and Lesbian Candidates, Elections, and Policy Representation.* Washington, DC: Georgetown University Press.

Hajnal, Zoltan L. 2007. *Changing White Attitudes toward Black Political Leadership.* New York: Cambridge University Press.

Jenkins, J. Craig, David Jacobs, and Jon Agnone. 2003. "Political Opportunities and African-American Protest, 1948–1997." *American Journal of Sociology* 109 (2): 277–303.

Katz, Jonathan. 1976. *Gay American History: Lesbians and Gay Men in the U.S.A.; A Documentary.* New York: Crowell.

Kollman, Ken. 1998. *Outside Lobbying: Public Opinion and Interest Group Strategies.* Princeton: Princeton University Press.

Levina, Marina, Craig R. Waldo, and Louise F. Fitzgerald. 2000. "We're Here, We're Queer, We're on TV: The Effects of Visual Media on Heterosexuals' Attitudes toward Gay Men and Lesbians." *Journal of Applied Social Psychology* 30 (4): 738–58.

Mazur, Michelle A., and Tara M. Emmers-Sommer. 2002. "The Effect of Movie Portrayals on Audience Attitudes about Nontraditional Families and Sexual Orientation." *Journal of Homosexuality* 44 (1): 157–81.

McAdam, Doug. 1995. "'Initiator' and 'Spinoff' Movements: Diffusion Processes in Protest Cycles." In *Repertoires and Cycles of Collective Action,* ed. Mark Traugott, 217–39. Durham: Duke University Press.

Meyer, David S., and Douglas R. Imig. 1993. "Political Opportunity and the Rise and Decline of Interest Group Sectors." *Social Science Journal* 30 (3): 253–70.

Meyer, David S., and Debra C. Minkoff. 2004. "Conceptualizing Political Opportunity." *Social Forces* 82 (4): 1457–92.

Meyerowitz, Joanne. 2002. *How Sex Changed: A History of Transsexuality in the United States.* Cambridge: Harvard University Press.

Minter, Shannon Price. 2006. "Do Transsexuals Dream of Gay Rights? Getting Real about Transgender Inclusion." In *Transgender Rights,* ed. Paisley Currah, Richard M. Juang, and Shannon P. Minter, 141–70. Minneapolis: University of Minnesota Press.

Nownes, Anthony J. 2010. "Density Dependent Dynamics in the Population of Transgender Interest Groups in the United States, 1964–2005." *Social Science Quarterly* 91 (3): 689–703.

Nownes, Anthony J. 2013. *Interest Groups in American Politics: Pressure and Power.* New York: Routledge.

Nownes, Anthony J., and Nathan Kelly. 2009. "Sex Change, Organizational Change: Boundary Change among American Gay and Lesbian Organizations." Unpublished manuscript. Available from the author.

Page, Benjamin I., and Robert Y. Shapiro. 1992. *The Rational Public: Fifty Years of Trends in Americans' Policy Preferences.* Chicago: University of Chicago Press.

Park, Madison. 2011. "What Fuels Transgender Backlash?" Retrieved December 3, 2012, from http://www.cnn.com/2011/09/30/health/transgender-discrimination/index.html.

Ranger-Moore, James, Jane Banaszak-Holl, and Michael T. Hannan. 1991. "Density-Dependent Dynamics in Regulated Industries: Founding Rates of Banks and Life Insurance Companies." *Administrative Science Quarterly* 36 (1): 36–65.

Raymond, Janice G. 1979. *The Transsexual Empire: The Making of the She-Male.* Boston: Beacon Press.

Riggle, Ellen D. B., Alan L. Ellis, and Anne M. Crawford. 1996. "The Impact of 'Media Contact' on Attitudes toward Gay Men." *Journal of Homosexuality* 31 (3): 55–69.

Rios, Simon. 2012. "Laughton Changes Mind Resigns as State Rep." *UnionLeader.com,* November 29. http://www.unionleader.com/article/20121130/NEWS06/121139944.

Salisbury, Robert H. 1984. "Interest Representation: The Dominance of Institutions." *American Political Science Review* 78 (1): 64–76.

Snow, David A., and Robert D. Benford. 1992. "Master Frames and Cycles of Protest." In *Frontiers in Social Movement Theory,* ed. Aldon D. Morris and Carol McClurg Mueller, 133–55. New Haven: Yale University Press.

Stimson, James A. 2008. "Mood Excel File, Mood5208.xls". Updated from James A. Stimson, *Public Opinion in America: Moods, Cycles, and Swings.* 2nd ed. Boulder: Westview Press, 1999. Retrieved December 4, 2012, from http://www.unc.edu/~jstimson/.

Strolovitch, Dara Z. 2007. *Affirmative Advocacy: Race, Class, and Gender in Interest Group Politics.* Chicago: University of Chicago Press.

Thomas, Sue. 1994. *How Women Legislate.* New York: Oxford University Press.

Transgender Law and Policy Institute. 2007. "Non-Discrimination Laws That Include Gender Identity and Expression." Retrieved February 14, 2008, from http://www.transgenderlaw.org/ndlaws/index.htm.

Transsexual Road Map. 2008. *Transgender Road Map, Info, Organizations.* Retrieved December 4, 2012, from http://www.tsroadmap.com/info/organizations.html.

West, Darrell M., and Burdett A. Loomis. 1998. *The Sound of Money: How Political Interests Get What They Want.* New York: W. W. Norton.

Wilson, Kimberly A. C. 2008. "Silverton Gives Its Vote to Transgendered Mayor." *Oregonian,* November 7. Retrieved December 4, 2012, from http://www.oregonlive.com/news/index.ssf/2008/11/post_9.html.

Wolbrecht, Christina, and David E. Campbell. 2007. "Leading by Example: Female Members of Parliament as Political Role Models." *American Journal of Political Science* 51 (4): 921–39.

Zaller, John. 1992. *The Nature and Origins of Mass Opinion.* New York: Cambridge University Press.

Jami K. Taylor and Daniel C. Lewis

4 | The Advocacy Coalition Framework and Transgender Inclusion in LGBT Rights Activism

The LGBT rights advocacy coalition is a diverse group with a wide variety of policy goals and concerns. From same-sex marriage to antibullying laws to transgender rights, the LGBT community deals with a large number of issues relative to the space that is available on the governmental and public agendas (e.g., Kingdon 1984). So, how does this coalition prioritize its advocacy agenda? Are some issues and segments of the community given greater weight and urgency than others? In particular, how do transgender advocacy efforts fit in with the priorities of the wider LGBT community?

The history of LGBT rights in Maryland provides an instructive example of how the movement's policy priorities and the limited agenda space may affect transgender advocacy efforts. At the behest of gay activists, the state's first gay-inclusive nondiscrimination bill was proposed in the 1970s. However, it got little support and the issue was dormant in the legislature for the next decade and a half. A similar measure was reintroduced in 1992. This bill had transgender-inclusive language. Over the next few years and with the help of the state's largest LGBT rights group, Free State Justice, support in the legislature gradually increased. However, the growing support for gay rights did not always extend to the transgender community. Their inclusion was often controversial (McClellan and Greif 2004).

The controversy over transgender inclusion exploded during the tenure of Governor Parris Glendening. He spent much political capital during his second term by trying to advance gay rights (Wagner and Mosk 2005). Glendening, whose gay brother had died of AIDS, vested the full weight of his office behind an attempt to pass a nondiscrimination measure during the 1999 legislative session. He even testified in support of the bill before legislative committees (Jansen 1999). As with the previous bills, transgendered identities were protected in the definition of sexual orientation. However, the House Judiciary Committee amended the measure to remove the transgender-inclusive language. The altered bill passed the House by a vote of 80–56, but it stalled in the Senate.

Although unsuccessful in 1999, Governor Glendening continued to press for a sexual-orientation-inclusive nondiscrimination bill in 2001. Given the problems at the committee level in previous sessions, the new nondiscrimination bill was not transgender inclusive. This was a huge disappointment for many transgender activists. A lobbyist for Equality Maryland (the successor organization to Free State Justice) later likened their treatment to "being thrown overboard." Yet, gay rights activists believed that removing transgender protections from the bill was an important tactical maneuver to overcome opposition to the bill. The new, narrower measure passed and it was signed into law by Governor Glendening in 2001. This sequence of events left the transgender community feeling betrayed by elected officials and by LGBT rights groups (McClellan and Greif 2004). The fight also demonstrated that gay and transgender activists might have different policy priorities and tactics, despite their mutual inclusion in LGBT activism.

LGB and T Activism?

Today, advocacy efforts on matters of sexual orientation and gender identity are commonly combined under the umbrella of LGBT rights activism. Despite these joint advocacy efforts, 21 states ban employment discrimination on the basis of sexual orientation while only 17 bar employment discrimination on the basis of gender identity (as of 2013).[1] Furthermore, several of the states that adopted the transgender protections did so years after the sexual orientation provisions were passed. So even though advocacy efforts are inclusive of transgender rights, policy outcomes sometimes do not reflect this inclusiveness.

Further, this discrepancy in state nondiscrimination policy breadth extends beyond the reasons why some initial policies only address sexual orientation to why states do not always quickly "come back" to transgender protections. Rather than immediately "coming back" to fight for transgender rights, state or regional LGBT rights groups sometimes pursue various types of partner recognition laws. For example, gay rights activists pushed Massachusetts to adopt a sexual-orientation-inclusive nondiscrimination law in 1989. In 2003, that state had a major court decision in *Goodridge v. Dept. of Health* that mandated same-sex marriage. This was not a spontaneous decision by the courts. It was the result of a legal strategy that was orchestrated by the region's leading LGBT rights groups (Gay & Lesbian Advocates & Defenders 2012). While the impetus for the new policy was judicial, the legislature was subsequently embroiled in an attempt by gay marriage opponents to ban same-sex marriage by amending the state's constitution. Groups such as MassEquality made blocking this amendment their legislative priority. MassEquality (2007; Bay Windows 2007a) explicitly stated that transgender protections were not on their agenda during the fight for marriage equality. Even after their victory was secured, MassEquality chose to focus on marriage protections in other New England states instead of basic nondiscrimination protections for the transgender community (Bay Windows 2007a, 2007b). The different policy priorities held by some gay and transgender activists led to the formation of the Massachusetts Transgender Political Coalition (MTPC) in 2001 (Massachusetts Transgender Political Coalition 2011).

These examples emphasize a hierarchy of policy priorities within the LGBT advocacy community. In fact, the policy priorities of some LGBT rights groups are starkly different from the policies (nondiscrimination and health care) desired by the transgender community (Grant, Mottet, and Tanis 2011, 178). In this chapter, we utilize the Advocacy Coalition Framework to explore how LGBT rights groups prioritize their causes relative to transgender equality. Through interviews and data analysis, we find that transgender exclusion from nondiscrimination law is affected by differing levels of attention to and familiarity with trans issues, the small size and resource base of the trans community, internal state political determinants, advocacy group resources, distributional concerns over the benefits of collective action, and the decision-making processes of advocacy groups.

Advocacy Coalitions and Transgender Protections

To explore how priorities are ranked within the LGBT rights social movement and how this affects the fight for transgender rights, we draw on insights from the Advocacy Coalition Framework (ACF) (Sabatier and Jenkins-Smith 1993, 1999; Sabatier and Weible 2007). The ACF analyzes the policy process at the level of policy subsystems. These subsystems include various coalitions (usually one to four) that compete to set policy. Within a policy subsystem, coalitions containing a wide array of political actors are organized around hierarchical belief systems that reflect members' values, perceptions of causality, and theories of how policies ultimately affect outcomes. At the broadest level, deep core beliefs include basic normative values, such as individual liberty and equality. Deep core beliefs are stable, with changes being analogous to religious conversions. Near core, or policy core beliefs are less abstract, constituting members' perceptions of causality and their basic strategies for achieving the goals that are informed by the deep core beliefs. For example, in a coalition with a deep core belief in equality, their perception of causality may require government regulation to ensure that discrimination does not occur. Policy beliefs tie an advocacy coalition together. At the bottom of the hierarchy are secondary beliefs that relate to instrumental decisions and the implementation of strategies to achieve policies that reflect near core beliefs. Secondary aspects of a coalition's belief system are the most malleable and susceptible to change.

Under the ACF, policy outcomes are determined by competition between coalitions to influence sovereign policymakers. From this perspective, policy change is driven by two mechanisms: changes external to the subsystem (e.g., elections, economic conditions, and focusing events) and policy-oriented learning within the system. Changes in external conditions have the potential to create near core policy shifts, but the impact of these changes is dependent on how they are incorporated into the policy subsystem by the coalitions. Internal dynamics around policy-oriented learning, meanwhile, tend to produce changes that reflect secondary aspects of coalitional belief systems.

Application to Transgender Policy

This chapter seeks to understand the policy process of transgender nondiscrimination protection and how this policy objective is prioritized by LGBT advocacy coalitions. In particular, we are interested in explaining why gender identity clauses have been removed from these nondiscrimination bills or why these transgender-inclusive provisions were not included in the first place. We justify this concern because of the importance that transgender persons attach to such nondiscrimination measures (Grant, Mottet, and Tanis 2011, 178). We begin by describing the policy subsystem in which these policies are considered. In general, nondiscrimination laws passed in recent decades have been debated under auspices of LGBT rights. As such, we identify two primary advocacy coalitions that are active in the LGBT policy subsystem: the LGBT rights community and social conservatives.

The LGBT rights coalition includes a variety of national, state, and local-level LGBT groups along with progressive lawmakers, researchers, and journalists. It is an outgrowth of a long effort to politically unite separate communities of gay men, lesbian women, bisexuals, and, later on, transgender people. In the United States, the drive for this sexual identity focused political advocacy harkens back to early sex- and class-based, largely incremental change-focused organizations, such as the Mattachine Society and the Daughters of Bilitis (D'Emilio 1983).[2] The subsequent influence of other identity-based civil rights movements (e.g., African Americans) and the rise of the New Left, led to a more aggressive, expansive, and liberationist tone in gay rights advocacy during the late 1960s (Adam 1995). However, as more radical groups, such as the Gay Liberationist Front, splintered and floundered in the early 1970s, a more institutionalist and assimilationist strain of gay rights advocacy returned to prominence (Rimmerman 2002, 2008). In this more conformist environment, lower-status identities, such as the gender variant, were marginalized (Minter 2006). Yet, the devastation from the AIDS crisis, governmental inaction, and a backlash against gay people during this era (1980s through early 1990s), brought a new wave of unconventional outsider politics to gay rights activism. This forced gay men and lesbian women to put aside their long-standing differences in the face of a common bigotry (Rimmerman 2002, 2008).

A common core experience of being subjected to similar types of bigotry is, in large part, what provided an opening for transgender people to make their claims for inclusion in what we now know as LGBT rights advocacy. As noted by Bornstein (1994, 104), gay men or women are not bashed because of who they have sex with. They are bashed because they "violate the rules of gender in this culture." Following a pattern identified in a review of social identity theory and group dynamics (Hogg and Reid 2006, 22), these arguments, along with consistent pressure, allowed transgender people to overturn the schism that had marginalized gender-variant identities within gay rights advocacy (Minter 2006; Denny 2006). It fostered a new normative consensus around LGBT advocacy.

The current LGBT coalition is united around core beliefs of equality and the near core (policy) beliefs of explicit governmental protections against discrimination and violence (e.g., Adam 1995, 162; Frye 2006). Since advocacy efforts have often been aimed at state governments, the groups active in the policy subsystem vary by jurisdiction.[3] Importantly, the coalitions tend to be dominated by groups that advocate on behalf of the entire spectrum of the LGBT community. Relatively few participants exclusively advocate for just gay or transgender rights. However, much of the funding and organizational direction of the groups is rooted in the gay rights movement rather than in transgender rights advocacy (Gallagher 1994; Minter 2006).

The social conservative coalition is built around evangelical and fundamentalist Protestant organizations and their members (see, e.g., Wald, Button, and Rienzo 1996; Haider-Markel 2001). Other coalition groups include nonprofit organizations advocating for conservative values (e.g., Focus on the Family and the National Organization for Marriage). In large part, the rise of this social conservative coalition is in reaction to the increased visibility of LGBT people and the advances of the gay rights movement (Adam 1995). The coalition's belief system is centered on the core values of moral and religious orthodoxy (see, e.g., Haider-Markel and Meier 1996). As such, the coalition's near core (policy) beliefs view homosexuality as an intolerable behavior and public recognition of LGBT rights would serve to degrade the standing of moral values in American society (Button, Rienzo and Wald 1997, 2000). As discussed in Barry Tadlock's chapter in this volume, the social conservative coalition tends to lump gender identity in with homosexuality as an immoral behavior. Thus, their near core (policy) beliefs toward transgender rights mirror those of their beliefs toward gay rights.

Since the policy subsystems under examination in this study largely target state governments, the external conditions affecting the policy subsystem—constitutional structure, socioeconomic conditions, governing regimes, and public opinion—vary by jurisdiction. As such, previous research has shown that LGBT rights policies are more likely to be adopted in some states and less likely in others (Haider-Markel and Meier 1996; Haider-Markel 2001; Lewis 2011a, 2011b). These contextual factors not only influence the passage of LGBT protections, but also influence the content of these policies (Taylor et al. 2012). Thus, the dynamics of the LGBT policy process should be driven, at least in part, by how the advocacy coalitions learn from and adapt to a state's political climate. This is important because LGBT rights policy is normally subsumed under the domain of morality politics. The sharp clash over fundamental values associated with this type of policy makes a state's internal factors decisive (Mooney and Lee 1995, 1999). Because LGBT rights policy is not a very technical area, we expect policy oriented learning to be focused on the political strategies and the political implications of the policies chosen by the advocacy coalitions (Haider-Markel and Meier 1996; Haider-Markel 2001, 2010).

Given the hierarchy of beliefs that bind the state-level and national LGBT coalitions together and the political focus of learning in this issue area, we expect that the LGBT coalitions will pursue and pass fully inclusive and comprehensive nondiscrimination policies when they believe that the political climate in the state is favorable. However, when they learn or begin with a belief that the political climate is less than favorable, we hypothesize that the coalition will compromise on secondary aspects of the policy—either in scope or in breadth—in order to achieve the primary policy goals that reflect their near core beliefs. Therefore, transgender protections may be left out or eliminated when conditions are unfavorable.

Methodology and Data

To investigate our research questions, we engage in two types of analysis. We begin with a qualitative analysis of archival data, interviews with LGBT coalition activists, and information about when nondiscrimination, hate crimes, and partner recognition laws (comprehensive domestic partner, civil union, and same-sex marriage) were adopted by American states. We then supplement our initial findings with an event history analysis that covers the period from 1982 to 2012. The foundation for both analyses is how gay and transgender-inclusive nondiscrimination laws have spread over time. Table 4.1 shows the adoption dates for all 21 states (as of 2012) that have passed a comprehensive nondiscrimination law covering sexual orientation, as well as the adoption dates for similar policies that include gender identity.[4] Since we are interested in exploring the hierarchical policy belief system of the LGBT coalition, we also present adoption dates for competing LGBT policy agenda items—partner recognition policies (e.g., same-sex marriage laws) and hate crimes laws.[5]

As seen in table 4.1, Wisconsin passed the nation's first statewide law banning employment discrimination against gays and lesbians in 1982. In the 30 years since the passage of that law, 21 states have passed similar laws. If we divide the years into decades, 1982–1992, 1993–2002, and 2003–2012, an interesting trend emerges. During the first decade, none of the seven states adopting such measures passed a fully inclusive nondiscrimination policy. Their initial policies only addressed sexual orientation (or preference, such as Wisconsin's policy). However, six of those seven states eventually passed laws addressing transgender discrimination in employment. Indeed, the average time between the passage of the gay rights law and the addition of a gender identity clause was seventeen years for this group. Further, of the six states that later passed gender identity laws, three of them (Massachusetts in 2011, Connecticut in 2011, and Vermont in 2007) added some form of partner recognition law (same-sex marriage, civil union, or comprehensive domestic partnership) first. All seven adopted a hate crime statute before returning to address gender identity protections. Only three of those hate crimes laws (Connecticut, Hawaii, and California) were made transgender inclusive prior to the state adopting gender identity nondiscrimination protections. Though it was a pioneer in passing the first nondiscrimination policy to include sexual orientation

TABLE 4.1. Nondiscrimination Policy Data

State	Sexual Orientation ND Law	Relationship Recognition Law	Hate Crime Law (Gay/ Trans)	Gender Identity ND Law	Years b/w Gay & Trans Laws	Relationship Recognition or Hate Crime Law before Gender Identity Law?
WI	1982	—	2002	—	—	Yes
MA	1989	2004	2002/2011	2011	22	Yes
CT	1991	2008	2004/2004	2011	20	Yes
HI	1991	2012	2003/2003	2011	20	Yes
CA	1992	2005	1999/1999	2003	11	Yes
NJ	1992	2007	2002/2008	2006	14	Yes
VT	1992	2000	2001/2001	2007	15	Yes
MN	1993	—	1993/1993	1993	0	Same Year
RI	1995	—	2001	2001	6	Same Year
NH	1997	2010	2002	—	—	Yes
NV	1999	2009	2001	2011	12	Yes
MD	2001	2012	2005/2005	—	—	Yes
NY	2002	2011	2002	—	—	Yes
NM	2003	—	2003/2003	2003	0	Same Year
IL	2005	2011	2001	2005	0	No
ME	2005	—	2001	2005	0	No
WA	2006	2008	1993/2009	2006	0	No
CO	2007	—	2005/2005	2007	0	No
IA	2007	2009	2002	2007	0	No
OR	2007	2008	2001/2008	2007	0	No
DE	2009	2012	2001	—	—	Yes

Source: National Gay and Lesbian Task Force (2011; 2012) and the Human Rights Campaign (2012).

Note: States not listed here do not have a nondiscrimination law that covers sexual orientation or gender identity. MO (2001) has a fully inclusive hate crimes statute. AZ (2003), FL (2001), KS (2002), KY (2001), LA (2002), NE (2002), TN (2001), and TX (2002) offer hate crimes protections for sexual orientation. MI (2002) requires the collection of data for crimes committed on the basis of sexual orientation.

and it subsequently passed a sexual-orientation-inclusive hate crimes statute in 2002, Wisconsin has yet to pass a partner recognition law or a transgender-inclusive measure.

During the second decade, six states passed sexual-orientation-inclusive nondiscrimination statutes, but only Minnesota was transgender inclusive from the outset; two others (Nevada in 2011 and Rhode Island in 2001) later added transgender protections. Three of the five states (Nevada, New York, and Maryland) that passed sexual orientation-only policies later adopted partner recognition laws. In each of these states, this occurred before the adoption of transgender nondiscrimination protections. As of 2013, Maryland and New York still have not passed a transgender-inclusive nondiscrimination measure. In Nevada and Rhode Island, the transgender community waited twelve and six years, respectively, for legislators to "come back" to the issue of gender identity protections. Four of the six states also passed hate crimes laws before addressing gender identity in their nondiscrimination policy. The two others passed their hate crimes policy during the same year that they added transgender nondiscrimination protections.[6]

In the most recent decade, seven of the eight states adopting sexual orientation provisions in their nondiscrimination statutes concurrently included gender identity protections. The only outlier in this group is Delaware. However, Delaware did enact a civil union measure in 2011 and a subsequent same-sex marriage law in 2013. A few months after the same-sex marriage law was adopted, it also passed a comprehensive statute banning discrimination based on gender identity. The same bill also established hate crimes protections for the transgender community.[7]

From these policy adoption patterns, we can see that, prior to 2002, states were much more likely to pass gay-focused nondiscrimination laws rather than opting for full LGBT coverage. For a significant portion of these states, LGBT advocacy then moved toward partner recognition for gay and lesbian couples and to hate crimes policies. This pattern suggests that transgender rights were often secondary concerns for many of the state coalitions during these early time periods. In addition, it looks as if these states prioritized other LGBT policies over extending nondiscrimination policies to trans individuals. In the most recent period (2003–2012), transgender exclusion occurred far less often. All parts of the LGBT community were more likely to receive protection from discrimination. This period also saw some of the early adopting gay rights states reinvent (Glick and Hays 1991) their nondiscrimination policies by "coming back"

TABLE 4.2. Interview Subjects

Organization	Number of Respondents
Catholic Church—Priest (NC)	1
Center for Lesbian and Gay Civil Rights (PA)	1
Delaware Legislature	1
Delaware Liberty Fund	1
Delaware Right to Marry	1
Equality Delaware	1
Equality Federation	2
Equality Georgia	1
Equality Illinois	1
Equality Maryland/Free State Justice	3
Equality Michigan	1
Equality North Carolina	4
Equality Ohio	2
Equality Pennsylvania	1
Gay & Lesbian Advocates & Defenders	2
Gender Rights Maryland	1
Historically African-American Denomination—Minister (NC)	1
John Locke Foundation (NC)	1
Lobbying Firm in Maryland	1
Massachusetts Transgender Political Coalition	1
National Black Justice Coalition	1
National Center for Lesbian Rights	1
National Center for Transgender Equality	1
National Gay and Lesbian Task Force	1
North Carolina Family Policy Council	1
North Carolina Legislature	2
NYAGRA (NY)	1
Political Consultants (NC)	2
Progressive Leadership Alliance of Nevada	1
PROMO (MO)	1
Toward Equality.Org (DE)	1
Transgender Law Center (CA)	1

Source: Authors.
Note: A few respondents had dual affiliations; each is classified separately. With few exceptions, interview subjects are board members, executive directors, or policy specialists; $n = 35$.

to make them fully inclusive. In the following section, we draw on our qualitative data and interviews with LGBT rights activists and policymakers to help explain these patterns further and to assess the applicability of the Advocacy Coalition Framework to battles for transgender rights.

Qualitative Analysis

We conducted telephone and e-mail interviews with more than 30 activists and policymakers in several states that have differing degrees of conflict over LGBT rights. This sample reflects approximately a 50 percent response rate from the solicitations that were sent to potential interviewees.[8] Interviews and archival work were conducted during two periods. The first period occurred between 2005 and 2007. The second period, which included follow-ups with several of the initial respondents, occurred during the spring of 2012. Table 4.2 provides limited information about the interview subjects.

The interviews revealed several themes that were consistently mentioned by respondents. The first issue affecting gender identity exclusion concerned the lack of attention to or understanding of transgender identities. While this has improved to some extent over time, it still hinders efforts to include transgender protections in legislation. Another theme dealt with the size of the transgender communities and its resources relative to those of the gay and lesbian communities. Gay or lesbian individuals almost always provide the majority of funding to national- and state-level LGBT rights groups. Trans individuals play a smaller role due to the size of their communities and the poverty that often afflicts them. This disparity in representation is evident in board membership, staffing, and volunteering. As such, trans persons often do not significantly affect group decision making and they rarely control vital organizational resources. These factors combine to create significant distributional concerns about the benefits of joint advocacy. Because there are many more gay persons than openly trans individuals, it is also less likely that members of the public or legislators know transgender persons. Social science research (e.g., Brewer 2008) has established that personal contact with minority group members decreases hostility toward them. As such, legislators are less certain when dealing with transgender issues and they may personally be uncomfortable with trans identities. While our interviews also uncovered some state-specific concerns, these themes represent the consensus of our respondents.

On the Outside, Looking In

When gays and lesbians first started to make policy advances at the state level, transgender rights were rarely included as policy concerns. In fact, there were active attempts to distance gender-variant and gender-nonconforming individuals from the gay and lesbian rights movement. Such individuals were viewed as a threat to assimilationist tendencies within the nascent gay rights movement (Minter 2006). This exclusion would last from the 1970s through the early 1990s (Gallagher 1994; Wilchins 2004). For example, one of the largest gay and lesbian advocacy organizations, the National Gay and Lesbian Task Force, did not fully embrace transgender rights until 1996 (National Gay and Lesbian Task Force 2010).

Thus, during this early period, transgender rights were likely not part of the policy core for many of the statewide groups. This likely explains why transgender protections were not addressed by the first states to adopt gay rights policies. As noted previously, none of the early adopters of sexual orientation nondiscrimination protections included provisions for transgender identities. Interviews with our policy expert at Gay & Lesbian Advocates & Defenders (GLAD) and a few current or former state advocacy group leaders echoed this theme about the lack of transgender inclusion in the policy core. In Massachusetts, local advocates noted that there was "little transgender political activism" in the state during the late 1980s. This lack of activism was evident in California as well, where one respondent noted a "lack of awareness" by policymakers, the public, and by gay activists. A GLAD staffer interviewed in 2007 summed it up best by saying that "transgender had not even been on the radar" during this period.

Joining the Coalition

Mobilization of gender-variant persons under the umbrella of the transgender community in the mid-1990s forced gay and lesbian groups nationwide to grapple with gender identity and gender expression (Denny 2006; Minter 2006). However, this was (and sometimes still remains) a slow process. While combined LGBT advocacy became increasingly common during this period, the transgender community had not become part of the policy core of many groups. An important exception to this appears to be Minnesota. That state had already seen its two largest cities (Minneapolis in 1975 and St. Paul in 1990) protect gender-variant individuals from employment discrimination (Transgender Law and Policy Institute 2012) when it passed the nation's first statewide transgender-inclusive employment nondiscrimination law in 1993. Minnesota was also the first state (also in 1993) to pass a transgender-inclusive hate crimes law (Human Rights Campaign 2012).

In many places where the gay community had long been mobilized, transgender persons were often not substantively included in the decision-making structure of many LGBT rights advocacy groups. In particular, respondents familiar with advocacy efforts in Maryland and New York noted the lack of transgender participation in Free State Justice (Maryland) and the Empire State Pride Agenda (New York). The former head of Free State Justice stated that trans people rarely participated in lobbying efforts. A contact with NYAGRA (New York Association for Gender Rights Advocacy) felt similar concerns with Empire State Pride Agenda during this era. While there may have been some mobilization of the transgender community, transgender individuals did not comprise a significant resource base to many statewide LGBT rights groups. Many of the respondents contend that this was due to the small size of the transgender community and the discrimination-related poverty that afflicts it. Nearly all of the state-level LGBT rights advocates noted that gay and lesbian individuals provide most of the money for the interest groups and they also supply the vast majority of the volunteer and staff labor.

Additionally, and as one board member of a North Carolina–based advocacy organization put it, "our major donors are gay and many of them are ambivalent about transgender rights." This contribution disparity raises distributional concerns (Sabatier and Jenkins-Smith 1999; Sabatier and Weible 2007) about the benefits of collective action. In other words, should those who provide the biggest share of the resources derive the primary benefits from collective action? One very experienced former state executive director found that this distributional issue can become pronounced because LGBT rights groups normally do not have the resources to focus on more than one policy goal in a legislative session. As such, transgender persons were and are sometimes still not viewed as a primary constituency of LGBT rights groups. The effects of not being a primary constituency, having limited coalition resources, and not fully integrating transgender rights into the policy core was clear when LGBT rights groups experienced difficult political environments.

Our interviews revealed that transgender inclusion in nondiscrimination bills was often negotiable when legislators expressed a reluctance to include transgender persons. In New York and Maryland, legislators specifically objected to coalition pressures to add gender identity to the list of enumerated protections. Coalition attempts were brushed back because the battles to get sexual orientation on the decision agenda had been long and hard fought. In Maryland, a lobbyist involved with the passage of their sexual-orientation-inclusive nondiscrimination measure in 2001 stated that while some legislators were not personally opposed to transgender inclusion, they often felt that it was "a bridge too far for their colleagues." In response, groups such as Free State Justice (now Equality Maryland) and Empire State Pride Agenda elected to take a "pragmatic" or "incremental" approach rather than wait for a fully inclusive policy. Thus, the evidence supports our hypothesis about transgender issues being secondary and negotiable concerns.

At the national level, the Human Rights Campaign and Democratic allies such as Rep. Barney Frank took a similar, but failed, approach with the Employment Nondiscrimination Act in 2007 (Murray 2007). Our contact with the National Center for Transgender Equality described the tendency to negotiate on transgender inclusion as the "flinch moment" for LGBT rights groups. As noted by Congressman Frank (Jost 2006; Murray 2007) and the former head of Empire State Pride Agenda (Foreman 2007), doing what was best for the majority of LGBT community (gay persons) was paramount in their decision making. While upsetting to many trans persons, the former director of Free State Justice said that these losses for transgender rights were important gains for gay and lesbian people.

Full Membership in the LGBT Coalition?

Our contact with the National Center for Transgender Equality observed that it is now uncommon for state-level nondiscrimination protections to be adopted if they are not fully LGBT inclusive. Yet despite the trend toward transgender inclusion between 2003 and 2012, there remain significant challenges. In states where gay rights policy battles have not been fully completed (e.g., Maryland and New York), transgender rights measures sometimes face competition from other gay rights policy issues. Distributional concerns and limited coalition resources still can relegate transgender rights to secondary issues. Like the Massachusetts Transgender Political Coalition, Gender Rights Maryland formed out of frustration with a long-running lack of attention to transgender concerns. It felt the impact of distributional concerns and limited coalition resources during the 2012 legislative session. A contact with Gender Rights Maryland stated that the governor and Senate leadership were only going to let a single LGBT rights bill advance during the session. In that case, the bill chosen for advancement allowed same-sex marriage.

As seen repeatedly in Maryland and New York, LGBT rights advocacy coalitions still face legislatures that are often not receptive to transgender rights. One of our contacts with Equality Ohio found that several legislators, particularly Republicans, might be personally okay with gay people but are sometimes repulsed by transgender individuals. Our contact with the Massachusetts Transgender Political Coalition stated that this was not a regional or party affiliation problem because his organization sometimes noticed that the parents of transgender persons were better advocates for transgender rights than were transgender individuals. As our contact said, "Legislators are often not comfortable with transgender persons unless they pass well." A Democratic state senator in North Carolina also echoed this sentiment. As such, transgender persons are able to achieve protections most easily when they can be included in bills that concurrently add protections for gays and lesbians. As more than one activist stated, it is easier to include gender identity and gender expression protections when it can be shown how that language is necessary to protect the entire gay community and some straight persons as well. One or two of our activists even said that they try to avoid any mention of transgender when lobbying. When faced with resistance, advocacy coalitions remain susceptible to being forced to choose between pragmatic incrementalism and full inclusion. In the struggle for transgender protections in Massachusetts (2011), the coalition chose to narrow the scope of nondiscrimination protections in a bill (eliminating public accommodations) rather than see the entire measure fall to defeat.

In 2009, Delaware chose to pass a sexual-orientation-inclusive nondiscrimination statute. Interviews with people knowledgeable about that situation, including a state senator who was heavily involved with passage of this measure and a later civil union statute, attribute this to legislator discomfort with transgender identities. She also noted that her colleagues "were not up to speed" on this issue and that even the bill's primary sponsor was against transgender inclusion. Hinting at the secondary nature of transgender issues in the policy core of the coalition, the senator further stated that there was very little transgender organizing and activism in the state. Trans persons were not active in the advocacy coalition. Each of the four Delaware contacts also stressed the "incremental" and "pragmatic" nature of policy making in the state by highlighting the fact that gay activists had also chosen to accept civil unions rather than pushing for full marriage equality. They based this decision on polling data that did not find sufficient support for same-sex marriage. While the Delaware activists and the state senator expressed a desire to later "come back" to transgender protections, there was consensus that the policy concerns of gay and lesbian individuals were priorities for the coalition. As such, after passage of the nondiscrimination bill, they chose to focus on civil unions rather than transgender protection.

However, Delaware's civil unions were only a short-term measure. In 2013, after historic same-sex marriage wins in several other states (including its neighbor, Maryland), Equality Delaware and their allies pursued full marriage rights. Only after these marriage rights were obtained (signed into law on May 7, 2013), did the full attention of LGBT activists "come back" to transgender policy priorities. Subsequently, the legislature passed and Governor Jack Markell (D) signed into law a measure adding comprehensive transgender nondiscrimination and hate crimes protections on June 19, 2013 (Human Rights Campaign 2013). In accordance with our hypothesis, the coalition learned from its environment and it did not push for secondary policy concerns until its primary goals were obtained.

Similar to the Delaware situation in 2009 or the earlier Maryland and New York examples, another such episode occurred in North Carolina during the 2005–06 legislative session. A conservative Democrat from a rural area introduced a measure banning sexual orientation based discrimination for employees of the legislature. According to our contacts, this senator did not speak with Equality North Carolina prior to submitting the bill. When later contacted by the organization regarding the inclusion of transgender persons, the senator refused to budge. He admitted to not being comfortable with transgender persons and he felt that his colleagues would not be accommodating. Equality North Carolina was forced to choose between working with what had been a nonsupportive but influential Democrat and transgender inclusion. After much heated discussion, the board of directors chose to push for the gay-only bill. At the time of the controversy, the organization did not have a transgender person on the board, on the staff, or in a leadership position.

The two cases above (Delaware and North Carolina) highlight the lack of transgender voices in many state-level groups and hint at the lack of organizationally relevant resources held by trans communities. Very few of the organizations contacted in this research (except the few that were explicitly transgender focused) had more than a single transgender board member. Only Equality Michigan had a transgender staffer in a key decision-making role. The lack of transgender input is keenly felt when it comes to organization funding. Most groups had no major transgender donors and few collected significant financial resources from trans communities. As noted by a few of our Equality North Carolina contacts, major donors are key constituencies for LGBT interest groups. One of those board members felt that the existing major donors were ambivalent about transgender inclusion. Although not openly opposed to trans rights, they would give "no ringing endorsement." Transgender volunteerism was more common across groups but even that paled in comparison to the efforts of gays and lesbians. While there is disparity in volunteer labor, one former executive director of a state group found that volunteers and activists tend to be more progressive and knowledgeable about transgender inclusion than most of the community. Indeed, many of the staff professionals who we interviewed were strongly committed to fully inclusive measures. In fact, a statewide director implied on more than one occasion that he would resign before doing something (transgender exclusion) that is "morally wrong." This sentiment was particularly true for our contacts in midwestern and southern states.

In the southern and midwestern states, there was a strong preference in each of these LGBT groups to advocate for full inclusion. Some organizations, such as Equality North Carolina and Equality Ohio, had explicit policies set by their board of directors to ensure that the organization would only support fully inclusive measures. However, it should be noted that the majority of those southern and midwestern states have seen little success in LGBT rights advocacy.[9] North Carolina, Georgia, Pennsylvania, Missouri, and Ohio are all states with substantial opposition to LGBT rights in their legislatures. With little prospect for any legislative policy advancement in the current climate, advocacy coalitions in those states do not (or rarely in the cases of Ohio and North Carolina) face tough choices between a perfect bill or less inclusive legislation. One activist pointed out that it is far easier to remain united behind a policy goal when pragmatism would not likely affect the outcome. According to our contact with Equality Georgia, this approach allows for "issue education." This appears to be needed because many of the contacts felt that "even our allies are all over the board" with respect to their knowledge and acceptance of transgender issues.

Event History Analysis of Adoption of Transgender Protection Policy

Our analysis of the timing of policy adoptions and the interviews with LGBT coalition activists point to two factors internal to the advocacy coalition that shape the decision to include gender identity in nondiscrimination policies. First, the coalitions and their belief systems were structured so that gender identity protections tended to be secondary aspects of their policy goals. As such, these could be compromised to achieve primary policy goals. This suggests that as the transgender community progressed toward full membership in the coalition, gender identity protections were less likely to be compromised. The second factor is also driven by the hierarchy of the coalition's belief system. If transgender rights tend to lag behind other gay rights policies, such as partner recognition and hate crimes laws, then the inclusion of gender identity protections would be pursued only after the adoption of the competing policies.

To further scrutinize the findings from our qualitative examination, we employ event history analysis using a Cox Proportional Hazards model.[10] The dependent variable is a binary indicator of whether a state adopts a gender identity clause in a state's nondiscrimination policy in each year. As with other event history models, once a state adopts a gender identity protection it is then dropped from the analysis in subsequent years because it is no longer "at risk" of adopting the policy again. However, since no state has adopted this policy without simultaneously or previously passing a sexual orientation protection, states do not enter our analysis (i.e., become "at risk" to experience the event) until they pass the latter type of law.[11] This approach allows us to focus our analysis on the states where gender identity inclusion is most likely. In effect, we ask: Given that the state has chosen to provide discrimination protection on the basis of sexual orientation, what factors affect the probability of also including a gender identity clause?

To test the changing nature of the LGBT coalition over time, we include a set of binary variables indicating the time period in which the state adopted their sexual-orientation-inclusive nondiscrimination policy. Since the transgender community was not a full partner in the advocacy coalition until at least the 2002–2012 time period, states adopting their nondiscrimination policy during this time period should be the most likely to extend the protections to gender identity.

To evaluate whether gender identity was prioritized behind other gay rights policies, binary indicators of whether a state has passed a partner recognition law and a hate crime policy that covers sexual orientation are included in the model. If prioritization of other policies is affecting the likelihood of passing transgender-inclusive nondiscrimination protections, then states that have passed these competing policies already should be more likely to adopt the lower-priority policy.

The models also account for other factors that are commonly found to be important in LGBT policy adoption research (e.g., Taylor et al. 2012). An indicator of divided party control of state government is included to control for the difficulty that divided governments face in passing legislation. States with a more liberal citizenry should also be more likely to pass a gender identity protection law. Citizen ideology is measured with the updated Berry et al. (1998) estimates.[12] Additionally, states with more organized LGBT communities should be more likely to pass these policies. We use the proportion of same-sex households in each state (based on the U.S. Census's 2000 count) as a proxy measure of interest group strength (see Smith and Gates 2001). We also include the 1980, 1990, and 2000 population rates of evangelical Christians to account for support for the competing advocacy coalition (Association of Statisticians of American Religious Bodies 2002).[13] Finally, a regional diffusion variable—measured as the proportion of states in a U.S Census Bureau–defined region with transgender protections—is included. We expect that states in regions with higher proportions of states with these laws will be more likely to pass their own versions (e.g., Berry and Berry 1990). The results of the analysis are presented in table 4.3.

The analysis shows that gender identity protections are more likely to be passed in a given year in states that adopted sexual orientation protections

TABLE 4.3. Adoption of Gender Identity Clauses among States with Sexual Orientation Inclusive Nondiscrimination Policies

Variable	Coefficient	P-Value
Hate Crime Law [+]	37.506	0.500
Partner Recognition Law [+]	−0.493	0.399
Divided Government [−]	0.134	0.917
Citizen Ideology [+]	−0.145	0.097
Same-Sex Households [+]	4.752	0.070
Evangelical Rate [−]	−0.098	0.308
Regional Diffusion [+]	9.127	0.032
Nondiscrimination Law: 1993–2002 [+]	−5.241	0.136
Nondiscrimination Law: 2003–2012 [+]	3.768	0.022
Observations = 192		
Log Likelihood	−9.670	0.000

Note: Coefficients are generated from a Cox proportional hazards analysis using the exact discrete method for ties. P-values are from one-tailed tests where appropriate; expected direction of coefficients in brackets. The dependent variable is the adoption of a state level nondiscrimination policy in a given year.

during the most recent decade. This is consistent with the argument that states that passed their original sexual-orientation-inclusive nondiscrimination policies during the past decade likely had LGBT coalitions that incorporated transgender rights into their near core policy beliefs rather than having these policy goals as secondary aspects of their belief system.

The model also shows that passing a partnership recognition law or a hate crime law does not significantly increase the probability of passing a gender identity protection law. This finding contrasts with the argument that transgender rights were farther down on the agendas of state LGBT rights coalitions. Though the coefficients are both positive, they do not come close to statistical significance. We do, however, want to be cautious in completely dismissing this policy priority effect. The hate crime law coefficient is quite large in magnitude and the pattern of policy adoptions seen in table 4.1 shows that all the states that passed a sexual orientation–only nondiscrimination policy in the first two periods and "came back" for gender identity later on, had passed a hate crime law in the intervening period. In this case, the standard errors may be inflated due to the lack of variation in the timing of the passage of the hate crimes policies.

Though the event history analysis produces results that are partly consistent with our story of an evolving LGBT coalition, it is important to also consider alternative explanations. Returning to the timing of the adoption LGBT rights policies presented in table 4.1, it is clear that nearly all gender-identity-inclusive nondiscrimination policies were passed after 2002. It is also evident that nearly all sexual-orientation-inclusive hate crimes laws were passed from 1999 to 2005. An alternative explanation for this pattern could be that shifts in public issue attitudes drove these policies on (and off) the national and state policy agendas at specific times (e.g., Downs 1972). State government subsequently responded to these demands during those specific time periods. This might explain why states that lead the way on inclusion of sexual orientation in their nondiscrimination policies were relative laggards on transgender protections. However, this explanation ignores the role that advocacy coalitions and policy entrepreneurs have in shaping the policy agenda (Kingdon 1984; Baumgartner and Jones 1993, Mintrom 1997). Nondiscrimination policy would have lacked salience to gay-rights-focused advocacy coalitions if they already had those statutory protections for the majority of their constituencies. Only when other priorities have been achieved has attention been focused on transgender policy issues. Although including public issue attitudes toward transgender rights would certainly bolster our analysis, the lack of these measurements should not undermine our findings.[14]

Conclusion

This chapter used the Advocacy Coalition Framework to explore policy priorities in LGBT rights activism as positioned in relation to transgender nondiscrimination. These nondiscrimination policies are ranked as a top priority for trans persons given the high levels of unemployment, under-employment, and poverty experienced by this marginalized group of people (Grant, Mottet, and Tanis 2011). However, there are some limitations to our study. Future tests of this phenomenon might look at each nondiscrimination bill in each of the 50 states over the past 30 years. We did not take this strategy because of the multitude of ways to not protect the transgender community in legislation (e.g., elimination in committee, conference committee, and not including it in the first place). Resource constraints and the reluctance of LGBT rights activists in some states to talk on the record also limited the number of interviews that could be conducted. However, we did reach the point of diminishing returns in our interviews.

Nonetheless, since our results were triangulated through qualitative and quantitative approaches, we are still confident in our core findings. Transgender nondiscrimination was not part of the policy core during early periods of LGBT rights activism. As such, many early adopting gay rights states eschewed transgender inclusion for an extended period. During the most recent decade, transgender concerns have moved toward the policy core in many state advocacy coalitions. Coalitions were much more likely to win passage of fully inclusive nondiscrimination statutes when these were adopted concurrently with sexual orientation measures. However, distributional concerns about the benefits of advocacy and a lack of familiarity with transgender issues and people remain significant hurdles. The pragmatic way that advocacy coalitions often operate highlights how these coalitions learn from and adapt to their environment.

NOTES

1. As of July 2013, 21 states statutorily ban employment discrimination against gay persons, while 17 states ban such discrimination against transgender persons. This research, because it focuses on advocacy coalition activity in a legislative context, avoids analysis of any transgender protections that may stem from various court interpretations of state or federal sex discrimination or disability statutes. We acknowledge that these court interpretations may affect coalition decision making, but such effects are likely to be minor given that nearly all state-level LGBT rights groups list statutory nondiscrimination protections as achievements or as primary goals.

2. See Rimmerman (2002) for an excellent history of the gay and lesbian advocacy movements.

3. We acknowledge the importance of federal and local policy changes. However, many key LGBT rights policy advances (e.g., nondiscrimination laws, same-sex marriage, and birth certificate amendment statutes for transsexual persons) have occurred at the state level. Local laws are of course facilitated by state home rule provisions.

4. The final edits to this chapter were made in the summer of 2013 and thus we do not have a full year's worth of data on 2013 policy adoptions. As such, our quantitative analysis only includes those policies adopted as of 2012. However, we do include policy changes enacted in early 2013 in Nevada and Delaware to our discussion. We find that these adoptions correspond well with the patterns identified in our analysis.

5. All statutory data along with information about the year of adoption was obtained from the National Gay and Lesbian Task Force (2011, 2012) and the Human Rights Campaign (2012).

6. In fact, of the 23 states passing a gay-inclusive hate crimes statute during this era, only four (California, Minnesota, Missouri, and Vermont) made these hate crimes laws fully inclusive from the outset. Six states (Delaware, Massachusetts, New Jersey, Nevada, Oregon, and Washington) added the transgender protections to their hate crimes statutes at a later date.

7. Sexual orientation was included under the Delaware hate crimes law in 2001.

8. Interviews were solicited via e-mail, telephone, and in person over the two periods of analysis. The response rate is a conservative approximation.

9. North Carolina passed a fully LGBT-inclusive antibullying policy in 2009.

10. Alternative approaches using parametric hazards models produce substantively similar results. We use the exact-discrete approximation for tied cases.

11. Since some states passed sexual orientation and gender identity policies simultaneously, states join the analysis during the year in which they pass the sexual orientation clause.

12. The updated Berry et al. (1998) ideology measures are available at http://www.bama.ua.edu/~rcfording/stateideology.html.

13. This data is from the 1980, 1990, and 2000 Religious Congregations and Membership surveys, available from Association of Religion Data Archives at www.thearda.

14. Unfortunately, state and national surveys do not consistently ask respondents about transgender policies in a way that would allow for the type of dynamic measurement of state-level issue attitudes necessary for our analysis. Alternative models that include static measures of support for sexual orientation protections (Lax and Phillips 2009) and annual estimates of tolerance of homosexuality (Lewis and Jacobsmeier 2014) do not change our results and do not add additional explanatory power.

REFERENCES

Adam, Barry. 1995. *The Rise of a Gay and Lesbian Movement, Revised Edition.* New York: Twayne.

Association of Statisticians of American Religious Bodies. 2002. "Religious Congregations and Membership Study, 2000." Nashville: Glenmary Research Center.

Baumgartner, Frank R., and Bryan D. Jones. 1993. *Agendas and Instability in American Politics*. Chicago: University of Chicago Press.

Bay Windows. 2007a. "MassEquality Plots Its Future." *Bay Windows*, July 25. Retrieved March 28, 2012, from http://www.baywindows.com/massequality-plots-its-future-58830.

Bay Windows. 2007b. "MassEquality: New England's LGBT Political Organization." *Bay Windows*, October 17. Retrieved March 28, 2012, from http://www.baywindows.com/massequality-new-englands-lgbt-political-organization-58272.

Berry, Frances Stokes, and William D. Berry. 1990. "State Lottery Adoptions as Policy Innovations: An Event History Analysis." *American Political Science Review* 84 (2): 395–415.

Berry, William D., Evan J. Ringquist, Richard C. Fording, and Russell L. Hanson. 1998. "Measuring Citizen and Government Ideology in the American States, 1960–93." *American Journal of Political Science* 42 (1): 327–48.

Bornstein, Kate. 1994. *Gender Outlaw: On Men, Women, and the Rest of Us*. New York: Routledge.

Brewer, Paul. 2008. *Value War: Public Opinion and the Politics of Gay Rights*. New York: Rowman and Littlefield.

Button, James W., Barbara Ann Rienzo, and Kenneth D. Wald. 1997. *Private Lives, Public Conflicts: Battles over Gay Rights in American Communities*. Washington, DC: CQ Press.

Button, James, Barbara Ann Rienzo, and Kenneth Wald. 2000. "Politics of Gay Rights at the Local and State Level." In *The Politics of Gay Rights*, ed. Craig Rimmerman, Kenneth Wald, and Clyde Wilcox. Chicago: University of Chicago Press.

D'Emilio, John. 1983. *Sexual Politics, Sexual Communities: The Making of a Homosexual Minority in the United States, 1940–1970*. Chicago: University of Chicago Press.

Denny, Dallas. 2006. "Transgender Communities of the United States in the Late Twentieth Century." In *Transgender Rights*, ed. Paisley Currah, Richard Juang, and Shannon Price Minter, 171–91. Minneapolis: University of Minnesota Press.

Downs, Anthony. 1972. "Up and Down with Ecology—the 'Issue-Attention Cycle.'" *Public Interest* 28: 38–50.

Foreman, Matt. 2007. "Reflections from a Previous Battle." Retrieved March 19, 2008, from http://www.thetaskforce.org/blog/20071026-matt-foreman-reflections.

Frye, Phyllis Randolph. 2006. "The International Bill of Gender Rights." In *Transgender Rights*, ed. Paisley Currah, Richard Juang, and Shannon Price Minter, 327–31. Minneapolis: University of Minnesota Press.

Gallagher, John. 1994. "For Transsexuals, 1994 Is 1969: Transgendered Activists Are a Minority Fighting to Be Heard within the Gay and Lesbian Community." In *Witness to Revolution: The* Advocate *Reports on Gay and Lesbian Politics, 1967–1999*, ed. Chris Bull. Los Angeles: Alyson Books.

Gay & Lesbian Advocates & Defenders. 2012. "Goodridge et al v. Department of Health." Retrieved March 30, 2012, from http://www.glad.org/work/cases/goodridge-et-al-v-dept-public-health/.

Glick, Henry R., and Scott P. Hays. 1991. "Innovation and Reinvention in State Policymaking: Theory and the Evolution of Living Will Laws." *Journal of Politics* 53 (3): 835–50.

Grant, Jaime, Lisa Mottet, and Justin Tanis. 2011. *Injustice at Every Turn: A Report of the*

National Transgender Survey. Washington, DC: National Gay and Lesbian Task Force. Retrieved March 28, 2012, from http://www.thetaskforce.org/downloads/re ports/reports/ntds_full.pdf.

Haider-Markel, Donald P. 2001. "Policy Diffusion as a Geographical Expansion of the Scope of Political Conflict: Same Sex Marriage Bans in the 1990s." *State Politics & Policy Quarterly* 1 (1): 5–25.

Haider-Markel, Donald P. 2010. *Out and Running: Gay and Lesbian Candidates, Elections, and Policy Representation.* Washington, DC: Georgetown University Press.

Haider-Markel, Donald P., and Kenneth J. Meier. 1996. "The Politics of Gay and Lesbian Rights: Explaining the Scope of the Conflict." *Journal of Politics* 58 (2): 332–49.

Hogg, Michael, and Scott Reid. 2006. "Social Identity, Self-Categorization, and the Communication of Group Norms." *Communication Theory* 16 (1): 7–30.

Human Rights Campaign. 2012. "State Hate Crimes Laws." Retrieved March 28, 2012, from http://www.hrc.org/files/assets/resources/hate_crime_laws-1.pdf.

Human Rights Campaign. 2013. "Delaware Governor Markell Signs Transgender Rights Bill into Law." Retrieved June 19, 2013, from http://www.hrc.org/blog/entry/dela ware-governor-markell-signs-transgender-rights-bill-into-law/.

Jansen, B. 1999. "Gov. Glendening Testifies for the First Time Endorsing Gay Rights." Associated Press State & Local Wire, March 12. Retrieved May 10, 2007, from Lexis-Nexis Academic.

Jost, Kenneth. 2006. "Transgender Issues." *CQ Researcher* 16 (17): 385–408. Retrieved August 2, 2006, from *CQ Researcher Online.*

Kingdon, John W. 1984. *Agendas, Alternatives, and Public Policies.* Boston: Little, Brown.

Lax, Jeffery R., and Justin H. Phillips. 2009. "Gay Rights in the States: Public Opinion and Policy Responsiveness." *American Political Science Review* 103 (3): 367–86.

Lewis, Daniel C. 2011a. "Bypassing the Representational Filter? Minority Rights Policies under Direct Democracy Institutions." *State Politics & Policy Quarterly* 11 (2): 198–222.

Lewis, Daniel C. 2011b. "Direct Democracy and Minority Rights: Same-Sex Marriage Bans in the U.S. States." *Social Science Quarterly* 92 (2): 364–83.

Lewis, Daniel C., and Matthew L. Jacobsmeier. 2014. "Gay Rights and Direct Democracy in the States: Testing Policy Responsiveness with Dynamic MRP Estimates and Multiprocess Models." Presented at State Politics and Policy Conference, May 15–17, Bloomington, IN.

Massachusetts Transgender Political Coalition. 2011. "Mission and Values." Retrieved March 28, 2012, from http://www.masstpc.org/about/mission-values/.

MassEquality. 2007. "About Us." Retrieved July 31, 2007, from http://www.massequality. org/about/.

McClellan, Daphne, and Geoffrey Greif. 2004. "Organizing to Amend Antidiscrimination Statutes in Maryland." *Journal of Gay & Lesbian Social Services* 16 (3–4): 55–68.

Minter, Shannon Price. 2006. "Do Transsexuals Dream of Gay Rights?" In *Transgender Rights,* ed. Paisley Currah, Richard Juang, and Shannon Price Minter, 141–70. Minneapolis: University of Minnesota Press.

Mintrom, Michael. 1997. "Policy Entrepreneurs and the Diffusion of Innovation." *American Journal of Political Science* 41 (3): 738–70.

Mooney, Christopher Z., and Mei-Hsien Lee. 1995. "Legislating Morality in the American States: The Case of Pre-*Roe* Abortion Regulation Reform." *American Journal of Political Science* 39 (3): 599–627.

Mooney, Christopher Z., and Mei-Hsien Lee. 1999. "Morality Policy Reinvention: State Death Penalties." *Annals of the American Academy of Political and Social Science* 566: 80–92.

Murray, Shailagh. 2007. "Quandary over Gay Rights Bill: Is It Better to Protect Some or None?" *Washington Post,* October 18. Retrieved March 28, 2012, from http://www. washingtonpost.com/wp-dyn/content/article/2007/10/17/AR2007101702164.html.

National Gay and Lesbian Task Force. 2010. "Task Force History." Retrieved March 13, 2011, from http://www.thetaskforce.org/about_us/history.

National Gay and Lesbian Task Force. 2011. "Relationship Recognition for Same-Sex Partners in the U.S." Retrieved February 29, 2012, from http://thetaskforce.org/downloads/reports/issue_maps/rel_recog_6_28_11_color.pdf.

National Gay and Lesbian Task Force. 2012. "State Nondiscrimination Laws in the U.S." Retrieved February 29, 2012, from http://thetaskforce.org/reports_and_research/nondiscrimination_laws.

Rimmerman, Craig. 2002. *From Identity to Politics: The Lesbian and Gay Movements in the United States.* Philadelphia: Temple University Press.

Rimmerman, Craig. 2008. *The Lesbian and Gay Movements: Assimilation or Liberation?* Boulder: Westview Press.

Sabatier, Paul A., and Hank Jenkins-Smith, eds. 1993. *Policy Change and Learning: An Advocacy Coalition Approach.* Boulder: Westview Press.

Sabatier, Paul, and Hank Jenkins-Smith. 1999. "The Advocacy Coalition Framework: An Assessment." In *Theories of the Policy Process,* ed. Paul A. Sabatier. Boulder: Westview Press.

Sabatier, Paul A., and Christopher M. Weible. 2007. "The Advocacy Coalition Framework: Innovations and Clarifications." In *Theories of the Policy Process,* ed. Paul A. Sabatier. 2nd ed. Boulder: Westview Press.

Smith, David M., and Gary J. Gates. 2001. "Gay and Lesbian Families in the United States: Same-Sex Unmarried Partner Households." Washington, DC: Human Rights Campaign.

Tadlock, Barry. 2014. "Issue Framing and Transgender Politics: An Examination of Interest Group Websites and Media Coverage." In *Transgender Rights and Politics: Groups, Issue Framing, and Policy Adoption,* ed. Jami Taylor and Donald Haider-Markel. Ann Arbor: University of Michigan Press.

Taylor, Jami, Daniel Lewis, Matthew Jacobsmeier, and Brian DiSarro. 2012. "Content and Complexity in Policy Reinvention and Diffusion: Gay and Transgender-Inclusive Laws against Discrimination." *State Politics & Policy Quarterly* 12 (1): 75–98.

Transgender Law and Policy Institute. 2012. "Nondiscrimination Laws That Include Gender Identity and Gender Expression." Retrieved March 4, 2012, from http://www.transgenderlaw.org/ndlaws/index.htm#jurisdictions.

Wagner, John, and Matthew Mosk. 2005. "Md. Bills Bolstering Gay Rights Approved." *Washington Post,* April 8, B1.

Wald, Kenneth D., James W. Button, and Barbara A. Rienzo. 1996. "The Politics of Gay Rights in American Communities: Explaining Antidiscrimination Ordinances and Policies." *American Journal of Political Science* 40 (4): 1152–78.

Wilchins, Riki Anne. 2004. *Queer Theory Gender Theory: An Instant Primer.* Los Angeles: Alyson Books.

The Diffusion and Implementation of Transgender-Inclusive Nondiscrimination Policy

Jami K. Taylor, Barry L. Tadlock,
Sarah J. Poggione, and Brian DiSarro

5 | Transgender-Inclusive Ordinances in Cities

Form of Government, Local Politics, and Vertical Influences

Gainesville, Florida, is a city with more than 120,000 residents and it is probably most famous for its economic engine, the University of Florida. However, in 2008 the city garnered national attention due to a high-profile fight over its discrimination laws. In January of that year, the Gainesville City Commission prepared to vote on a proposal to add transgender-inclusive language to its citywide nondiscrimination ordinance. Although the city already had extensive protections for gay persons, the new gender-identity-inclusive language prompted outrage from parts of the religious and business communities (Rolland 2008a, 2008b). In particular, there were concerns about restroom and locker room access for transgender females. Despite the outcry, the commission passed the ordinance by a narrow 4–3 vote (Rolland 2008c). But the battle was not over; opponents of the ordinance, under the guise of a group called Citizens for Good Public Policy, collected enough signatures to challenge the measure via a proposed charter amendment. With the help of a Michigan-based special interest group, the Thomas More Law Center, opponents placed a measure on the ballot that would "prohibit the city from offering resident protections except those included in Florida's Civil Rights Act" (Fisher 2008). Beyond overturning the transgender protections, this charter amendment would have also stripped the city's gay community of their legal protections.

As the vote approached, amendment supporters aired a controversial TV commercial in which a little girl at a playground walks into a bathroom and is followed in by a suspicious-looking man. Subsequently, a black screen flashed the words, "Your City Commission made this legal" (Rolland 2008d). Michelle Ott, a member of the steering committee for

Equality is Gainesville's Business (a pro-LGBT rights group), responded to the ad by noting that "regardless of anything you have heard to the contrary, there has been no public safety issue connected to any of them," referring to the transgender-inclusive nondiscrimination protections enacted in other jurisdictions (Ott 2008). *The Gainesville Sun* (2009) also editorialized in opposition to the amendment:

> We subscribe to "Rise of the Creative Class" author Richard Florida's contention that the most successful communities in America today, and the most desirable to live in, are those that embrace and celebrate diversity, not shun and fear it. Amendment 1 would destroy Gainesville's reputation as a city of inclusiveness. It would damage the University of Florida's ability to recruit new talent. It would make us a meaner, less tolerant community.

On March 24, 2009, the amendment was defeated 58–42 percent (Rolland 2009).

In this chapter, we examine city policymaking on transgender-inclusive nondiscrimination laws. This is important because cities and other types of municipalities are key policymaking venues for transgender rights. For instance, Minneapolis enacted its transgender-inclusive nondiscrimination ordinance in 1975, much earlier than any transgender-inclusive, state-level nondiscrimination law. To date, more than 140 American municipalities have ordinances that offer these protections to transgender individuals (Transgender Law and Policy Institute 2012). In the following sections, we briefly review the literature on policy innovation/diffusion and on city-level morality policy. With event history analysis, we then investigate the adoption of transgender-inclusive nondiscrimination ordinances in American cities with populations greater than 100,000. We also utilize case studies, like the brief one presented above about Gainesville, to further explore the dynamics that affect policy adoption. Our goal is to uncover the factors that affect the adoption of transgender-inclusive city ordinances.

Morality Policy Innovation and Diffusion in Cities

Governments adopt policies in response to internal or external forces (Gray 1994). Internal forces include economic, social, or political influences. External pressures include policy learning, competition, imitation, and coercion (Shipan and Volden 2008). Some polices, such as highly technical regulatory issues, are more amenable to policy learning across communities. Others, such as morality and governance policies, are susceptible to sudden policy outbreaks that are orchestrated by interest groups (Boushey 2010).

Although much of the work on policy diffusion provides important insights or methodological advances for the study of state-level policymaking (e.g., Walker 1969; Gray 1973; Berry and Berry 1990), localities are not immune from these internal or external influences when adopting policy. For instance, in their study of California gun control laws, Godwin and Schroedel (2000) find evidence of regional policy diffusion effects among localities via policy learning. Interestingly, local policy adoptions can even influence state policymaking through a process of "bottom-up diffusion" (Shipan and Volden 2006). Yet, while localities may learn from other cities and respond to vertical influences, municipality characteristics may determine which local governments engage in policy innovation. For instance, in a study of policies made by California counties, Percival, Johnson, and Neiman (2009) find that citizen ideology affects policies that generate high degrees of conflict (e.g., redistributive policies). Additionally, Krause (2011) finds that these types of internal determinants are the drivers of local government climate policies. Thus, factors associated with the policy and a municipality's characteristics are important determinants of local policy adoption.

In this chapter, we focus on a type of morality policy, transgender nondiscrimination law. Morality policies are not complex and they involve sharp clashes over fundamental values (Mooney and Lee 1995, 1999). As such, not all communities are equally likely to adopt a given morality policy (Boushey 2010). Sharp (2005) finds that the type of morality policy (gay rights, abortion, gambling, and others) affects which internal or external factors are important in policy adoption. Primarily, she notes that the local subculture (conventional or unconventional) or economic considerations affect how local governments respond to morality issues.[1] This is contingent on whether the policy in question concerns a purely morality-related issue or whether it affects material concerns. In Sharp's view, the sociopolitical subculture drives pure morality policies like drug laws. Economic ramifications might have a larger effect on the regulation of sexually explicit businesses or gambling.

With regard to local LGBT rights laws, an "urbanism/social diversity model" (Wald, Button, and Rienzo 1996) has been used to explain how the mobilization of gay rights interest groups is an important internal social/

political force that spurs cities to adopt sexual-orientation-inclusive non-discrimination ordinances. Similarly, Colvin (2008) finds these forces at work in his study of local transgender-inclusive nondiscrimination policies. City education levels, the percentage of same-sex households, racial diversity, and population levels are statistically significant predictors in his model. Sharp (2005) describes gay rights as a hybrid policy (that is, one that contains aspects of both pure morality policies and material policies). Her research notes that gay rights policy is mostly affected by a jurisdiction's subculture but that economic considerations sometimes matter.

Sharp (2005) also finds that institutional characteristics and intergovernmental influences might have an effect on the adoption of local morality policies. With respect to institutional characteristics, Sharp (2005) suggests that the differential impact of reformed versus nonreformed city government is relevant.[2] In council-manager cities (a reformed government structure), an appointed executive provides expertise that heavily influences council-level policymaking (Svara 1985, 1998). Council-manager arrangements centralize decision making and reduce access points for pressure groups (Lineberry and Fowler 1967). Cities with council-manager or similar institutional forms of government engage in more consensus-oriented policymaking because the city manager's position is only as secure as his or her support on the council (Nelson and Nollenberger 2011). Collectively, characteristics of reformed cities allow professionalized managers to serve citywide (nonparochial), nonpartisan interests (Sharp 2005). Institutional structures like the council-manager system "serve to reduce the impact of socio-economic cleavages and minority voting blocs in local politics" (Lineberry and Fowler 1967, 702). Thus, business and middle-class groups are relatively more influential in cities with these reform structures (Northrop and Dutton 1978). When compared to reformed cities, unreformed cities are more responsive to the policy demands of organized minority groups (Karnig 1975; Mladenka 1989). As such, it is not surprising that Sharp (2005) finds unconventional cities with (nonreformed) mayor-council governments to be susceptible to the influence of politically mobilized gay rights activists.

Intergovernmental (state or federal) influences might also have an effect on local morality policy; for example, Sharp (2005) finds that a city with an unconventional political subculture might engage in compensatory policymaking favorable to gay constituents if there is state-level policy inaction. However, states give localities varying degrees of authority to manage local affairs. Some states heavily restrict local authority to enact policies by following what is commonly known as Dillon's Rule. This principle, which restricts localities to powers expressly granted, exists because local governments have no constitutional authority at the national level. In contrast to this highly restrictive approach, the majority of states give their localities some degree of home rule authority (Dalmat 2005). In general, home rule powers allow local governments to manage their affairs without obtaining express permission from the state. Yet, there are different approaches to home rule. Some states restrict this authority to purely local governance matters while others provide for a fuller devolution of powers to municipalities (Wood 2011; Krane, Rigos, and Hill 2000). Yet even where municipal discretion exists, states can preempt local laws with state legislation (Krane, Rigos, and Hill 2000). For instance, a state could block localities from passing local minimum wage ordinances that are more generous than state law (Dalmat 2005). Alternatively, a more expansive state law could alleviate the need or pressure for local action.

Based on the literature, we provide the following research hypotheses:

Hypothesis 1: Transgender-inclusive nondiscrimination ordinances are more likely to be adopted in cities with unconventional political subcultures.

Hypothesis 2: In the presence of mobilized activists, transgender-inclusive nondiscrimination ordinances are more likely to be adopted in cities with nonreformed government structures.

Hypothesis 3: In states where there are no statewide transgender protections, localities are more likely to compensate for the lack of a statewide policy by adopting compensatory transgender-inclusive protections.

Data and Methods

To investigate our research questions, we use event history analysis to determine what factors lead a locality to adopt a transgender-inclusive nondiscrimination ordinance in a given year. Our data contain information on all cities in the United States with a population over 100,000 (as of 2011) and our analysis covers policy adoptions that occurred between 1990 and 2011. We omit cities with a population smaller than 100,000 because some other studies that address form of local government or mayoral policymaking have used this cut off point in their research (e.g., Wolman,

Strate and Melchior 1996; Ebdon and Brucato 2000). While a small number of cities adopted these transgender-inclusive ordinances prior to 1990, we restrict our analysis because the Census Bureau did not collect information on a key variable in our model, same-sex partner households, prior to its 1990 census.[3] We supplement the event history analysis with case studies of transgender rights battles in Nashville, Tennessee, and Anchorage, Alaska, to provide more contextual information about local-level policymaking on this issue.

The dependent variable in our model is a binary indicator of whether a city has adopted a transgender-inclusive nondiscrimination ordinance in a given year. Because the process of policy adoption is influenced by factors that may vary across place and over time, we use event history analysis to account for how this process unfolds over time in different cities.[4] In this type of analysis, once a city adopts such a policy, it is no longer in the process of determining policy on this issue and it drops from the dataset. Policy information for this variable was collected from records maintained by the Transgender Law and Policy Institute (2012) and the National Gay and Lesbian Task Force (2012). We also supplement this information through searches of city websites.

The independent variables that we use in the model reflect the factors thought to be important in the adoption of local LGBT policies. Guided by Sharp's (2005) analysis of morality policymaking in cities, we consider how sociopolitical subculture, institutional, intergovernmental, and economic forces influence the adoption of local transgender-inclusive nondiscrimination ordinances. Based on Sharp's (2005) approach to measuring the local subculture, we extract or otherwise interpolate from U.S. Census data the following subculture variables for all localities with populations of at least 100,000:

1. Same-sex partner households (percentage of all households)
2. Nonfamily households (percentage of all households)
3. Percentage of females in labor force
4. Percentage of the civilian population age 16 and up employed in management, business, science, and arts occupations.[5]

We expect positive relationships between the dependent variable and each of these subculture measures. As the subculture of a locality becomes less traditional or conventional, it should be more likely to adopt transgender-inclusive nondiscrimination ordinances. As another measure of the local political climate, we assess community religiosity (Sharp 2005). Based upon Erickson, Wright, and McIver (1993), we include a variable that captures the percentage of the population that is a member of an evangelical or Latter-Day Saints congregation. Religious adherent data was constructed from county-level estimates obtained from the Association of Religion Data Archives (2012).[6] Because of variations in the way this data was collected over the years, it is held constant at 2000 levels. We also include the percentage of the population that is white and whether or not the locality is located in a southern state as additional measures of the sociopolitical culture. Given the more traditional views associated with these characteristics, we expect negative relationships between these three variables and the adoption of transgender-inclusive ordinances.

To assess the institutional influences of reformed/nonreformed city government, we utilize form of government data obtained from Nelson and Svara (2010). Nonreformed cities with variations on the mayor-council form of government are scored as a 1 in this binary indicator and reformed cities utilizing a city manager are scored 0.[7] While we do not expect that nonreformed local governments will consistently favor or oppose a transgender-inclusive policy because of the importance of the local subculture, we do expect that these nonreformed governments will be more permeable by political interests than their reformed counterparts. As a result, we expect that LGBT activists will be more successful in promoting their views to the more politically responsive mayor-council systems of government than with city managers. While we do not have a direct measure of LGBT activism at the local level, the proportion of same-sex partner households at the local level serves as proxy for local LGBT activism. With the inclusion of a multiplicative interaction of same-sex partner households with the form of local government, we can determine whether particular types of local government institutions afford policy activists a more favorable context. In taking this approach of interacting the form of government with the percentage of same-sex partnered households, we follow work by Mladenka (1989) who finds that the effect of nonreformed government on municipal employment of African Americans was conditioned by the size of the local African American community.

To assess the role of intergovernmental influences, we include two variables. First, we add a binary indicator of whether a state has a transgender-inclusive nondiscrimination law. State policy data was collected from the National Gay and Lesbian Task Force (2012). While we expect that localities may be less active in this area if the state has already initiated a policy, state action does not preclude the adoption of local transgender-inclusive nondiscrimination ordinances as symbolic statements. As a result, we do not drop localities from the analysis after state action; rather, we model state action and inaction to account for Sharp's (2005) insights that state inaction might prompt action by local governments and state action might reduce local intervention. We also include a variable that addresses the scope of state home rule laws. Data for this continuous variable was taken from Wood (2011). His study of municipal discretion addresses the degree of structural, functional, and fiscal discretion along with the legal definition of home rule in each state. Higher scores indicate greater levels of discretion in municipal affairs. As such, we expect a positive relationship with the dependent variable.

We also assess the possibility that local ordinances are adopted in response to regional policy diffusion. We calculated the percentage of cities with more than 100,000 residents that have transgender-inclusive ordinances in each of the nine U.S. Census defined regional divisions. We use the nine regional divisions because cities should be more likely to learn from nearby localities. Because cities would have to observe policy adoption in order to learn from the example of others, this variable is lagged by one year. If policy learning does occur, a positive relationship should exist with the dependent variable.

Although Sharp (2005) finds no relationship between economic factors and gay rights ordinances, we control for local economic pressures in our analysis but do not hypothesize specific relationships between these variables and local policy adoption. Following Sharp (2005), we measure local economic factors by extracting or otherwise computing from editions of U.S. Census data the following:

1. Percentage population change between years
2. Median household income (in thousands of dollars)
3. Unemployment rate for the population age 16 and older

Results

Table 5.1 presents the results of our event history analysis. Note that the chi-square statistics for the full model suggests that our model does provide significant explanatory power about the propensity of localities to adopt transgender-inclusive nondiscrimination provisions. We use a number of variables to assess aspects of the sociopolitical subculture but only one is statistically significant at traditional levels. As the percentage of the local population employed in management, business, science, and arts occupations increases, municipalities are more likely to adopt transgender-inclusive ordinances. A 1 percent increase in employment in these areas would increase the propensity of a locality adopting such an ordinance in a given year by 15 percent. Even though the remaining measures of sociopolitical culture do not have statistically significant effects, it is important to note that the effects of same-sex partner households cannot be evaluated without considering its associated interaction with the type of local government institution.

Although it does not appear that the type of local government institu-

TABLE 5.1. Adoption of Transgender Inclusive Nondiscrimination Ordinances (1990–2011)

	Cox Model[a]		
	Coefficient	St. Error	Hazard Ratio
Sociopolitical Subculture			
Same Sex Partner Households	−.26	(.99)	
Nonfamily Households	.00	(.06)	1.00
Women in Labor Force	−.05	(.07)	.95
Employment in Business, Management, Science, and Arts	0.14**	(.05)	1.15
Evangelical/LDS Adherents	−.04	(.02)	.96
White Population	.00	(.01)	1.00
South	−.41	(.57)	.66
Local Government Institution			
Nonreformed Institution (mayor/council)	−1.14	(.89)	
Same-Sex Households*Nonreformed Institution	1.96*	(.96)	
Intergovernmental Context			
Transgender Inclusive State Law	−1.65*	(.84)	.19
Home Rule	.02	(.02)	1.02
Regional Diffusion	−.54	(2.82)	.58
Economic Pressures			
Population Change	−3.72	(2.25)	.02
Median Household Income	−.09*	(.04)	.91
Unemployment	.00	(.12)	1.00
Log Likelihood	−135.04		
Model χ^2	78.80***		
N observations	4,938		

Note: The analysis includes 264 localities over 21 years.
[a]Cell entries present coefficient estimates of the Cox proportional hazard rate model, exact partial method for resolving ties, with standard errors in parentheses and associated hazard rates in final column. The dependent variable is whether a city adopted a transgender inclusive nondiscrimination ordinance.
*$p < .05$, **$p < .01$, and ***$p < .001$, two-tailed tests

tion influences the adoption of transgender-inclusive nondiscrimination ordinances, its effects also cannot be fully understood without accounting for the interaction term. Given the significance of the interaction term, we can conclude that same-sex partner households do impact the likelihood of local adoption in a given time in localities with nonreformed local governments, and that nonreformed local governments are more likely to adopt these policies when the local population includes a greater percentage of same-sex partner households. The hazard ratio for same-sex partner households is calculated at 0.77 for localities with reformed governments employing some type of city manager. This means that a 1 percentage point increase in same-sex partner households in a locality with a city manager would result in no increase in the odds of adopting a transgender-inclusive nondiscrimination ordinance; in fact, this increase in same-sex partner households would decrease the odds of adoption by about 23 percent. In comparison, the hazard ratio associated with same-sex partner households for nonreformed localities with nonreformed mayor-council governments is 5.47. This means that a 1 percentage point increase in same-sex partner households in a nonreformed locality would make it about five and half times more likely to adopt the ordinance. It appears that LGBT rights activists are more successful in influencing local government policy when the form of local government is more conducive to political influence. These findings favorably compare with those from studies of other minority groups, which show that large, politically active minorities can successfully lobby mayor-council governments in order to obtain desired policies (e.g., Lineberry and Fowler 1967; Karnig 1975; Stein 1986; Mladenka 1989).

Similarly, the hazard ratio for the form of local government when no same-sex partner households are present in the local population (the lowest value observed in the data) is 0.32. This means that nonreformed local governments are far less likely than reformed local governments to adopt such ordinances under these conditions. However, when the percentage of same-sex households is 2.8 percent (the highest value observed in the data) the hazard ratio is 77.32. Under these conditions, nonreformed governments appear far more likely to respond to mobilized LGBT interests than reformed governments. In the presence of mobilized activists, localities run by mayors and city councils are 77 times more likely than those with city managers to adopt transgender-inclusive ordinances.

Intergovernmental context also influences local government policy decisions in this area. Localities in states with a transgender-inclusive state law are far less likely than those in states without such a law to adopt a local ordinance. It appears that state action reduces the propensity for local action, and that inaction at the state level encourages a local response.

Of the three measures of local economic pressures, only median household income has a statistically significant effect. It may be that increased economic pressures drive municipalities to adopt policies that are more inclusive. However, it is also possible that wealthier municipalities indicate more conservative policy preferences and result in a lower propensity to adopt transgender-inclusive protections.

Case Studies

Along with the earlier discussion of a transgender rights policy battle in Gainesville, Florida, the following short case studies highlight themes found in our quantitative models.

Nashville

Nashville, Tennessee, is a large consolidated city that has a mayor-council form of government. The city has been granted substantive home-rule provisions by the state. Although located in the South, terrain generally considered hostile to LGBT rights, the Council of Metropolitan Nashville and Davidson County (known as the "Metro Council") enacted fully LGBT-inclusive nondiscrimination ordinances in 2009 and 2011. The first policy dealt with city employees. The second proposal was titled the Contract Accountability and Non Discrimination Ordinance (CANDO). It required companies doing business with the City of Nashville or Davidson County to add sexual orientation and gender identity to their written nondiscrimination policies. Upon its introduction by members of the council, CANDO immediately drew the support of Mayor Karl Dean. He said, "I think as a city we are opposed to discrimination. We want people to be treated fair. We want people to be treated the same under the law. And I said if this particular ordinance passes, I would sign it" (Cannon 2011a).

Despite enthusiastic support from the LGBT community and some national businesses like Nike, the bill met with strong opposition from the Nashville Area Chamber of Commerce. They raised serious concerns about the bill and its impact on local businesses. The Chamber of Commerce sent a letter to the Council saying "the legislation does not reflect a process in which diligent and responsible research has been conducted." CANDO also drew opposition from religious and right-leaning "family values" groups, such as the Family Action Council of Tennessee. Despite the opposition, the measure passed the council on a 21–15 vote (Cannon 2011b). However, the victory was short lived. Demonstrating the preemptive power of the state over its localities, the Republican-dominated Tennessee state legislature and Republican governor Bill Halsam very quickly enacted a state law that overturned Nashville's ordinance and forbade localities from passing nondiscrimination policies that are more expansive than those of the state (McWhirter 2011).

This case highlights the preemptive power of state governments over their localities. Furthermore, it shows that some localities may engage in compensatory policymaking until directed otherwise by the state. The Nashville case also illustrates how LGBT rights groups can successfully advocate for policy change in localities that have mayor-council forms of government.

Anchorage

Anchorage is a growing medium-sized city. It has a mayor-council form of government. The state affords the city some home-rule powers. Alaska also does not have a state law barring discrimination based on sexual orientation or gender identity. As such, local groups, such as One Anchorage, have pushed the city to enact these measures. In 2009, a proposal to extend nondiscrimination protections to LGBT residents of Anchorage was passed by the Anchorage Assembly (the city council), only to be vetoed by Mayor Dan Sullivan. Sullivan said he saw no evidence of discrimination, therefore he felt the ordinance was unnecessary (Grove 2011).

In 2011, One Anchorage pushed for such protections again. However, instead of focusing on the Assembly, they decided to gather signatures to place the matter on the April 2012 municipal election ballot. The campaign to secure nondiscrimination protections in Anchorage was unique in several ways. First, the initiative would have added "sexual orientation" and "transgender identity" to the city's existing nondiscrimination laws covering employment, housing, and public accommodations (Shinohara 2011). Second, unlike many other ballot questions related to these issues, the side bringing the issue to a public vote was in favor of LGBT civil rights. One Anchorage had many powerful backers within Alaska's political establishment, including U.S. Senator Mark Begich (D), former two-term governor Tony Knowles (D), and five former mayors of Anchorage (including Knowles, who was mayor in the 1980s) (Shinohara 2011; Boots 2011a).

During the period leading up to Mayor Sullivan's veto, opponents argued that Anchorage was already a tolerant community and that such laws were not needed. Moreover, they argued that this initiative would actually produce discrimination, because those who opposed homosexuality on moral/religious grounds would be effectively discriminated against for their views, thus violating their religious freedom (Minnery 2011). Jim Minnery, president of the Alaska Family Council, said, "It's not clear that there is any widespread discrimination against the gay community. What is clearer is that this is a true threat to religious liberties" (Shinohara 2011). Minnery added that, "If someone thinks homosexuality is wrong, they shouldn't 'check their beliefs at the church door' and be forced to provide services to gays or lesbians" (Grove 2011). Others in the religious community, including Catholic archbishop Roger Schwietz (2011) of the Archdiocese of Anchorage, shared his concerns. Echoing an oft-used slogan that opponents of gay rights have used for decades, opponents of the initiative also argued that it would give LGBT individuals "special rights" (Jenkins 2011).

To counter Minnery's claims on the supposed lack of discrimination in Anchorage, One Anchorage released a survey conducted by Identity, Inc., the Alaska LGBT Community Survey Task Force, and the University of Alaska–Anchorage Justice Center, which found that 70 percent of LGBT respondents hid their sexual orientation to avoid workplace discrimination (Boots 2011b). Moreover, the survey also found that there were "significant levels of verbal harassment, threats of physical violence and workplace and school harassment" of LGBT individuals (Boots 2011b). Opponents criticized the methodology of the survey, as well as the timing (it was released only two weeks before the vote on the initiative).

Supporters of the initiative largely relied on appeals to fairness. For instance, Trevor Storrs, spokesman for One Anchorage, said, "I wish we lived in a world where everyone was automatically treated the same regardless of whether we agreed or disagreed with who they are as people. The reality is a person who works hard and does a good job can be fired simply because they are gay" (Shinohara 2011). In another example, the *Anchorage Daily News* (2012), which editorialized in favor of the initiative, said, "There is no justification for discrimination against law-abiding, contributing members of the community. . . . How can it not be obvious and easy to understand that no one should have the right to deny a man a job, a woman a promotion or a couple an apartment solely because of who they have chosen to love?"

In the waning days of the campaign, opponents of the initiative began airing inflammatory television and radio ads claiming that the initiative "would require day care centers to hire transvestites or face jail time" (Boots 2011c). In the ads, "a cartoon transvestite who wants to work at a day care is drawn as a man with a jutting jaw and body hair, wearing a short pink dress, red high heels and lipstick. If Prop 5 passes, the narrator of the ad says, 'it will be illegal for Carol to refuse a job to a transvestite who wants to work with toddlers'" (Boots 2011c). In response, Trevor Storrs of One Anchorage called the imagery "an offensive, stigmatizing and distorted representation of a transgender person" and called on those running the ads to pull them from the airwaves (Boots 2011c). Jim Minnery and others defended the ads, claiming that there was no clear definition of "transgender identity" and that adding those words to the nondiscrimination code could very well require day care centers to hire transvestites (Boots 2011c). In the end, the initiative was defeated by a margin of 58–42 percent (Boots 2011d).

This case demonstrates that the presence of a mayor-council system and mobilized LGBT rights groups are not sufficient conditions to gain nondiscrimination protections. The local political culture affects adoption of these ordinances and when that political culture is more traditional, passage is unlikely. In this instance and despite a form of government that is amenable to minority group pressures, local religious leaders demonstrated their influence. These religious leaders and groups, who typify conventional political culture, were able to derail passage of an LGBT-inclusive nondiscrimination ordinance by successfully petitioning the mayor for a veto. This demonstrated the responsiveness of mayor-council governments not just to minority interests but also to all organized interests. Subsequently, religious groups and leaders were able to defeat a pro-LGBT rights ballot initiative. To do so, they utilized inflammatory anti-transgender language and imagery in their advertising campaign.

Conclusion

This chapter explores transgender rights policymaking at the local level. In order to enact transgender-inclusive ordinances, localities must be granted the power to do so by their state. Thus, cities in states that follow Dillon's Rule or jurisdictions that are subject to other types of preemptive state action are not likely to enact enforceable transgender-inclusive ordinances. Our quantitative analysis and our Nashville case study demonstrate the power that states have over their localities. If states provide home-rule powers to their localities, these jurisdictions may sometimes engage in compensatory policymaking in the face of state inaction. The possibility of policy adoption is enhanced when LGBT rights activists can organize and exert pressure under mayor-council or similar nonreformed government structures. However, as demonstrated in our Anchorage case study, religious groups can also mobilize and exert pressure on elected leaders. Thus, a nonreformed government structure also offers opportunities for the opponents of transgender rights.

It is also not surprising that our model shows that the local political subculture matters in transgender rights policymaking. The effect of subculture is likely to be decisive when the voters have a say via a referendum or initiative process. We saw the powerful interaction of voter referendums and local political culture in our Anchorage and Gainesville case studies. Cities with unconventional subcultures, like the university town of Gainesville, are more likely to support transgender rights. Interestingly, we see similar effects in places such as Kalamazoo (Michigan), Montgomery County (Maryland), and Bowling Green (Ohio) where similar transgender-inclusive measures were put to a vote. The fact that Kalamazoo and Bowling Green host large state universities relative to their municipalities' size likely fostered favorable unconventional political subcultures that facilitated victories for LGBT rights forces. The diversity inherent in large and urban Montgomery County likely had a similar effect.

Despite providing some interesting insights, our analysis does have some limitations. First, the measure of local religious adherence is based on county-level estimates and thus it may not reflect denominational patterns within the city. Despite following the lead of the political literature, our measure also ignores opposition that may come from other theologically conservative denominations, such as the Roman Catholic Church. Due to data limitations, this measure was also held constant and therefore does not reflect changes over time. A second weakness is found in our case studies. In Gainesville (at the referendum stage), Anchorage, and Nashville, transgender rights were packaged with protections for sexual orientation. As such, these cases cannot solely explore the politics of transgender rights. However, in each case, transgender inclusion was a prime target for opponents. Our quantitative model also does not explore the possibility that sexual orientation protections were being addressed at the same time that gender identity protections were included. Thus, it is possible that in some cases, transgender inclusion was subsumed under a broader LGBT rights discussion. On a related point, our binary dependent variable cannot capture differences in policy content across the cities and it does not assess gender-identity-inclusive nondiscrimination policies that cover municipal employees only. While we have some of that data, we did not have years of adoption for these internal policies.

Despite these concerns, this study confirms much of the existing literature on local morality policy. Moreover, it points to the importance of organized activists and the context in which they operate in determining the outcome of local nondiscrimination policy battles. Our work suggests that such activists and their allies should be most successful when targeting localities with home rule powers, nonreformed government structures such as the mayor-council system, and unconventional political subcultures. In the absence of federal action, this sort of targeted activism should ensure that cities remain on the cutting edge of transgender rights.

NOTES

1. Sharp (2005) utilizes six indicators in order to assign cities to a conventional/unconventional typology. They are same-sex-partner households per 100,000 households; percentage of individuals not living in households with married parents and children under age 19; percentage of women in the labor force; percentage of the workforce in professional, scientific, technical, or educational categories; percentage of the over-age-25 population with a B.A. or higher; and percentage of the county population not adhering to a church.

2. Reformed and nonreformed city governments differ in three areas: (a) chief executives (often called a city manager) versus mayors; (b) at-large city council districts versus single-member districts; and (c) nonpartisan versus partisan ballots.

3. Localities adopting these measures prior to 1990 are not included in the risk set.

4. We estimate the model presented here using the exact partial likelihood method for resolving ties. Use of the Breslow method for resolving tied failures produces very similar results. Given that our results are not sensitive to the choice of method and the greater accuracy of approximating the partial likelihood with the exact partial likelihood method (Box-Steffensmeier and Jones 2004), we present only these results here.

5. As noted previously, Sharp (2005) includes education levels (percentage of the population age 25 and older with at least a bachelor's degree). However, this indicator has an extremely strong correlation ($r = .8997, p < .001$) with the percentage of the civilian population age 16 and older employed in management, business, science, and arts occupations. Thus, we exclude education levels to avoid concerns about multicollinearity. We obtain similar results if we retain education levels and exclude the other variable.

6. County-level data was averaged when cities were located in more than one county.

7. Nelson and Svara (2010) note evolution from the classic mayor-council and council-manager forms of government. They identify seven variations on these two constructs. Form of government data was obtained courtesy of those authors and we rely on their interpretation of whether localities are nominally mayor-council or council-manager in classification. In order to assist with interpretation of our findings, we use

this dichotomous classification. A more expansive testing of the Nelson and Svara classification proved problematic because of the distribution of the dependent variable across the seven classes, the highly uneven distribution of forms of government across the seven classes, the necessity of adding six dummy variables to the model, and the multitude of interactions necessary given our hypotheses. Following the Nelson and Svara (2010) coding scheme for their government form scale, the small number of localities with a commission style of government are treated as missing data. We also attempted to use their data as a seven-point ordinal scale (Nelson and Nollenberger 2011). This approach was not fruitful because of the distribution of the data across the classes. Four of the seven classes have two or fewer cities that have adopted these measures.

REFERENCES

Anchorage Daily News. 2012. Editorial. "Our View: Equal Rights." *Anchorage Daily News,* March 31. Accessed June 8, 2012, http://www.adn.com/2012/03/31/2401322/our-view-equal-rights.html.

Association of Religion Data Archives. 2012. "U.S. Congregational Membership: State Maps." Accessed August 2, 2012, http://www.thearda.com/mapsReports/maps/StateMaps.asp.

Berry, Frances Stokes, and William D. Berry. 1990. "State Lottery Adoptions as Policy Innovations: An Event History Analysis." *American Political Science Review* 84 (2): 395–415.

Boots, Michelle Theriault. 2012a. "5 Former Anchorage Mayors Back Gay Rights Initiative." *Anchorage Daily News,* February 4. Accessed June 8, 2012, http://www.adn.com/2012/02/03/2298868/4former-mayors.html.

Boots, Michelle Theriault. 2012b. "Survey Indicates Sexual-Orientation Discrimination in Anchorage." *Anchorage Daily News,* March 23. Accessed June 8, 2012, http://www.adn.com/2012/03/22/2386145/new-survey-reveals-sexual-discrimination.html.

Boots, Michelle Theriault. 2012c. "Supporters of Prop 5 Ask Opponents to Pull Broadcast Ads." *Anchorage Daily News,* March 28. Accessed June 8, 2012, http://www.thenewstribune.com/2012/03/27/2084601/proposition-5-backers-ask-opponents.html.

Boots, Michelle Theriault. 2012d. "Voters Reject Sexual Orientation Initiative." *Anchorage Daily News,* April 4. Accessed June 8, 2012, http://www.adn.com/2012/04/03/2406275/voters-reject-gay-rights-initiative.html.

Boushey, Graeme. 2010. *Policy Diffusion Dynamics in America.* Cambridge: Cambridge University Press.

Box-Steffensmeier, Janet M., and Bradford S. Jones. 2004. *Event History Modeling: A Guide for Social Scientists.* Cambridge: Cambridge University Press.

Cannon, Chris. 2011a. "Non-Discrimination Bill Passes 2nd Reading at Metro Council." NewsChannel5.com, February 15. Accessed October 15, 2012, http://www.newschannel5.com/story/14036500/non-discrimination-bill-passes-2nd-reading-at-metro-council.

Cannon, Chris. 2011b. "Non-Discrimination Bill Passes on 3rd Reading." NewsChannel5.com, April 5. Accessed October 15, 2012, http://www.newschannel5.com/story/14389865/council-passes-non-discrimination-bill-on-3rd-reading.

Colvin, Roddrick. 2008. "Innovations in Non-discrimination Laws: Exploratory Research on Transgender-Inclusive Cities." *Journal of Public Management & Social Policy* 14 (1): 19–34.

Dalmat, Darin M. 2005. "Bringing Economic Justice Closer to Home: The Legal Viability of Local Minimum Wage Laws under Home Rule." *Columbia Journal of Law and Social Problems* 39 (1): 93–147.

Ebdon, Carol, and Peter Brucato. 2000. "Government Structure in Large U.S. Cities: Are Forms Converging?" *International Journal of Public Administration* 23 (12): 2209–35.

Erikson, Robert S., Gerald C. Wright, and John P. McIver. 1993. *Statehouse Democracy: Public Opinion and Policy in the American States.* Cambridge: Cambridge University Press.

Fisher, Lise. 2008. "City Reluctantly Advances Sexual Orientation Amendment." *Gainesville Sun,* October 2. Accessed June 8, 2012, http://www.gainesville.com/article/20081002/NEWS/810039969.

Gainesville Sun. 2009. Editorial. "No on Amendment 1." *Gainesville Sun,* March 8. Accessed June 8, 2012, http://www.gainesville.com/article/20090308/OPINION01/903070972.

Godwin, Marcia, and Jean Reith Schroedel. 2000. "Policy Diffusion and Strategies for Promoting Policy Change: Evidence from California Local Gun Control Ordinances." *Policy Studies Journal* 28 (4): 760–76.

Gray, Virginia. 1973. "Innovation in the States: A Diffusion Study." *American Political Science Review* 67 (4): 1174–85.

Gray, Virginia. 1994. "Competition, Emulation, and Policy Innovation." In *Perspectives on American Politics,* ed. L. Dodd and C. Jillson, 230–48. Washington, DC: CQ Press.

Grove, Casey. 2011. "Anti-Discrimination Law Is in Spotlight Once Again." *Anchorage Daily News,* September 2. Accessed June 8, 2012, http://www.adn.com/2011/09/01/2044149/group-files-initiative-petition.html.

Jenkins, Paul. 2012. "Prop 5 Creates Unnecessary Patchwork of Special Rights." *Anchorage Daily News,* April 1. Accessed June 8, 2012, http://www.adn.com/2012/04/01/2401425/prop-5-creates-unnecessary-patchwork.html.

Karnig, Albert. 1975. "Private-Regarding Policy, Civil Rights Groups, and the Mediating Impact of Municipal Reforms." *American Journal of Political Science* 19 (1): 91–106.

Krane, Dale, Platon Rigos, and Melvin Hill. 2000. *Home Rule in America: A Fifty State Handbook.* Washington, DC: CQ Press.

Krause, Rachel. 2011. "Policy Innovation, Intergovernmental Relations, and the Adoption of Climate Change Protection Initiatives by U.S. Cities." *Journal of Urban Affairs* 33 (1): 45–60.

Lineberry, Robert, and Edmund Fowler. 1967. "Reformism and Public Polices in American Cities." *American Political Science Review* 61 (3): 701–16.

McWhirter, Cameron. 2011. "Law Riles Gay Rights Group." *Wall Street Journal Abstracts,* May 25. Retrieved October 17, 2012, from LexisNexis Academic.

Minnery, Jim. 2011. "Measure Would Harm Religious Freedom." *Anchorage Daily News,* December 28. Accessed June 8, 2012, http://www.adn.com/2011/12/28/2236970/measure-would-harm-religious-freedom.html.

Mladenka, Kenneth. 1989. "Blacks and Hispanics in Urban Politics." *American Political Science Review* 83 (1): 165–91.

Mooney, Christopher Z., and Mei-Hsien Lee. 1995. "Legislating Morality in the American States: The Case of Pre-*Roe* Abortion Regulation Reform." *American Journal of Political Science* 39 (3): 599–627.

Mooney, Christopher Z., and Mei-Hsien Lee. 1999. "Morality Policy Reinvention: State Death Penalties." *Annals of the American Academy of Political and Social Science* 566:80–92.

National Gay and Lesbian Task Force. 2012. "Jurisdictions with Explicitly Transgender Inclusive Nondiscrimination Laws." Accessed August 2, 2012, http://www.thetask force.org/downloads/reports/fact_sheets/all_jurisdictions_w_pop_6_12.pdf.

Nelson, Kimberly, and Karl Nollenberger. 2011. "Conflict and Cooperation in Municipalities: Do Variations in Form of Government Have an Effect?" *Urban Affairs Review* 47 (5): 696–720.

Nelson, Kimberly, and James Svara. 2010. "Adaptation of Models versus Variations in Form: Classifying Structures of City Government." *Urban Affairs Review* 45 (4): 544–62.

Northrop, Alana, and William Dutton. 1978. "Municipal Reform and Group Influence." *American Journal of Political Science* 22 (3): 691–711.

Ott, Michelle. 2008. "Not Too Late to Revoke Your Signature." *Gainesville Sun,* August 2. Accessed June 8, 2012, http://www.gainesville.com/article/20080802/OPINION03/787584560.

Percival, Garrick, Martin Johnson, and Max Neiman. 2009. "Representation and Local Policy: Relating County Level Public Opinion to Policy Outputs." *Political Research Quarterly* 62 (1): 164–77.

Rolland, Megan. 2008a. "Transgender Ordinance Backlash." *Gainesville Sun,* February 3. Accessed June 8, 2012, http://www.gainesville.com/article/20080203/NEWS/802030312.

Rolland, Megan. 2008b. "Transgender Debate Draws Crowd." *Gainesville Sun,* January 29. Accessed June 8, 2012, http://www.gainesville.com/article/20080129/NEWS/801290319.

Rolland, Megan. 2008c. "City Passes Transgender Ordinance." *Gainesville Sun,* January 30. Accessed June 8, 2012, http://www.gainesville.com/article/20080130/NEWS/801300328.

Rolland, Megan. 2008d. "Transgender Petition Branded 'Anti-Gay.'" *Gainesville Sun,* July 23. Accessed June 8, 2012, http://www.gainesville.com/article/20080723/news/924201154.

Rolland, Megan. 2009. "City Votes Down Amendment 1." *Gainesville Sun,* March 24. Accessed June 8, 2012, http://www.gainesville.com/article/20090324/ARTICLES/903249997.

Schwietz, Roger. 2012. "Prop 5 Will Encourage Discrimination." *Anchorage Daily News,* March 31. Accessed June 8, 2012, http://www.adn.com/2012/03/31/2401321/prop-5-will-encourage-discrimination.html.

Sharp, Elaine. 2005. *Morality Politics in American Cities.* Lawrence: University Press of Kansas.

Shinohara, Rosemary. 2011. "Gay Rights Initiative Likely Headed to Ballot." *Anchorage Daily News,* December 9. Accessed June 8, 2012, http://www.adn.com/2011/12/08/2209015/gay-rights-initiative-likely-headed.html.

Shipan, Charles, and Craig Volden. 2006. "Bottom-Up Federalism: The Diffusion of Antismoking Policies from U.S. Cities to States." *American Journal of Political Science* 50 (4): 825–43.

Shipan, Charles, and Craig Volden. 2008. "The Mechanisms of Policy Diffusion." *American Journal of Political Science* 52 (4): 840–57.

Stein, Lana. 1986. "Representative Local Government: Minorities in the Municipal Workforce." *Journal of Politics* 48 (3): 694–713.

Svara, James. 1985. "Dichotomy and Duality: Reconceptualizing the Relationship between Policy and Administration in Council-Manager Cities." *Public Administration Review* 45 (January–February): 221–32.

Svara, James. 1998. "The Politics-Administration Dichotomy Model as Aberration." *Public Administration Review* 58 (1): 51–58.

Transgender Law and Policy Institute. 2012. "Non-discrimination Laws That Include Gender Identity and Expression." Accessed August 2, 2012, http://www.transgenderlaw.org/ndlaws/index.htm.

Wald, Kenneth D., James W. Button, and Barbara A. Rienzo. 1996. "The Politics of Gay Rights in American Communities: Explaining Antidiscrimination Ordinances and Policies." *American Journal of Political Science* 40 (4): 1152–78.

Walker, Jack L. 1969. "The Diffusion of Innovations among the American States." *American Political Science Review* 63 (September): 880–99.

Wood, Curtis. 2011. "Understanding the Consequences of Municipal Discretion." *American Review of Public Administration* 41 (4): 411–27.

Wolman, Harold, John Strate, and Alan Melchior. 1996. "Does Changing Mayors Matter?" *Journal of Politics* 58 (1): 201–23.

Daniel C. Lewis, Jami K. Taylor, Brian DiSarro,
and Matthew L. Jacobsmeier

6 | Is Transgender Policy Different?

Policy Complexity, Policy Diffusion, and LGBT
Nondiscrimination Law

Transgender policies are rarely discussed on their own terms. Instead, they are often lumped together with policies related to gay rights. In some ways, grouping transgender issues with gay rights makes sense—advocates for transgender rights normally collaborate with gay, lesbian, and bisexual rights groups. Indeed, the community in which transgender advocates find themselves—the LGBT community—often explicitly links transgender policies to gay rights policies. However, by linking transgender policies to gay rights via the LGBT advocacy community, public officials, citizens, and even scholars often assume that the politics of the two policy areas are the same. In this chapter we test this assumption: Are the politics of transgender rights the same as those of gay rights? Do the factors that affect the policy process for gay rights issues also affect transgender rights?

A review of state-level gay and transgender nondiscrimination laws in the United States suggests that the assumption about the same politics affecting the two types of policy might be flawed. Figure 6.1 shows a large discrepancy in the number of states with comprehensive protections for gay and transgender individuals.[1] While these differences may be explained by the later emergence of gender identity as a valid protection class, it is possible that there are differences in the factors that affect policy adoption. A similar discrepancy is seen in figure 6.2, which compares the number of states in 2011 that provide protections in seven components of nondiscrimination policy. Whereas there is substantial variation in the number of states that have adopted the various types of sexual orientation protections, when states adopt gender identity protections they typically do so in a more comprehensive manner and they adopt many or all of the

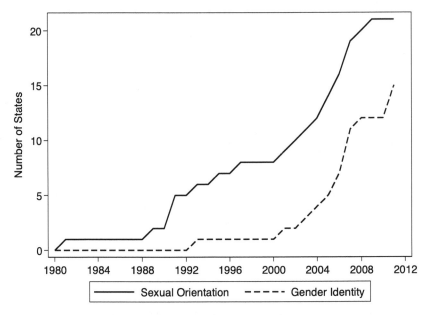

Fig. 6.1. States with comprehensive nondiscrimination protections, 1980–2011. (Data compiled by the authors.)

component protections simultaneously. Again, the pattern of nondiscrimination policy adoption suggests that the factors underlying transgender protections may differ from sexual orientation protections.

In addition to the empirical patterns seen in figures 6.1 and 6.2, the literature on LGBT politics and the policy process in the United States also suggests that transgender policy and politics is likely to be distinct from the politics and policy of gay rights. In the following sections, we examine this body of scholarship. We then test our arguments about differences in gay and transgender policy empirically by using a multiple component, simultaneous event history analysis to examine the effects that a variety of political factors have on the adoption of LGBT-inclusive nondiscrimination policies in the American states. Lastly, we explore the unique challenges faced by transgender rights advocates in state-level policy battles via short case studies.

Innovation, Diffusion, and Policy Complexity

One common approach to exploring the reasons that states adopt a given policy is to use a policy innovation and diffusion perspective (Walker

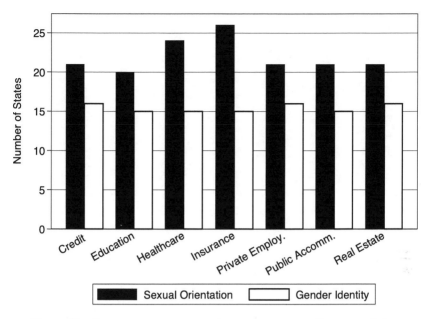

Fig. 6.2. Nondiscrimination protections by component, 2011. (Data compiled by the authors.)

1969). Policy innovations occur when states adopt new policies. What factors drive governments to innovate? Existing literature on policy innovation and diffusion has explored both external factors—geographic diffusion, policy networks, policy entrepreneurs, vertical diffusion—and internal factors, including a state's economic, social, and political characteristics (Gray 1973; Grossback, Nicholson-Crotty, and Peterson 2004; Haider-Markel 2001; Mintrom 1997; Welch and Thompson 1980; Berry and Berry 1990).

The policy innovation and diffusion literature typically utilizes event history analyses to empirically test their arguments (e.g., Berry and Berry 1990; Shipan and Volden 2006). While this analytical approach has allowed for broad testing of a variety of internal and external determinants simultaneously while also accounting for temporal dynamics, it is has been limited in its ability to cope with policy complexity. Most event history analyses use a binary indicator of whether or not a state has passed a policy of a certain type. This assumes that all policies of that type are identical. Thus, traditional event history modeling can tell us a great deal about how policies are diffused, but can tell us very little about the content of the policies that ultimately are adopted (Clark 1985; Karch 2007; Boehmke 2009). This limitation is important because policies addressing the same issue might vary substantially (Mintrom and Vergari 1998; Volden 2006; Taylor et al. 2012). For instance, in two states offering nondiscrimination protections to the LGBT community, one state might offer comprehensive protections, including housing, public accommodations, and employment, while the other might only protect on the basis of discrimination in employment. Additionally, one state might protect the entire LGBT community while the other extends coverage only to the gay community.

The literature on policy reinvention provides evidence that policies of similar types often vary in their particular content. As states become familiar with the effects and political consequences of a particular policy, they often "reinvent" the policy, adding additional components or only keeping the most successful portions of a policy (Glick and Hays 1991; Volden 2006; Volden, Ting, and Carpenter 2008). A traditional event history analysis cannot account for this kind of policy complexity.

Another vein of political science research, the literature on policy typologies (e.g., Wilson 1980; Lowi 1964; Peterson 1981), also emphasizes the differences in the policy process across different policies. This literature categorizes policies based on various characteristics and dimensions and theorizes how the policy process varies across different policy types. For example, James Q. Wilson (1980) categorizes policies based on the distribution of costs and benefits. The politics of a policy with concentrated costs and dispersed benefits (e.g., environmental regulation) are likely to vary significantly from one with dispersed costs and concentrated benefits (e.g., agricultural subsidies). Furthermore, the characteristics of the policy might affect whether there is a rapid outbreak of adoption or whether there is a slower process of diffusion (Boushey 2010). More complex regulatory policies are likely to slowly diffuse while morality and governance policy appear to be more susceptible to policy outbreaks. However, Boushey (2010) cautions that despite the susceptibility of morality policy to outbreaks, this is conditioned on the policy target and state-level factors that may affect receptiveness. Thus, policies giving a stigmatized group more rights are not likely to experience outbreaks of adoption.

Regardless of the particular theoretical framework utilized, the key point of this research is that the factors that influence policy outcomes are likely to vary by the content of the policy. Even within a particular policy area, such as LGBT politics, variations in content should affect the factors that influence outcomes—especially when those variations affect the scope and breadth of the policy. For example, the factors that explain the adoption of laws allowing same-sex marriage may differ from those that explain bans on discrimination based on sexual orientation.

Gay and Transgender Rights Policies

At first glance, one might not expect that the factors influencing the adoption of gay and transgender-inclusive laws to differ. Despite some disagreements over policy concerns and policy priorities, the gay and transgender communities are engaged in common advocacy under the LGBT banner. The public also sometimes conflates these identities. Additionally, morality politics is thought to affect the adoption of most LGBT-related legislation (Meier 1994; Mooney and Lee 1995; Mooney 2001; Haider-Markel and Meier 1996). Policies that fit this type, such as abortion and capital punishment, are characterized by moral, rather than utilitarian, arguments undergirded by core values. As such, the politics of morality policies are often divisive and publicly salient, and the adoption of these types of policies tend to be driven by state-specific political and social factors and affected by national policy networks (Mooney and Lee 1995, 1999; Boushey 2010). Indeed, Colvin (2008) found that factors affecting which cities adopt transgender-inclusive policies were similar to those that drive gay inclusion. Social factors believed to be relevant to LGBT-inclusive laws include citizen education levels and the percentage of the state that are adherents to various evangelical Christian denominations. Partisan and ideological differences on LGBT issues and which sides control key political institutions are important political determinants. Despite a conservative bias in policy on LGBT issues, there is responsiveness to public opinion (Lax and Phillips 2009).

However, in their expansive analysis of LGBT policies ranging from restrictions on sodomy to same-sex marriage, Lax and Phillips (2009) noted that there are varying levels of public support and policy responsiveness for the diverse set of policies advocated for by sexual minorities. As such, one should question whether each LGBT rights issue can be analyzed in the same way. While the policy target matters, so do the characteristics of the policy (Boushey 2010). Even within the same set of policies (e.g., nondiscrimination), Taylor et al. (2012) found subtle differences in the factors that might cause states to adopt certain aspects of policies. They also found some differences between the factors that appeared to drive gay versus transgender nondiscrimination policies. However, those analyses only included policy adoption before 2009. Taylor, Tadlock, and Poggione (2014) also addressed a policy that uniquely benefits the transgender community: birth certificate amendment laws. Unlike most other LGBT rights policies, morality politics does not fully explain the adoption of this type of policy. In this chapter, we examine the differences between gay and transgender policy adoption with an expanded analysis of non-discrimination policies in the American states. Based on the literature on policy complexity, policy reinvention, and the growing body of scholarship on LGBT rights, we test the following research hypothesis:

> *Hypothesis 1:* The factors that affect the adoption of sexual orientation policies differ from those that affect the adoptions of transgender-inclusive law.

In addition to the differences between gay and transgender policies, studies on policy complexity suggest that there may be differences across the various components that comprise complex policies (Taylor et al. 2012; Boehmke 2009). However, Taylor et al. (2012) find more cross-component variation in sexual-orientation-inclusive nondiscrimination policies than in comparable transgender-inclusive policies. Therefore, along with differences in the types of factors that affect the adoption of gay and transgender nondiscrimination policies, we also expect there to be differences in the variation across components. Thus, we also test the following hypotheses regarding cross-component differences:

> *Hypothesis 2:* The factors that drive adoption of specific policy components in gay nondiscrimination law differ from those that drive adoption of the same components in transgender-inclusive nondiscrimination law.

> *Hypothesis 3:* The adoption of gay-inclusive nondiscrimination policies will show more cross-component variation than the adoption of transgender-inclusive nondiscrimination policies.

To assess our hypotheses, we utilize both quantitative and qualitative approaches. We begin with a multiple component simultaneous event history analysis of the adoption of state nondiscrimination policies covering sexual orientation and gender identity. We expand the event history approach by creating fourteen separate models—one for each of the seven policy components of nondiscrimination policies for both sexual orientation and gender identity—simultaneously. Separating out the component pieces of state nondiscrimination policy allows us to account for variation in *what* is being protected (i.e., public accommodations) as well as *who* is being protected by the policies (gay and/or transgendered individuals). We then present qualitative case studies of policy battles for transgender rights in Maryland, Massachusetts, and Hawaii that supplement the quantitative results.

Multiple Component Event History Analysis

The dataset used in the event history analysis was constructed by content analysis of all state codes as of 2011 to identify nondiscrimination policies pertaining to seven components areas: credit, education, health care, insurance, private employment, public accommodations, and real estate. Our research identified the years that these sexual orientation and gender identity (or expression) protections were passed. To verify the accuracy of our coding, we compared adoption dates with those listed on the Human Rights Campaign website.

The analysis begins in 1981, with the adoption of the first state nondiscrimination policy by Wisconsin, and ends in 2011. In the dataset, 29 states provide some type of discrimination protection on the basis of sexual orientation and 16 states provide statutory protection on the basis of gender identity. There is much more variation in the number of components that states with sexual orientation policies protect. Eight states, like Ohio, provide sexual orientation protections for only one component—either insurance or health care.[2] The remaining 21 states have comprehensive coverage, but several passed different protection components at different times—exhibiting a pattern consistent with policy reinvention (Glick and Hays 1991). Most states with transgender protections have comprehensive coverage.

As with traditional event history analysis, the dependent variables are binary indicators of whether the state adopted the component in a particular year. Once a state adopts a component, it is dropped from that model for future years since it is no longer "at risk" of experiencing the event (i.e., adopting the policy). In essence this approach allows us to ask, "For a state that has not yet adopted a particular component of a nondiscrimination policy that includes sexual orientation or gender identity, what is the probability that it will adopt this policy component in a given year?" With 14 policy components, we estimate 14 separate event history models using logistic regression. We then link the models together to jointly estimate standard errors, which allows for statistical testing of differences in coefficients across the different policy components.[3]

The independent variables in each model cover a wide range of political and socioeconomic factors demonstrated to be significant influences on policy innovation and diffusion. The models include up to four variables to account for various diffusion and reinvention factors. Often, policymakers emulate policies from neighboring and nearby states due to their similar political and socioeconomic characteristics (see, e.g., Daley and Garand 2005). This kind of geographic diffusion may also be driven by policy and political learning and regional networks. Thus, the models include a variable indicating the proportion of states in the Census-defined subregion that have previously adopted the nondiscrimination component in question. To account for the tendency of early innovators to subsequently expand the scope of their existing policy, we include a variable indicating whether a state has previously adopted the same class of protections for another component (Glick and Hays 1991). We also include a variable measuring the average level of protections for that group (gay or transgendered individuals) nationally. As the number of states that have nondiscrimination laws increases, along with the scope of those policies, states with limited protections or no protections should be more likely to pass nondiscrimination policies. For the transgender policy models, we also include a variable indicating whether the state has previously provided protections for that component on the basis of sexual orientation. To control for other regional effects, we include regional indicators, with the South serving as the reference category. However, these regional controls must be omitted from the gender identity model because they perfectly predict nonadoption.

The models also include several internal political factors. The ideological orientation of the state is assessed with an annual measure of ideological identification, created using a three-year running average of estimates from a multilevel regression and poststratification technique (Pacheco 2011). More liberal states should be more likely to pass these policies. We also expect that states with direct democracy institutions, such as direct initiatives and popular referenda, to be more responsive to public preferences (Gerber 1996; Burden 2005; Lewis 2011, 2013). Thus, we include a measure of a state's ballot measure use (logged) and interact it with the citizen ideology variable.

The models also account for partisan influences. The Democratic Party has tended to be more supportive of LGBT rights, so legislatures with a higher percentage of Democrats should be more likely to pass these nondiscrimination policies (Haider-Markel 2000; Herrick 2008). Divided governments may be less likely to pass any policy, particularly policies that invoke morality politics. The final party variable accounts for the competitiveness of a state's party system. We include a folded Ranney index and expect that states with more competition between the two parties are more likely to pass these policies as they try to reach out to new constituencies in order to gain an electoral advantage (Ranney 1976).

We also account for the effects of organized interests in the state. This policy area pits LGBT rights groups against conservative Christian groups (Haider-Markel 2000, 2001; Wald, Button, and Rienzo 1996). We assess the organizational capacity of LGBT rights groups with estimates of the per capita budgets of state-level LGBT organizations as reported by the Equality Federation (Taylor et al. 2012).[4] The strength of the conservative Christian movement is gauged by the rate of evangelical adherents in a state since organizations in this movement tend to be membership groups.[5]

Finally, the models include a variable measuring educational attainment. Education has proven to be a consistent predictor of political tolerance (see, e.g., McClosky and Brill 1983). States with a higher proportion of college graduates should be more likely to pass these policies.

Results and Discussion

The results from the seven sexual orientation models are presented in table 6.1. Positive coefficients indicate that an increase in that variable is associated with an increase in the likelihood of a state adopting that policy component in a given year. Negative coefficients indicate a decreased likelihood of policy adoption. While there is certainly variation in the coefficients across the different components, some general patterns do emerge. Diffusion and reinvention factors, for the most part, do not significantly affect the likelihood of passing nondiscrimination policies covering sexual orientation. Instead, as suggested by the morality politics literature (e.g., Boushey 2010), internal political factors tend to drive these policy adoptions. Citizen ideology does not seem to affect policy adoption for non-direct-democracy states, but it is a significant predictor in states that use ballot measures. The results also show that the partisan makeup of the legislatures affects the likelihood of policy adoption in three of the models. Finally, the capacity of LGBT rights groups has a significant impact on whether a state passes sexual orientation protections.

The results for the seven gender identity models are presented in table 6.2 and should be interpreted similarly to the first seven models. Unlike the sexual orientation components models, these models show a significant reinvention effect. States that previously passed a gender identity protec-

TABLE 6.1. Event History Analysis of the Adoption of Sexual Orientation–Inclusive Nondiscrimination Policy Components, 1981–2011

Variable	Credit	Education	Health Care	Insurance	Private Employ.	Public Accom.	Real Estate
Diffusion	0.298	−3.544	1.868	−1.737	−0.545	0.147	−0.613
	(2.517)	(3.867)	(2.940)	(1.841)	(2.757)	(2.675)	(2.698)
Prior Passage	0.180	0.440	0.959	1.095	1.281*	0.653	0.101
	(0.600)	(0.912)	(0.672)	(0.888)	(0.765)	(0.639)	(1.007)
Avg. Protection	2.585	0.363	−0.423	−2.550	0.776	2.714	2.559
	(2.304)	(1.565)	(1.912)	(1.999)	(2.397)	(2.278)	(1.756)
Citizen Ideology	−5.641	7.748	−14.182	1.037	−13.944	−5.900	−5.697***
	(12.489)	(18.974)	(11.561)	(15.263)	(10.855)	(12.677)	(12.166)
Initiative Use	−4.120*	−1.785*	−2.207*	−0.088	−3.791**	−4.064*	−4.510***
	(2.334)	(0.951)	(1.274)	(0.913)	(1.788)	(2.286)	(1.439)
Ideology × Initiative Use	15.066*	6.182	8.728*	0.894	13.894**	14.918*	17.367*
	(9.033)	(3.919)	(5.270)	(3.941)	(7.054)	(8.887)	(6.030)
% Democrats (logged)	3.913*	3.492	5.773***	1.459	5.536**	3.970	5.111
	(2.072)	(3.482)	(2.190)	(1.118)	(2.661)	(2.228)	(3.014)
Divided Gov't.	−0.251	0.062	−0.009	0.986	−0.528	−0.223	0.051
	(0.942)	(0.878)	(0.861)	(0.825)	(0.844)	(0.961)	(0.923)
Party Competition	−0.314	5.860	2.804	−4.714	3.291	0.678	4.412
	(7.153)	(6.662)	(6.033)	(4.430)	(7.377)	(7.103)	(8.577)
LGBT Group Capacity	27.576***	18.473**	17.981***	20.930***	10.940	26.456***	20.588**
	(9.768)	(7.458)	(6.126)	(6.292)	(8.034)	(9.450)	(9.032)
Evangelicals	−0.212	−0.227	0.007	−0.049	−0.439*	−0.200	−0.223
	(0.151)	(0.177)	(0.041)	(0.038)	(0.257)	(0.152)	(0.161)
Educational Attainment	0.118	−0.008	0.125	0.095	0.180	0.133	0.141
	(0.149)	(0.095)	(0.103)	(0.108)	(0.175)	(0.154)	(0.095)
Northeast	1.527	1.239	2.799**	0.595	1.500	1.874	1.757
	(1.825)	(2.355)	(1.368)	(1.046)	(1.622)	(1.847)	(1.674)
Midwest	4.004***	3.209***	2.604***	1.627*	4.964***	4.162***	3.978***
	(1.246)	(0.979)	(0.772)	(0.909)	(1.076)	(1.160)	(0.793)
West	2.741***	1.603	0.821	0.938	6.009***	2.705**	3.077**
	(1.052)	(1.215)	(0.686)	(0.950)	(1.683)	(1.057)	(1.212)

TABLE 6.1.—*Continued*

Year	−0.116	0.188	0.185	0.313	0.065	−0.136	−0.106
	(0.276)	(0.163)	(0.261)	(0.192)	(0.327)	(0.279)	(0.228)
N	1,247	1,283	1,229	1,106	1,212	1,248	1,237
Log Likelihood	−56.434	−59.710	−71.224	−88.907	−54.543	−56.127	−57.516
McFadden's R^2	0.449	0.421	0.354	0.256	0.442	0.452	0.438

Note: Cell entries are logistic regression coefficients. Simultaneously estimated robust standard errors, clustered on the state, are presented in parentheses.
* $p < 0.1$; ** $p < 0.05$; *** $p < 0.01$

tion are significantly more likely to pass a subsequent protection. In fact, previous adoption of a prior gender identity protection perfectly predicts the ensuing passage of private employment and real estate protections. Partisan factors are also significant in most of the gender identity models. However, in contrast to the findings regarding sexual orientation components, divided government and party competition significantly affect the likelihood of adoption of gender identity components. Another apparent difference between the gender identity models and the sexual orientation models is that the state-level organized interest variables do not significantly affect the likelihood of adopting gender identity protections.

Although the results presented in tables 6.1 and 6.2 certainly appear to show differences between gay and transgender policies in the types of factors that significantly affect the likelihood of policy adoption, simple comparisons of significance levels can be misleading. To test the differences more robustly, we ran pairwise chi-squared tests of the differences between corresponding sexual orientation and gender identity components.[6] Table 6.3 lists the variables that have statistically significant ($p < 0.10$) differences between corresponding coefficients, accounting for nearly half of all the variables (for the full table, see the appendix, table 6.6). The differences are most consistently significant for the prior passage coefficients, initiative use, the interaction between initiative use and citizen ideology, divided government, and LGBT group capacity. From these results, it is apparent that the politics of transgender rights fits less well in the morality politics typology, relative to gay rights politics. Whereas sexual orientation protections are driven by internal party and interest group factors, the adoption of gender identity provisions are influenced by reinvention factors, the absence of divided government, and levels of party competi-

TABLE 6.2. Event History Analysis of the Adoption of Gender Identity–Inclusive Nondiscrimination Policy Components, 1981–2011

Variable	Credit	Education	Health Care/Public Accomm.	Insurance	Private Employment	Real Estate
Diffusion	3.058	1.776	2.863	3.928*	2.262	3.179
	(2.300)	(2.163)	(2.449)	(2.032)	(2.003)	(2.199)
Prior Passage	3.992***	2.670***	4.242***	5.250***	—	—
	(1.109)	(0.936)	(1.204)	(1.127)	—	—
Avg. Protection	−3.057	−2.130	−3.208*	−3.584**	−3.990	−3.541*
	(1.907)	(1.621)	(1.659)	(1.783)	(2.486)	(2.022)
Prior S.O.	−1.621	−0.450	−0.837	−0.701	−1.083	−0.879
Component	(1.675)	(1.168)	(1.307)	(1.233)	(0.886)	(1.139)
Citizen Ideology	17.326	9.476	18.961	18.918	12.121	16.742
	(18.386)	(20.327)	(19.770)	(18.986)	(16.412)	(15.815)
Initiative Use	0.822	0.667	1.001	0.691	0.665	0.539
	(1.052)	(0.938)	(1.015)	(1.073)	(1.124)	(1.056)
Ideology ×	−4.360	−2.509	−4.917	−3.538	−2.385	−1.955
Initiative Use	(4.205)	(3.900)	(4.355)	(4.513)	(4.694)	(4.402)
% Democrats	4.644**	5.188***	4.275**	4.232**	6.577***	6.069***
(logged)	(1.916)	(1.925)	(1.869)	(1.878)	(2.063)	(1.992)
Divided	−2.185***	−1.243	−2.254*	−2.176**	−2.416***	−1.983***
Government	(0.836)	(0.872)	(0.901)	(0.884)	(0.782)	(0.727)
Party	7.638*	8.989*	8.716*	8.878*	12.077**	9.920**
Competition	(4.502)	(5.229)	(4.664)	(4.668)	(5.260)	(5.030)
LGBT Group	6.759	3.014	5.182	3.898	2.068	−0.058
Capacity	(4.433)	(4.965)	(4.168)	(4.265)	(3.333)	(4.111)
Evangelicals	−0.064	−0.075	−0.064	−0.065	−0.070	−0.058
	(0.050)	(0.052)	(0.044)	(0.043)	(0.050)	(0.045)
Educational	−0.106	−0.093	−0.144	−0.151	−0.051	−0.054
Attainment	(0.112)	(0.105)	(0.111)	(0.110)	(0.096)	(0.100)
Year	0.532	0.450	0.512*	0.532*	0.666	0.587*
	(0.330)	(0.290)	(0.279)	(0.302)	(0.458)	(0.347)
N	1,459	1,467	1,459	1,457	1,459	1,454
Log Likelihood	−48.905	−52.035	−48.975	−46.471	−49.733	−51.793
McFadden's R^2	0.445	0.410	0.414	0.444	0.436	0.412

Note: Cell entries are logistic regression coefficients. Simultaneously estimated robust standard errors, clustered on the state, are presented in parentheses.

*$p < 0.1$; **$p < 0.05$; ***$p < 0.01$

TABLE 6.3. Statistically Significant Differences in Coefficients between Gender Identity and Sexual Orientation Equations

Policy Component	Gender Identity > Sexual Orientation	Gender Identity < Sexual Orientation
Credit	Prior Passage (+/+) Initiative Use (+/−)	Average Protection (−/+) Ideology × Initiative Use (−/+) Divided Government (−/−) LGBT Capacity (+/+)
Education	Diffusion (+/−) Initiative Use (+/−)	Ideology × Initiative Use (−/+) Divided Government (−/+) LGBT Capacity (+/+)
Health Care	Prior Passage (+/+) Citizen Ideology (+/−) Initiative Use (+/−)	Ideology × Initiative Use (−/+) Divided Government (−/−) LGBT Capacity (+/+) Educational Attainment (−/+)
Insurance	Diffusion (+/−) Prior Passage (+/+) % Democrats (+/+) Party Competition (+/−)	Divided Government (−/+) LGBT Capacity (+/+) Educational Attainment (−/+)
Private Employment	Citizen Ideology (+/−) Initiative Use (+/−)	Ideology × Initiative Use (−/+) Divided Government (−/−)
Public Accommodations	Prior Passage (+/+) Initiative Use (+/−) Year (+/−)	Average Protection (−/+) Ideology × Initiative Use (−/+) Divided Government (−/−) LGBT Capacity (+/+)
Real Estate	Initiative Use (+/−) Year (+/−)	Average Protection (−/+) Ideology × Initiative Use (−/+) Divided Government (−/−) LGBT Capacity (−/+)

Note: Statistical significance determined with χ^2 tests ($p < 0.1$); direction of corresponding coefficients in parentheses (gender identity/sexual orientation).

tion. Thus, we find that the factors affecting the adoption of sexual orientation and gender identity protections differ significantly.

A large number of the comparisons between the sexual orientation coefficients and the gender identity coefficients show significant differences, but comparisons across the different policy components within those two groups revealed relatively less variation.[7] Tables 6.4 and 6.5 list the variables that have statistically significant differences ($p < 0.1$) across the different policy components (for the full tables, see the appendix, tables 6.7 and 6.8). Only 14.58 percent of the comparisons were statistically significant. The cross-component differences are seen most often in the magnitude of the impact of citizen ideology and national reinvention pressures. Partisanship and interest group effects also differed significantly across some components. Though the cross-component variation was not as extensive as the variation between sexual orientation and gender identity, we nonetheless find support for Hypothesis 2 (concerning differences between similar gay and transgender policy components) for sexual orientation policies.

Hypothesis 3, which states that there will be more cross-component variation for sexual-orientation-inclusive policies relative to gender-identity-inclusive policies, is also supported by the analyses. Only 5.47 percent of the comparisons in the gender identity models reached traditional levels of statistical significance. The main sources of cross-component variation for gender-identity-inclusive policies are the effects of internal reinvention pressure, partisanship in the legislature, and interest group influence. However, these tests reveal very little variation across the various components, suggesting that the content of each component is less important in terms of the factors affecting policy adoption than is evident for sexual-orientation-inclusive policies.

Case Studies

Though the event history analyses showed support for our hypotheses, especially the difference between sexual orientation and gender identity, it is not immediately evident how these differences manifest themselves. To further explore how the two classes of protections have been considered by different states, we conducted qualitative case studies of three states: Hawaii, Maryland, and Massachusetts. Using interviews and newspaper and magazine accounts, these case studies explore how and why certain components of nondiscrimination policy were blocked in the respective states.

These states were selected because they offered opportunities to study transgender policymaking in different regions of the country (West, Northeast, and Mid-Atlantic), over time, and under different political conditions. Hawaii exhibits periods of divided and unified Democratic control of state government, while our Maryland and Massachusetts cases feature Democratic control of state institutions. The cases also allow us to look at fully LGBT-inclusive proposals (Hawaii and Maryland) and transgender specific ones (Hawaii, Maryland, and Massachusetts). Importantly, each of these states engaged in incremental LGBT nondiscrimination policymaking. In other words, the states chosen did not adopt sexual orientation and gender identity provisions together in a comprehensive manner.

Maryland

For most of the past few decades, Maryland has experienced unified Democratic control. The exception to this trend was the tenure of Republican governor Robert Ehrlich Jr. (2003–7). Despite long periods of one-party rule, the General Assembly has experienced division based on financial disputes between the haves and have-nots (Barone, Lilley, and DeFranco 1998). There are also ideological cleavages in the state's Democratic Party, but conservative Democrats have seen their influence dwindle in recent years.

During the past 20 years, LGBT rights have often featured prominently in the state's political battles. In the 1999 legislative session, a fully LGBT-inclusive nondiscrimination measure was submitted to the legislature (HB 315); it was heavily backed by Democratic governor Parris Glendening. Following attempts to enact similar measures in the 1990s (McClellan and Greif 2004), this bill protected transgender persons under the definition of sexual orientation. However, the House Judiciary Committee struck the transgender-inclusive language. The altered bill passed in the House by a vote of 80–56, but it stalled in the Senate. The proposal did not have the support of the Judicial Proceedings Committee chairperson, Walter Baker, a conservative Democrat who represented to the rural Eastern Shore (Kelly 2002).

While unsuccessful in 1999, Gov. Glendening and the LGBT advocacy group Free State Justice (later Equality Maryland) continued to press for a sexual-orientation-inclusive nondiscrimination bill in 2001. Given problems at the committee level in previous sessions, the new nondiscrimination bill (SB 205) was not transgender inclusive. This was a huge disappointment for many transgender activists.

TABLE 6.4. Statistically Significant Differences in Coefficients across Policy Component Equations—Sexual Orientation

	Education	Health Care	Insurance	Private Employment	Public Accomm.	Real Estate
Credit	—	Prior Passage (+ > +) % Democrats (+ < +) West (+ > +) Year (− < +)	Avg. Protection (+ > −) Year (− < +)	Avg. Protection (+ > +) Citizen Ideology (− > −) LGBT Capacity (+ > +) West (+ < +)	—	—
Education		—	Initiative Use (− < −)	Initiative Use (− > −) Ideology × Initiative Use (+ < +) West (+ < +)	—	Initiative Use (− > −) Ideology × Initiative Use (+ < +)
Health care			% Democrats (+ > +)	Evangelicals (+ > −) Midwest (+ < +) West (+ < +)	Avg. Protection (− < +) Midwest (+ < +) West (+ > −) Year (+ > −)	Avg. Protection (− < +) Initiative Use (− > −) Ideology × Initiative Use (+ < +) West (+ < +) Year (+ > −)

Insurance	Initiative Use (− > −) Ideology × Initiative Use (+ < +) % Democrats (+ < +) Divide Government (+ > −)	Avg. Protection (− < +) Midwest (+ < +) Year (+ > −)	Avg. Protection (− < +) Initiative Use (− > −) Ideology × Initiative Use (+ < +) Midwest (+ < +)
	LGBT Capacity (+ > +) Midwest (+ < +) West (+ < +)		Year (+ > −)
Private Employment		Avg. Protection (+ < +) LGBT Capacity (+ < +) West (+ > +)	LGBT Capacity (+ < +) West (+ > +)
Public Accom.			—

Note: Statistical significance determined with χ^2 tests ($p < 0.1$); direction of corresponding coefficients and inequalities in parentheses (row < > column).

Although eliminating transgender protections from the bill was important in gathering support, the Senate's Judicial Proceedings Committee remained a formidable hurdle to passage. Glendening intensely lobbied Chairperson Baker (Associated Press 2001). Important to changing Baker's mind was the precedent set by several localities. Four of the largest jurisdictions in the state already had nondiscrimination policies that were inclusive of gays and lesbians. Changes in committee composition also shaped the dynamics. Senator Norman Stone (D), an opponent of the bill from relatively conservative Baltimore County, was replaced on the Judicial Proceedings Committee by Senator Perry Sfikas (D-Baltimore City), a key sponsor of the bill, at the start of the 2001 session (Associated Press 2001). Baker's change of heart and the replacement of Senator Stone allowed the Judicial Proceedings Committee to pass the measure on a 6–5 vote.

While transgender people were not protected by the legislation, they remained part of the discussion. During the floor debate, Senator Alex Mooney (R-Frederick and Washington Counties), a staunch opponent of LGBT rights, attempted to pass an amendment that would have explicitly

TABLE 6.5. Statistically Significant Differences in Coefficients across Policy Component Equations—Gender Identity

	Education	Health Care/ Public Accom.	Insurance	Private Employment	Real Estate
Credit	—	—	Prior Passage (+ < +) LGBT Capacity (+ > +)	—	LGBT Capacity (+ > −)
Education		—	Prior Passage (+ < +)	—	—
Healthcare/ Public Accom.			Prior Passage (+ < +) Initiative Use (+ > +) Ideology × Initiative Use (− < −)	% Democrats (+ < +)	% Democrats (+ < +)
Insurance				% Democrats (+ < +)	% Democrats (+ < +)
Private Employment					—

Note: Statistical significance determined with χ^2 tests ($p < 0.1$); direction of corresponding coefficients and inequalities in parentheses (row < > column).

allowed employers to regulate dress in a manner consistent with an employee's biological sex. This proposal was rejected, 14–30. The sexual-orientation-inclusive nondiscrimination bill passed the Senate by a vote of 32–14. It passed the House, 90–47, and was signed by Governor Glendening.

Subsequently, some advocacy groups began lobbying the state's Human Relations Commission to cover transgender people under existing prohibitions on sex and gender discrimination (McClellan and Greif 2004). Additionally, and as noted during our interview with their lobbyist, Free State Justice/Equality Maryland agreed to later back a gender-identity-inclusive nondiscrimination bill. This stance was necessary to heal divisions within their membership.

In 2007, after a period where Republicans held the governor's mansion, Equality Maryland's highest legislative priority was passing a gender-identity-inclusive nondiscrimination bill. Supporters in the Senate, notably Senator Richard Madaleno (D-Montgomery County), expected a good reception because of the increased visibility of transgender issues. Our lobbyist contact with Equality Maryland noted that legislators and the public were more familiar with the issues because transgender people were increasingly in the news, portrayed more favorably in popular culture, and were testifying before legislative committees.

Given these developments, legislative prospects seemed good. The lobbyist stated that opponents who had worked against previous bills did not organize for this fight. The only significant opposition came from a single retail trade group, the Maryland Retailers Association. They were concerned about restroom issues, but were willing to compromise with Equality Maryland. Given that the newly elected governor, Martin O'Malley (D), had signed a transgender-inclusive nondiscrimination ordinance in the City of Baltimore, everything seemed in place. However, the bill ran aground in a familiar place, the Senate's Judicial Proceedings Committee. SB 516 failed on a 6–5 vote. All of the Republicans voted against the measure. Additionally, recently elected Senator C. Anthony Muse (D-Prince George's County) and Senator Stone (who had returned to the committee) voted against it. According to Equality Maryland's executive director and their lobbyist, the committee troubles occurred because leadership did not want the bill on the floor. The lobbyist noted that the Senate leadership was worried about the potential for electoral backlash given the state's pending high court decision on same-sex marriage. This may have been why the Senate Democrats installed Senator Muse, a prominent minister who was a known opponent of LGBT rights (Concerned Women for America 2004), and Senator Stone on the Judicial Proceedings Committee.

Since the surprising defeat in 2007, transgender activists and their allies have managed to have nondiscrimination bills introduced in each legislative session. However, there were no votes taken until 2011. In that year, a controversial measure, HB 235, was introduced. Unlike previous bills, public accommodations protections were not included in the measure. This was a strategic decision made by Equality Maryland and their legislative allies in response to tepid support for that provision (Najafi 2011). Some transgender activists subsequently opposed the bill (Najafi 2011). It passed the House on a vote of 86–52. After a campaign by Equality Maryland to keep the bill from being killed by the senate's Rules Committee (Chibbaro 2011), the bill later received a favorable report from the Senate's Judicial Proceedings Committee. On the Senate floor, Senator Muse questioned whether the Boy Scouts would have to hire transgender persons or whether people could avoid transgender roommates (Chibbaro 2011). Senator James DeGrange (D-Anne Arundel County) then made a motion to recommit the bill to committee. With the support of Senate president Mike Miller (D-Prince George's and Calvert Counties), the motion prevailed 27–20. According to our contact with Gender Rights Maryland, a transgender-focused interest group, competition from the issue of same-sex marriage, divisions in the LGBT advocacy community, and the high-profile bathroom/locker room issue continue to block transgender rights in the state.

This case demonstrates that legislative opposition to gay- and transgender-inclusive laws is likely to come from Republicans, Democrats in conservative areas, or those who base their opposition on theological grounds. In that regard, gay- and transgender-inclusive policymaking is similar. This finding is quite consistent with our quantitative analyses showing few differences between gay and transgender policy adoption in the effects of legislative partisanship.

However, this case also highlights the difficulty of treating gay and transgender rights or all provisions of LGBT nondiscrimination law in the same manner. During the 2001 session, state legislators were uncomfortable with linking transgender rights to gay rights. Thus, the decision to remove transgender protections in 2001 provides support for Hypothesis 1.

We also find some support for Hypothesis 2 during the 2001 and 2011 debates. During the early debate, Senator Mooney's attempted amendment raised concerns about the ability of employers to regulate dress. In 2011, public accommodations protections were eliminated from the bill as a strategic tactic to mitigate concerns about restroom issues. The real estate provisions showed similar strategic considerations, with Senator

Muse raising questions about the rights of landlords. In each of these situations, legislators demonstrate more discomfort with transgender identities than they do with gay persons. Still, our analyses suggest that political strategies that differentiate between components of gender identity protections are less successful compared to similar tactics used to pass targeted components of sexual orientation protections.

Massachusetts

Massachusetts is generally viewed as a very liberal state. This is particularly true for LGBT issues. In 1989, it became one of the first states to ban discrimination on the basis of sexual orientation. In 2004, Massachusetts became the first state in the United States to legalize same-sex marriage. Yet, despite these accomplishments, progress on transgender issues moved much more slowly in the Bay State.

Until 2011, LGBT advocates were unsuccessful in securing statewide nondiscrimination protections for transgendered individuals through the legislature. Despite the overwhelming dominance of the Democratic Party in the legislature, a transgender-inclusive nondiscrimination bill had failed to advance for three consecutive years (Chabot 2011). Moreover, lesser packages of protections for the transgender community (in a variety of forms) had been stalled for six years (Chabot 2011). Each time hearings on such protections were held, strong opposition arose. Opponents of transgender civil rights often used heated rhetoric to express their opposition. In some cases, they characterized transgendered people as "sexual predators" (Scott and Suffredini 2011).

Some portions of the state's transgender community had achieved limited employment and education protections via statutory interpretations of sex and disability discrimination laws in *Robert Lie aka Allie Lie v. Sky Publishing Corporation* (2002) and *Doe v. Yunits* (2001). However, a broader-level protection was implemented on February 17, 2011, when Governor Deval Patrick (D) quietly issued an executive order to ban employment discrimination on the basis of gender identity and expression (Cheney 2011). This order extended to all jobs, programs, and services within state government, and also obliged any contractors working with the Commonwealth to refrain from this type of discrimination in their own organizations (Levenson 2011).

Governor Patrick's move was hailed by civil rights activists and was widely seen as an important step to providing broader protections for the transgender community. Beth Boland, former president of the state Women's Bar Association, said the move was "a powerful step that's going to help us get the bill passed," referring to the Transgender Equal Rights Bill making its way through the legislature (Levenson 2011). Arline Issacson, the co-chairperson of the Massachusetts Gay and Lesbian Political Caucus, agreed. She noted that once the public saw no ill consequences from extending these protections to state workers and vendors, they would be more willing to extend these protections to everyone (Levenson 2011).

While opponents were caught off guard, they soon responded. According to the *Boston Herald*, "the event didn't appear on his [Patrick's] public schedule and his press office issued no statement on the signing" (Cheney 2011). Critics derided it as an "end run" around lawmakers (Chabot 2011), and House Minority Leader Bradley Jones (R) said, "This is going to set off a firestorm, and it's certainly something the governor should have given us a heads up on" (Chabot 2011).

Opponents were also quick to characterize the broader nondiscrimination bill in the legislature as a "bathroom bill" that would allow crossdressing males access to women's restrooms and locker rooms. This stoked fears about sexual assaults against women and child molestation targeting young girls. Kris Mineau, president of the Massachusetts Family Institute and a staunch opponent of the bill, characterized it as "a stealth bathroom bill, opening bathrooms, locker rooms, and showers to any gender in all government-controlled facilities, including public schools down to kindergarten. . . . There's no doubt that it will impact public schools. . . . This would directly impact vulnerable children, as well as the safety, modesty, and decorum of all citizens" (Chabot 2011).

At a public hearing on the bill conducted by the Massachusetts Legislature's Judiciary Committee on June 8, 2011, opponents continued to raise fears of sexual assaults facilitated by unisex restrooms and locker rooms, while proponents stressed the importance of added protections for the transgender community. Among those testifying in favor of the bill was state Attorney General Martha Coakley. The *Boston Globe* also editorialized in favor of the bill:

> A proposed ban on discrimination against transgender people would have virtually no effect on most people in Massachusetts. But it would enormously improve the lives of a small minority, whose ability to find jobs and places to live is compromised by the fact that their gender identity differs from their sex at birth. . . . Passing the bill would continue this Commonwealth's long tradition of equal rights; to do otherwise would be a deeply ungenerous

act toward people who are far more exposed to bias than many other groups protected by anti-discrimination statutes. (*Boston Globe* 2011)

The *Globe* went on to call opponents' fears "ludicrous," and said expression of such concerns was "nothing but a cheap way to play on some legislators' unease about the subject."

Near the end of the legislative session, the bill was brought to a vote. Critics were quick to pounce on the timing. State Rep. Mark Lombardo (R) said, "I think the ultra left-wing interest groups here are making a push in conjunction with Transgender Awareness Week, and, unfortunately, the leaders are actually giving in to it" (Cassidy 2011). Mineau called the legislature's action a "midnight end run to try to push this radical bill through" (Cassidy 2011). Jennifer Levi of the Transgender Rights Project countered by saying, "The idea that this is being rammed through is preposterous.... I think the opponents would look at their calendar and pick 'never' as the right time to address the protections in this bill" (Cassidy 2011).

Yet, in a blow to transgender advocates, an amendment was added to the bill to eliminate protections in public accommodations. This was done is order to blunt some of the "bathroom bill" arguments. The amended bill was passed by a vote of 95–58 in the House and by a voice vote in the Senate. While hailing passage of the bill, transgender political leaders were disappointed by the lack of public accommodations protections. Gunner Scott of the Massachusetts Transgender Political Coalition said, "You don't always get everything you'd like from the beginning" (Cassidy 2011). Kara Suffredini, executive director of MassEquality, said, "We are looking forward to working with the governor and lawmakers in getting a public accommodations law passed that will also protect transgender people from discrimination in public places like restaurants, grocery stores, trains and buses, and other places where daily life is routinely conducted" (Grindley 2012).

Like the Maryland case, this foray into Massachusetts policymaking demonstrates how some provisions of transgender rights laws meet heavy resistance. While opposition often comes from predictable partisan and ideological sources, advocates of transgender rights face special challenges. In this instance, given uneasiness over restroom issues, the public accommodations provisions were eliminated from consideration. This was important in obtaining passage of bias protections in areas such as employment and real estate. Interestingly, these protections were dropped in the same

year as those in the Maryland case. The effectiveness of differentiating between the policy components stands in contrast to the event history analyses and suggests that while there is little cross-component variation in gender identity politics, the content of the components does have the potential
to significantly affect the dynamics of policy adoptions. Moreover, the fact
that transgender identities were not protected under the 1989 statute that
added sexual orientation protections provides support for Hypothesis 1 during the early period of the LGBT rights movement.

Hawaii

The story of transgender civil rights in Hawaii is also a case study in piecemeal progress. It begins in 2005 with the passage of two bills by the Hawaii
Legislature. One bill would have prohibited housing discrimination based
on sexual orientation and gender identity and expression. The other bill
would have prohibited employment discrimination based on gender identity and expression. In regards to the latter type of discrimination, gay
persons had been protected in employment since 1991. Republican governor Linda Lingle decided to sign the bill related to housing discrimination, after an exemption was added for housing provided by religious organizations. This provision was the result of strong lobbying by officials
from Brigham Young University–Hawaii. On that point, Governor Lingle
said, "The housing bill was the result of many, many years of debate, discussion and an ultimate compromise with the Church of Jesus Christ of
Latter-day Saints . . . I felt it was important to honor that compromise"
(Reyes 2005). However, Lingle decided to veto the employment discrimination bill, saying that it addressed issues that were already covered by
other parts of Hawaii law (namely, prior rulings of the state's Civil Rights
Commission that provided certain protections to people based on gender
identity). Despite very large Democratic Party majorities in both chambers, the legislature was unable to override Lingle's veto of the transgender
nondiscrimination bill. Yet, they did override Governor Lingle on twelve
other bills during the 2005 legislative session (Borreca 2005).

The following year, in 2006, the legislature passed a bill prohibiting
discrimination in public accommodations on the basis of sexual orientation and gender identity/expression. According to the National Center for
Transgender Equality, this public accommodations law covered "any facil-
ity whose operations affect commerce, such as hospitals, shops, hotels,
restaurants, museums, theaters, and schools." The bill passed into law
without Governor Lingle's signature (National Center for Transgender
Equality 2006).[8]

Five years later, in 2011, a law to ban employment discrimination on the basis of "gender identity and expression"—a proposal nearly identical to the 2005 bill vetoed by Governor Lingle—was passed by overwhelming majorities in both legislative chambers and signed by Democratic governor Neil Abercrombie. This bill enjoyed strong support from LGBT civil rights groups and the Hawaii Civil Rights Commission (Mikesell 2011). Alan Spector, cochair of Equality Hawaii, said, "Providing employment protections to transgender people in Hawaii is a victory for civil rights. The people of this state should be judged on the quality of work they do and not on who they are—that's what this legislation guarantees."

In this case, when transgender protections were bundled with gay rights measures in the area of public accommodation and real estate, they were either signed by a Republican governor or were enacted without her signature. This seems to run counter to Hypothesis 1 because the same factors explain passage of gay and transgender law. However, the 20-year gap between the adoption of sexual-orientation and gender-identity-inclusive employment protections points to differences in how these issues have been viewed and the underlying factors that influenced the adoption of both policies. Additionally, given that gender identity protections in employment, public accommodations, and real estate were enacted in such an incremental approach, we find some support for Hypothesis 2.

Conclusion

This chapter examined differences between policymaking in gay- and transgender-inclusive nondiscrimination law. Using a novel methodological approach that provided a way to address shortcomings in other policy innovation and diffusion research, we were able to better analyze the content of these policies throughout the policymaking process. Our quantitative modeling was supplemented by case studies of policy adoption in Hawaii, Maryland, and Massachusetts. On the whole, we found support for each of our research hypotheses. Thus, the factors that explain policy adoption in gay and transgender law do appear to vary by whom the law protects and what it covers. Partisanship, with Democrats being more supportive, is important for both gay- and transgender-inclusive policies against discrimination. Yet there are significant differences. In particular, gay rights nondiscrimination policy seems much more driven by typical morality policy explanations whereas transgender policy is, in part, driven by reinvention pressures. Additionally, when compared to gay-inclusive nondiscrimination law, there might be less variation in the explanatory factors across aspects of transgender policy.

Of course, our analyses do have some limitations. Since comprehensive LGBT-inclusive nondiscrimination measures in general and transgender-inclusive measures in particular have been adopted in comparatively few states, it is possible that the explanatory factors affecting policy adoption will change over time. After all, public opinion studies find increasing acceptance of the LGBT community (e.g., Brewer 2008). An additional limitation in our work is found in the quantitative modeling and data. Our approach does not allow for policy reinvention within policy components. For instance, if a state passed a very narrow nondiscrimination policy that addresses a type of insurance policy bias and it later enacted a comprehensive insurance protection, our model does not capture this phenomenon. Thus, the power of some explanatory factors might be over- or underestimated. We were also unable to directly account for the strength of national issue networks, as suggested by Boushey (2010). However, the analyses do include a temporal trend variable that produced a significant positive effect for four of the seven gender identity protection components. This effect is consistent with a national issue network that has increased in strength over time. We also expect that the capacity of state-organized interest groups is correlated with national organizational strength, and the state-level variable should tap the effects of the national networks to some degree.

Nonetheless, we were able to triangulate our findings with multiple approaches. Our data and case studies note important changes in transgender nondiscrimination policymaking. Nondiscrimination policies advocated for or adopted prior to 2003 were less likely to include transgender protections. In the past decade, many of these early state adopters have undergone nondiscrimination policy reinvention in order to develop transgender-inclusive policies. However, when some of these early adopters sought to include transgender individuals, challenges to specific components of nondiscrimination protections were sometimes raised. Each of our case studies demonstrated this problem. In particular, public accommodations drew fire from opponents. Public accommodations measures in Maryland and Massachusetts drew intense push-back over restroom access in 2011. It is possible that this represents a growing vulnerability for transgender rights advocacy—and transgender rights advocates need to recognize this issue.

The public accommodations vulnerability can be avoided by including transgender-inclusive polices when gay rights measures are passed. As noted in our Hawaii case study (and with the experience of states such as Iowa, Washington, and New Mexico), transgender-inclusive measures fare much better when they are attached to similar gay-inclusive proposals. With only a handful of states remaining that have nondiscrimination policies that solely address sexual orientation, future battles for transgender rights are likely to increasingly benefit from such bundling. However, transgender rights advocates will need to be vigilant against attempts to jettison gender identity inclusion.

APPENDIX

TABLE 6.6. Tests of Differences of Coefficients between Sexual Orientation-Inclusive and Gender Identity-Inclusive Equations

Variable	Credit	Education	Health Care	Private Insurance Employment		Public Accommodations	Real Estate
Diffusion	0.226	**0.072**	0.754	**0.054**	0.398	0.279	0.222
Prior Passage	**0.001**	0.100	**0.007**	**0.001**	—	**0.002**	—
Avg. Protection	**0.041**	0.171	0.227	0.673	0.125	**0.032**	**0.004**
Citizen Ideology	0.131	0.915	**0.045**	0.299	**0.099**	0.120	0.127
Initiative Use	**0.019**	**0.028**	**0.025**	0.561	**0.004**	**0.022**	**0.001**
Ideology × Initiative Use	**0.024**	**0.056**	**0.024**	0.420	**0.008**	**0.027**	**0.002**
% Democrats (logged)	0.749	0.581	0.547	**0.078**	0.729	0.897	0.750
Divided Government	**0.030**	**0.063**	**0.013**	**0.001**	**0.028**	**0.033**	**0.027**
Party Competition	0.274	0.671	0.348	**0.025**	0.213	0.270	0.497
LGBT Group Capacity	**0.009**	**0.012**	**0.036**	**0.008**	0.212	**0.010**	**0.006**
Evangelicals	0.377	0.423	0.195	0.772	0.176	0.416	0.349
Educational Attainment	0.119	0.418	**0.050**	**0.088**	0.189	0.114	0.160
Year	0.102	0.358	0.348	0.514	0.241	**0.082**	**0.058**

Note: Cell entries are *p*-values from χ^2 tests of coefficients across the indicated equations. Bold regions highlight $p < 0.1$.

TABLE 6.7. Tests of Differences of Coefficients across Sexual Orientation–Inclusive Policy Component Equations

Variable	1/2	1/3	1/4	1/5	1/6	1/7	2/3	2/4	2/5	2/6	2/7	3/4	3/5	3/6	3/7	4/5	4/6	4/7	5/6	5/7	6/7
Diffusion	0.27	0.52	0.40	0.58	0.60	0.58	0.19	0.66	0.49	0.29	0.45	0.24	0.40	0.51	0.41	0.63	0.45	0.63	0.64	0.97	0.64
Prior Passage	0.76	0.16	0.37	0.22	0.29	0.92	0.54	0.48	0.47	0.78	0.68	0.88	0.68	0.45	0.22	0.82	0.61	0.40	0.34	0.25	0.34
Average Protection	0.30	**0.07**	**0.04**	**0.07**	0.53	0.99	0.70	0.23	0.85	0.27	0.25	0.27	0.50	**0.06**	**0.05**	0.17	**0.03**	**0.00**	**0.06**	0.27	0.92
Citizen Ideology	0.30	0.19	0.48	**0.09**	0.67	0.99	0.12	0.65	0.13	0.28	0.30	0.21	0.98	0.20	0.26	0.12	0.47	0.53	0.12	0.22	0.96
Initiative Use	0.22	0.28	0.10	0.75	0.74	0.78	0.70	**0.08**	**0.09**	0.21	**0.01**	0.14	0.23	0.27	**0.05**	**0.05**	0.10	**0.00**	0.78	0.49	0.75
Ideology × Init. Use	0.22	0.34	0.14	0.77	0.83	0.68	0.56	0.18	**0.09**	0.22	**0.01**	0.17	0.29	0.34	**0.06**	**0.07**	0.14	**0.01**	0.79	0.38	0.65
% Democrats (logged)	0.86	**0.09**	0.16	0.19	0.80	0.36	0.37	0.53	0.43	0.83	0.37	0.19	0.86	0.11	0.68	**0.09**	0.18	0.18	0.20	0.75	0.34
Divided Gov't.	0.66	0.44	0.12	0.46	0.58	0.17	0.92	0.31	0.44	0.69	0.98	0.13	0.15	0.51	0.87	**0.07**	0.14	0.26	0.42	0.12	0.23
Party Comp.	0.36	0.36	0.43	0.43	0.37	0.28	0.64	0.12	0.76	0.43	0.86	0.63	0.91	0.49	0.74	0.15	0.33	0.18	0.52	0.64	0.35
LGBT Group Capacity	0.18	0.17	0.40	**0.04**	0.39	0.35	0.94	0.72	0.36	0.23	0.79	0.32	0.21	0.19	0.64	**0.08**	0.47	0.96	**0.04**	**0.00**	0.41
Evangelicals	0.85	0.10	0.28	0.19	0.51	0.92	0.16	0.31	0.19	0.73	0.97	0.32	0.60	0.13	0.14	0.14	0.32	0.27	0.15	0.24	0.81
Educational Attainment	0.32	0.93	0.89	0.31	0.45	0.78	0.24	0.45	0.20	0.28	0.18	0.82	0.60	0.91	0.77	0.66	0.82	0.71	0.40	0.73	0.92
Northeast	0.85	0.34	0.60	0.97	0.21	0.87	0.42	0.77	0.87	0.69	0.75	0.13	0.30	0.47	0.43	0.55	0.47	0.47	0.58	0.82	0.93
Midwest	0.50	0.17	0.11	0.36	0.40	0.98	0.55	0.23	0.15	0.41	0.23	0.38	**0.04**	**0.09**	0.10	**0.02**	**0.07**	**0.03**	0.41	0.32	0.84
West	0.34	**0.05**	0.20	**0.05**	0.89	0.62	0.51	0.67	**0.01**	0.31	0.11	0.92	**0.01**	**0.04**	**0.02**	**0.01**	0.21	0.18	**0.05**	**0.06**	0.49
Year	0.15	**0.09**	**0.09**	0.14	0.48	0.95	0.99	0.58	0.64	0.14	0.14	0.55	0.58	**0.09**	**0.08**	0.40	**0.09**	**0.03**	0.11	0.38	0.84

Note: Cell entries are *p*-values from χ^2 tests of coefficients across the indicated equations. Bold regions highlight
$p < 0.1$. Equation numbers: (1) Credit; (2) Education; (3) Health care; (4) Insurance; (5) Private Employment; (6) Public
Accommodations; (7) Real Estate.

TABLE 6.8. Tests of Differences of Coefficients across Gender Identity–Inclusive Policy Component Equations

Variable	1/2	1/3	1/4	1/5	1/6	2/3	2/4	2/5	2/6	3/4	3/5	3/6	4/5	4/6	5/6
Diffusion	0.28	0.59	0.66	0.71	0.96	0.35	0.26	0.81	0.52	0.60	0.79	0.90	0.19	0.58	0.48
Prior Passage	0.20	0.29	**0.00**	—	—	0.12	**0.02**	—	—	**0.03**	—	—	—	—	—
Mean Protection	0.30	0.72	0.17	0.27	0.48	0.23	0.13	0.17	0.19	0.19	0.48	0.67	0.70	0.96	0.64
Prior S.O. Policy	0.22	0.23	0.15	0.66	0.68	0.62	0.74	0.49	0.75	0.47	0.79	0.98	0.63	0.90	0.85
Citizen Ideology	0.43	0.50	0.45	0.44	0.94	0.33	0.35	0.82	0.55	0.98	0.38	0.79	0.29	0.77	0.31
Initiative Use	0.82	0.39	0.53	0.77	0.62	0.53	0.97	0.99	0.86	**0.08**	0.52	0.35	0.96	0.77	0.74
Ideology*Initiative Use	0.50	0.47	0.37	0.44	0.31	0.32	0.73	0.97	0.88	**0.09**	0.35	0.22	0.65	0.49	0.76
% Democrats (logged)	0.58	0.24	0.25	0.11	0.17	0.34	0.37	0.18	0.48	0.81	**0.05**	**0.09**	**0.05**	**0.08**	0.54
Divided Government	0.28	0.71	0.94	0.44	0.55	0.26	0.31	0.17	0.39	0.53	0.70	0.53	0.52	0.61	0.21
Party Competition	0.48	0.39	0.33	0.13	0.35	0.88	0.95	0.31	0.75	0.83	0.31	0.66	0.28	0.67	0.11
LGBT Group Capacity	0.19	0.14	**0.05**	0.20	**0.07**	0.44	0.77	0.80	0.39	0.33	0.30	0.11	0.57	0.24	0.19
Evangelical Rate	0.62	0.95	0.93	0.63	0.70	0.70	0.74	0.87	0.59	0.91	0.70	0.65	0.76	0.65	0.35
Education Rate	0.86	0.41	0.26	0.36	0.59	0.32	0.24	0.54	0.66	0.54	0.18	0.31	0.12	0.26	0.95
Year	0.34	0.76	0.99	0.40	0.53	0.47	0.37	0.29	0.19	0.59	0.47	0.53	0.47	0.58	0.58

Note: Cell entries are p-values from χ^2 tests of coefficients across the indicated equations. Bold regions highlight $p < 0.1$. Equation numbers: (1) Credit; (2) Education; (3) Health Care/Public Accommodations; (4) Insurance; (5) Private Employment; (6) Real Estate.

NOTES

1. States with "comprehensive protections" in their nondiscrimination policies provide explicit protection in seven component areas—credit, education, health care, insurance, private employment, public accommodations, and real estate. For further information on the varying components of nondiscrimination policy, see Taylor et al. 2012.

2. Nebraska, Mississippi, and Tennessee only provide protection for health care. Florida, Ohio, Kentucky, Montana, and Arizona only provide protection for insurance. These protections are very narrow in scope. For instance, some of these states only have viatical settlement protections.

3. This approach combines the parameter estimates and variance-covariance matrices into a single parameter vector and simultaneous covariance matrix in order to jointly estimate robust standard errors clustered by state (Weesie 1999; White 1982, 1994).

4. Each state's interest group budgets were averaged with outliers being excluded. These were then linearly calculated back to 1980. See Taylor et al. (2012) for more about the creation of this measure.

5. We use the evangelical rates from the 1980, 1990, and 2000 Religious Congregations and Membership surveys, available from Association of Religion Data Archives at www.thearda.com and collected by Association of Statisticians of American Religious Bodies. Following Erikson, Wright, and McIver (1993), we include membership in the Church of Jesus Christ of Latter Day Saints as part of this measure.

6. The p-values from these tests are presented in table 6.6 in the appendix.

7. The p-values from these tests are presented in tables 6.7 and 6.8 in the appendix.

8. The Hawaii constitution allows passed legislation that is not signed by the governor or returned to the legislature within a certain amount of time (10 or 45 days) to become law.

REFERENCES

Associated Press. 2001. "Glendening Savors Gays Rights Bill Victory." *Capital,* April 12, A4.

Barone, Michael, William Lilley, and Laurence DeFranco. 1998. *State Legislative Elections: Voting Patterns and Elections.* Washington, DC: Congressional Quarterly Press.

Berry, Frances Stokes, and William D. Berry. 1990. "State Lottery Adoptions as Policy Innovations: An Event History Analysis." *American Political Science Review* 84 (2): 395–415.

Boehmke, Frederick J. 2009. "Approaches to Modeling the Adoption and Diffusion of Policies with Multiple Components." *State Politics and Policy Quarterly* 9 (2): 229–52.

Borreca, Richard. 2005. "Legislature Overturns a Dozen Lingle Vetoes, Tying a Record," *Honolulu Star-Bulletin,* July 13. Accessed June 8, 2012, http://archives.starbulletin.com/2005/07/13/news/index3.html.

Boston Globe. 2011. Editorial, "A Matter of Simple Justice." *Boston Globe,* June 8. Accessed June 8, 2012, http://www.boston.com/bostonglobe/editorial_opinion/editorials/articles/2011/06/08/a_matter_of_simple_justice.

Boushey, Graeme. 2010. *Policy Diffusion Dynamics in America.* Cambridge: Cambridge University Press.

Brewer, Paul. 2008. *Value War: Public Opinion and the Politics of Gay Rights.* New York: Rowman and Littlefield.

Burden, Barry C. 2005. "Institutions and Policy Representation in the States." *State Politics and Policy Quarterly* 5 (4): 373–93.

Cassidy, Chris. 2011. "Transgender Rights Bill Timing Attacked." *Boston Herald,* November 15. Accessed June 8, 2012, http://bostonherald.com/news/politics/view/2011_1115transgender_rightsbill_timing_attacked.

Chabot, Hillary. 2011. "Deval Patrick Signs 'Bathroom Bill,' Sets Off 'Firestorm.'" *Boston Herald,* February 18. Accessed June 8, 2012, http://bostonherald.com/news/politics/view/2011_0218deval_signs_bathroom_bill_sets_off_firestorm.

Cheney, Kyle. 2011. "Patrick Orders Protections for Transgender State Workers, Applicants." *Boston Herald,* February 17. Accessed June 8, 2012, http://bostonherald.com/news/us_politics/view/20110217patrick_orders_protections_for_transgender_state_workers_applicants.

Chibbaro, Lou. 2011. "Maryland Senate Kills Trans Rights Bill." *Washington Blade,* April 14. Accessed July 10, 2012, http://www.washingtonblade.com/2011/04/14/maryland-senate-kills-trans-rights-bill/.

Clark, Jill. 1985. "Policy Diffusion and Program Scope: Research Directions." *Publius: The Journal of Federalism* 15 (4): 61–70.

Colvin, Roddrick. 2008. "Innovations in Non-discrimination Laws: Exploratory Research on Transgender-Inclusive Cities." *Journal of Public Management & Social Policy* 14 (1): 19–34.

Concerned Women for America. 2004. "African American Pastors Fight for Marriage." Accessed May 30, 2007, http://www.cwfa.org/articles/6330/CWA/family/index.htm.

Daley, Dorothy M., and James C. Garand. 2005. "Horizontal Diffusion, Vertical Diffusion, and Internal Pressure in State Environmental Policymaking, 1989–1998." *American Politics Research* 33 (5): 615–44.

Doe v. Yunits, 15 Mass. L. Rep. 278 (Mass. Super. 2001).

Erikson, Robert S., Gerald C. Wright, and John P. McIver. 1993. *Statehouse Democracy: Public Opinion and Policy in the American States.* Cambridge: Cambridge University Press.

Gerber, Elisabeth R. 1996. "Legislative Response to the Threat of Popular Initiatives." *American Journal of Political Science* 40 (1): 99–128.

Glick, Henry R., and Scott P. Hays. 1991. "Innovation and Reinvention in State Policymaking: Theory and the Evolution of Living Will Laws." *Journal of Politics* 53 (3): 835–50.

Gray, Virginia. 1973. "Innovation in the States: A Diffusion Study." *American Political Science Review* 67 (4): 1174–85.

Grindley, Lucas. 2012. "A Milestone in Massachusetts: Trans Rights Bill Signed." *Advocate,* January 20. Accessed June 8, 2012, http://www.advocate.com/news/daily-news/2012/01/20/milestone-massachusetts-trans-rights-bill-signed.

Grossback, Lawrence J., Sean Nicholson-Crotty, and David A. M. Peterson. 2004. "Ideology and Learning in Policy Diffusion." *American Politics Research* 32 (5): 521–45.

Haider-Markel, Donald P. 2000. "Lesbian and Gay Politics in the States: Interest Groups, Electoral Politics, and Public Policy." In *The Politics of Gay Rights,* ed. Craig A. Rimmerman, Kenneth D. Wald, and Clyde Wilcox. Chicago: University of Chicago Press.

Haider-Markel, Donald P. 2001. "Policy Diffusion as a Geographic Expansion of the Scope of Political Conflict: Same-Sex Marriage Bans in the 1990s." *State Politics & Policy Quarterly* 1 (1): 2–26.

Haider-Markel, Donald P., and Kenneth J. Meier. 1996. "The Politics of Gay and Lesbian Rights: Expanding the Scope of the Conflict." *Journal of Politics* 58 (2): 332–49.

Herrick, Rebekah. 2008. "The Responsiveness of State Legislatures and Their Agenda Concerning Gay, Lesbian, Bisexual, and Transgender Interests." *Social Science Journal* 45 (4): 659–72.

Karch, Andrew. 2007. "Emerging Issues and Future Directions in State Policy Diffusion Research." *State Politics & Policy Quarterly* 7 (1): 54–80.

Kelly, E. 2002. "Some Key Legislators Say This May Be the Last Session." *Daily Record,* April 10. Retrieved June 12, 2007, from LexisNexis Academic.

Lax, Jeffery R., and Justin H. Phillips. 2009. "Gay Rights in the States: Public Opinion and Policy Responsiveness." *American Political Science Review* 103 (3): 367–86.

Levenson, Michael. 2011. "Transgender State Workers Get Aid from Governor." *Boston Globe,* February 18. Accessed June 8, 2012, http://www.boston.com/news/politics/articles/2011/02/18/patrick_gives_protection_to_transgender_state_workers.

Lewis, Daniel C. 2011. "Direct Democracy and Minority Rights: Same-Sex Marriage Bans in the U.S. States." *Social Science Quarterly* 92 (2): 364–83.

Lewis, Daniel C. 2013. *Direct Democracy and Minority Rights: A Critical Assessment of the Tyranny of the Majority in the American States.* New York: Routledge.

Lowi, Theodore J. 1964. "Review: American Business, Public Policy, Case Studies, and Political Theory." *World Politics* 16 (4): 677–715.

McClellan, Daphne, and Geoffrey Greif. 2004. "Organizing to Amend Antidiscrimination Statutes in Maryland." *Journal of Gay & Lesbian Social Services* 16 (3–4): 55–68.

McClosky, Herbert, and Alida Brill. 1983. *Dimensions of Tolerance: What Americans Believe about Civil Liberties.* New York: Russell Sage Foundation.

Meier, Kenneth J. 1994. *The Politics of Sin: Drugs, Alcohol, and Public Policy.* Armonk, NY: M. E. Sharpe.

Mikesell, Chris. 2011. "Transgender Rights Bill Awaits Governor's OK." *Honolulu Star-Advertiser,* April 20. Accessed June 8, 2012, http://archives.starbulletin.com/2005/07/13/news/index3.html.

Mintrom, Michael. 1997. "Policy Entrepreneurs and the Diffusion of Innovation." *American Journal of Political Science* 41 (3): 738–70.

Mintrom, Michael, and Sandra Vergari. 1998. "Policy Networks and Innovation Diffusion: The Case of State Education Reforms." *Journal of Politics* 60 (1): 126–48.

Mooney, Christopher Z. 2001. *The Public Clash of Private Values: The Politics of Morality Policy.* New York: Chatham House.

Mooney, Christopher Z., and Mei-Hsien Lee. 1995. "Legislative Morality in the American States: The Case of Pre-*Roe* Abortion Regulation Reform." *American Journal of Political Science* 39 (3): 599–627.

Mooney, Christopher Z., and Mei-Hsien Lee. 1999. "Morality Policy Reinvention: State Death Penalties." *Annals of the American Academy of Political and Social Science* 566:80–92.

Najafi, Yusef. 2011. "Community Debates Gender Identity Bill." *Metro Weekly,* March 11. Accessed July 10, 2012, http://www.metroweekly.com/news/?ak=6074.

National Center for Transgender Equality. 2006. "News 2006." Accessed June 8, 2012, http://transequality.org/news06.html.

Pacheco, Julianna. 2011. "Using National Surveys to Measure Dynamic State Public Opinion: A Guideline for Scholars and an Application." *State Politics & Policy Quarterly* 11 (4): 415–39.

Peterson, Paul E. 1981. *City Limits.* Chicago: University of Chicago Press.

Ranney, Austin. 1976. "Parties in State Politics." In *Politics in the American States: A Comparative Analysis,* ed. H. Jacob and K. N. Vines. Boston: Little, Brown.

Reyes, B. J. 2005. "Democrats Evaluating Veto List to Decide on Targets for Override." *Honolulu Star-Bulletin,* July 12. Accessed June 8, 2012, http://archives.starbulletin.com/2005/07/12/news/story9.html.

Robert Lie aka Allie Lie v. Sky Publishing Corporation (15 Mass. L Rep 412; 2002).

Scott, Gunner, and Kara Suffredini. 2011. "Commentary: Transgender Bill Debate Should Remain Civil." *Quincy Patriot-Ledger,* June 6. Accessed June 8, 2012, http://www.patriotledger.com/opinions/x1375389689/COMMENTARY-Transgender-bill-debate-should-remain-civil.

Shipan, Charles R., and Craig Volden. 2006. "Bottom-Up Federalism: The Diffusion of Antismoking Policies from U.S. Cities to States." *American Journal of Political Science* 50 (4): 825–43.

Taylor, Jami K., Daniel C. Lewis, Matthew L. Jacobsmeier, and Brian DiSarro. 2012. "Content and Complexity in Policy Reinvention and Diffusion: Gay and Transgender-

Inclusive Laws against Discrimination." *State Politics & Policy Quarterly* 12 (1): 92–115.

Taylor, Jami K., Barry Tadlock, and Sarah Poggione. 2014. "State LGBT Rights Policy Outliers: Transsexual Birth Certificate Laws." *American Review of Politics* 34 (Winter 2013–14): 245–70.

Volden, Craig. 2006. "States as Policy Laboratories: Emulating Success in the Children's Health Insurance Program." *American Journal of Political Science* 50 (2): 294–312.

Volden, Craig, Michael M. Ting, and Daniel P. Carpenter. 2008. "A Formal Model of Learning and Policy Diffusion." *American Political Science Review* 102 (3): 319–32.

Wald, Kenneth D., James W. Button, and Barbara A. Rienzo. 1996. "The Politics of Gay Rights in American Communities: Explaining Antidiscrimination Ordinances and Policies." *American Journal of Political Science* 40 (4): 1152–78.

Walker, Jack L. 1969. "The Diffusion of Innovations among the American States." *American Political Science Review* 63 (3): 880–99.

Welch, Susan, and Kay Thompson. 1980. "The Impact of Federal Incentives on State Policy Innovation." *American Journal of Political Science* 24 (4): 715–29.

Weesie, Jeroen. 1999. "Seemingly Unrelated Estimation and the Cluster-Adjusted Sandwich Estimator." *Stata Technical Bulletin* (52): 34–47.

White, Halbert. 1982. "Maximum Likelihood Estimation of Misspecified Models." *Econometrica* 50 (1): 1–25.

White, Halbert. 1994. *Estimation, Inference, and Specification Analysis.* Cambridge; New York: Cambridge University Press.

Wilson, James Q. 1980. *The Politics of Regulation.* New York: Basic Books.

Mitchell D. Sellers

7 | Executive Expansion of Transgender Rights

Electoral Incentives to Issue or Revoke Executive Orders

Efforts to expand employment protections to transgender individuals are usually focused on the legislative arena. However, all three branches of government hold promise for the transgender movement. For example, the civil rights movement gained significant headway in the 1950s and 1960s through the court system (Greenberg 1994). In the legislative arena, the 1964 Civil Rights Act banned discrimination on the basis of race and sex, but the executive branch's Equal Employment Opportunity Commission was responsible for its implementation. Thus, each branch has played a role in aiding previous social movements and the same potential exists for the transgender rights movement. As such, we must look beyond the legislative arena in order to understand the opportunity structure for the achievement of transgender-inclusive protections. In this chapter, I focus on state governors and their use of executive orders.

In the United States, most governors and the president can issue executive orders protecting transgender individuals from discrimination in the public sphere. Additionally, the executive branch can promulgate regulations or establish departments to carry out nondiscrimination policies pursuant to executive orders or statutes. For example, the Equal Employment Opportunity Commission under the Obama administration interpreted the term "sex" in the 1964 Civil Rights Act to encompass gender identity and expression (Human Rights Campaign 2012). Although the Obama administration has focused on the needs of transgender citizens more than any previous administration, the majority of the progress for the lesbian, gay, bisexual, and transgender movement in the United States has occurred at the state and local levels of government (see Button, Rienzo, and Wald 1997; Haider-Markel 2000; Taylor et al. 2012). Because the United States has a federal system, each state is able to develop policies and institutions as long as it upholds the Constitution and abides by relevant federal laws. State governments confront similar issues to the federal government, but they face different constituencies and institutional constraints, which causes public policies to differ significantly across jurisdictions.

Transgender rights present an excellent opportunity to understand why certain governors issue executive orders to protect citizens, while others do not. The transgender movement did not gain national attention until the 1990s, although pop culture has incorporated transpeople for decades. These portrayals have often involved "othering" or stereotyping, and these negative images continue to enter political debates regarding transgender issues (Stryker 2008). As discussed in this volume's chapter on advocacy coalitions (chapter 4), transgender nondiscrimination statutes are particularly hard to pass because they are contentious. When attempting to pass nondiscrimination bills, discourse shifts to morality politics or access to sex-segregated facilities, which eventually leads to resistance to the entire bill or the omission of transgender individuals as a protected class (Stone 2009). Governors in eleven states have elected to use executive orders to protect transgender individuals in public employment. One drawback of executive orders versus statutes, however, is that these protections are less stable since successors do not have to continue the protections. For example, upon entering office, Kentucky Republican governor Ernie Fletcher discontinued his predecessor's executive order that protected LGBT individuals (Human Rights Campaign 2006).

Executive orders are forms of position taking that contribute to a governor's overall social policy stance. Therefore, governors are strategic in their deployment of these orders. A governor evaluates prospective voters and his or her partisan base before adding or removing protections, and acts rationally to secure future electoral goals (Bishin 2000; Downs 1957). This chapter focuses on the motivations of governors, particularly the electoral incentives they consider, when issuing or revoking executive orders that protect transpeople. This analysis provides insight into governors' behavior, as well as a basis for exploring the motivations of presidents to support LGBT protections or to resist their expansion. This chapter finds that partisanship, divided government, and citizen ideology effects governors' use of executive orders to protect transgender people.

Public Opinion and Voter Information

Like all elected officials, a governor is accountable to the public. Citizens in the United States vote their executives into office and they can remove them. Some states allow for a recall vote prior to the completion of a governor's term, but reelection bids can also serve as a referendum on an administration. Therefore, governors must be cautious because citizens can hold officeholders accountable for policy decisions.

In this context, every policy alteration is a political action because it is taken with the understanding that it can potentially shape one's electoral prospects. There exists a possibility for backlash when breaking with the party platform or going against the desires of the prospective constituency.[1] Voters continuously update their perceptions of politicians based on new information provided by the media, by outside interests, or by the politicians themselves (Milburn 1991; Partin 2001; Zaller 1992). This constantly evolving conception of governors "ultimately . . . may help shape and affect vote choice" when selecting between candidates (Partin 2001, 133).

This chapter assumes that governors seek either reelection or aspire to higher office, so they will act strategically to ensure their electoral goals. One of the key ways that elected officials do this is by position taking (Mayhew 1974). Advocating for and signing particular pieces of legislation, public pronouncements on issues, and employing executive orders are some of the ways in which governors can take positions. They can also claim credit for policy victories. Regardless of how the executive advocates, position taking signals the governor's policy preferences to the public or rewards key constituencies, or both, in an effort to generate or maintain a favorable image (Mayhew 1974). Because there are variations in political attentiveness in the electorate (Zaller 1992), elected officials can judiciously advance policies that lack salience with the public (Geer 1996). This could be used to reward important supporters in their party's base. More salient policies might be used to attract swing voters. Although governors might not be able to reach certain parts of the electorate because of fixed partisan allegiances (Campbell et al. 1960), independents and those with weaker partisan affiliations can form part of the prospective constituency (Schaffner and Streb 2002). Through good performance and the strategic use of wedge issues, swing voters can be turned in an incumbent's favor (Edsall 2006).

As noted previously, this chapter focuses on the use of executive orders. Although gubernatorial powers vary by state, all governors retain some ability to issue executive orders (Donovan, Mooney, and Smith 2011). This tool allows the governor to enact policies unilaterally and to expeditiously change policies that relate to the administration of state government. Governors seeking reelection issue or remove executive orders based on their evaluation of two groups: (1) their prospective constituency, and (2) their partisan base. Loss of support from either constituency harms their probability of reelection, so governors are careful not to offend either. The governor acts strategically when there are clear benefits to adding, removing, or amending an executive order. Instituting or removing employment protections for specific groups are political acts that help to define values that politicians support within their administration and these actions indicate likely future activity (Partin 2001). This is a powerful heuristic for voters because "the past becomes a guide to future action" in terms of social policy (King 2001, 386).

With respect to social policies, the main parties in the United States have different priorities. The Republican platform favors "traditional values" and policies that frequently are at odds with LGBT rights. Due to the parties' contrasting stances on LGBT rights, a politician's position on LGBT rights is highly correlated with his or her party (e.g., Lublin 2005). Legislatures with more Democrats have an increased likelihood of adopting sexual-orientation and gender-identity-inclusive nondiscrimination laws (Haider-Markel 2000; Soule and Earl 2001; Taylor et al. 2012). Politicians are expected to issue or revoke executive orders in line with their party's values.

If the Republican base takes any position, it tends to be in opposition to LGBT protections and in favor of traditional values, so Republican governors have little motivation to issue executive orders that protect LGBT people (Edsall 2006). Consequently, extending protections could be at odds with the socially conservative views of their base—particularly, the Christian Right (Wilcox and Robinson 2011). Due to their political clout in some states, this transgression can hamper reelection prospects in the primary and general elections by motivating their partisan base to defect in support of a challenger. Therefore, there is little incentive for a Republican governor to issue an executive order. However, there is incentive to remove already existing executive orders in an effort to win favor with voters. Republican governors appear to risk little by reversing executive orders of previous governors because they can always point to the need for legislative action. The first hypothesis is:

Hypothesis 1: Republican governors are more likely to revoke existing transgender-inclusive executive orders signed by previous governors.

The electoral incentives for Democratic governors are not as clear. Democratic governors might have to appeal to a more conservative constituency in some states, such as those in southern or more rural states. Issuing an executive order in a more conservative state might appeal to the partisan base, but not to the prospective constituency. A strategic governor would not issue an executive order in this scenario. Still, other Democratic governors have reason to issue executive orders. Unlike Republican governors, issuing executive orders can be favorable to part of their partisan base, so such action can increase popularity and enhance the possibility of reelection. Executive orders also might not receive as much widespread media attention as legislation, making it less likely that the governor's action would repel prospective constituents. In certain instances, ensuring LGBT protections is a means of distinguishing an executive from his or her predecessor or it might even be a campaign promise (Gasper and Reeves 2010). If this is true, a change in partisan control of the executive should increase the probability that the governor will issue an executive order. This leads to two hypotheses:

Hypothesis 2: Democratic governors are more likely to sign transgender-inclusive executive orders.

Hypothesis 3: Governors are more likely to issue executive orders on transgender protections when the executive branch changes from Republican to Democratic control.

Finally, because of the party differences on LBGT rights (e.g., Lublin 2005), legislatures that are primarily controlled by Republicans should be less likely to pass gender-identity-inclusive nondiscrimination laws than those that are composed mostly of Democrats (Taylor et al. 2012). When Democratic governors are faced with this prospect, and they desire to engage in position taking and credit claiming aimed at shoring up support in the LGBT-supportive portion of their partisan base, they might choose to issue a transgender-inclusive executive order rather than wait for passage of legislation. Representatives in the legislature are unlikely to pass transgender protections unless the electorate pushes for it or if the electorate is unlikely to retaliate. A governor that is relatively more liberal than the state legislature may have motivation to press for transgender-inclusive protections, but may fail in the legislative arena or circumvent dealing with the legislature by adjusting the policy unilaterally. For example, a slightly liberal Democratic governor in a moderate state may want to extend protections via legislation, but is thwarted in the legislative arena by a more conservative legislature. The legislature does not support the policy in this instance, nor is the electorate pushing representatives to act. Legislation is not likely to pass, so the governor may elect to issue an executive order. These scenarios are more likely during divided government; specifically, when the executive in office is a Democrat. Therefore, divided government should encourage Democratic governors to issue protections when the electorate is more conservative.

Issuing an executive order allows governors to provide protections, albeit limited, to transgender employees. This allows them to simultaneously engage in position taking, as well as fulfilling a campaign promise. For two reasons, this heightened motivation for governors to issue protections during divided government dissolves as citizen ideology becomes more liberal. First, the representatives in the legislature of more liberal states have greater motivation to pass legislation because their voters are more agreeable to these protections. The need for the governor to act is reduced because the legislature may take action that renders an executive order unnecessary or moot. Second, with an increasingly liberal electorate, *all* governors can gain from issuing protections and standing against discrimination—potentially a political move that a socially liberal constituency would support. Therefore, divided government should have an overall positive effect on governors issuing protections; however, this relationship is muted as the ideology of the constituency becomes more liberal. The following two hypotheses test this argument:

> *Hypothesis 4:* Democratic governors are more likely to issue executive orders banning discrimination against transgender public sector workers when there is divided government.

> *Hypothesis 5:* Divided government will be less influential on the probability that governors will issue an executive order as constituent ideology increases (becomes more liberal).

Data and Methods

To explore the hypotheses, I use descriptive statistics and event history analysis. The dataset is composed of state political factors (Klarner 2012), state ideological factors (Fording 2012), and the years that nondiscrimination policies are established (executive orders and statute adoption).[2] Governments with nondiscrimination policies were identified by the Human Rights Campaign (2012) and the National Gay and Lesbian Task Force (2012), and substantiated through each state governmental website.

Two types of cases are identified in the data: (1) issuing, and (2) removing an executive order. The first occurs when a governor issues an executive order that prohibits gender identity or gender-expression-based discrimination in public sector employment when no such protections existed immediately before issuing it. This means that executive orders issued by governors will be included in the analysis only if the governor is adding protections that did not previously exist. Because the event history analysis is focused on factors that initially lead to issuing protections, states drop from analysis once an executive order is in place. The second type of case included is when a governor removes protections that were in place. This generally occurs when a new governor enters office and discontinues protections for transgender individuals. In effect, the protections are revoked by the executive choosing to suspend former policies. Table 7.1 shows the fourteen cases identified—twelve instances of governors adding protections and two of governors removing protections.

The hypotheses are asking: Which governors issue or revoke executive orders to protect transgender individuals and under what conditions? The hypotheses first consider the governor in office when the status quo is changed, and then the executive's predecessor. Event history analysis allows for evaluation of the factors that lead governors to issue an executive

TABLE 7.1. Governors' Issuance or Removal of Executive Orders

State	Issue		Remove	
	Cases	Year	Cases	Year
Delaware	1	2009		
Indiana	1	2004		
Iowa	1	1999	1[a]	2000[a]
Kansas	1	2007		
Kentucky	2	2003; 2008	1	2006
Maryland	1	2007		
Massachusetts	1	2011		
Michigan	1	2007		
New York	1	2009		
Ohio	1	2007	1	2011
Pennsylvania	1	2003		
Total	12		2	

Source: Human Rights Campaign (2013); National Gay and Lesbian (2012).
[a]Iowa's Supreme Court nullified this executive order in 2000.

order. In event history analysis, each state has an observation for every year under analysis. For this analysis, the state drops from the model once an executive order is issued. A binary indicator assessing whether the governor in a state issued a transgender-inclusive nondiscrimination executive order in a given year is the dependent variable in the event history models.

The event history analysis runs from 1999[3]—the first year that a gender-identity-inclusive executive order was issued—to 2010. These models test Hypotheses 2 through 5.[4] Each model provides standard errors clustered by state. In addition to states dropping from the risk set when the governor issues an executive order, they also drop from the risk set when a gender-identity-inclusive employment nondiscrimination statute is adopted.[5] The first model tests the influence of gubernatorial partisanship on the probability of issuing executive orders. The variable *Democratic Governor* is expected to be positive and statistically significant because Democratic governors are expected to be more likely to issue an executive order. The second model includes the variable *Republican to Democrat*[6] to test Hypothesis 3. It is also expected to be positive and statistically significant. Republican to Democrat is coded 1 in years that partisan control of the executive changes from Republican to Democrat, but 0 in all other regime changes. I expect that shifting executive control from Republican to Democratic will increase the probability of issuing executive orders. However, this variable only considers the year that the executive changes. This drastically reduces the number of observations, but tests the notion that Democratic governors will issue executive orders to distinguish themselves from their predecessor or to fulfill a campaign promise. If a governor wants to do either of the above, he or she will most likely issue an executive order early in his or her tenure to set the tone of the administration. Motivation may differ if a governor issues an executive order toward the end of the term. Therefore, Hypothesis 3 is more directly tested by including only years that the executive changes.

To test Hypotheses 4 and 5, *Divided Government* is included as a binary variable. Divided government is expected to increase the likelihood of issuing executive orders because greater Democratic control of the legislature increases the odds of adopting statutes (Taylor et al. 2012). Divided government limits the number of Democrats in office, which increases the probability that an executive order is needed. When different parties control the executive and legislative branches, this variable is coded as a 1. Because of the responsiveness of state policy to public opinion on LGBT issues (Lax and Phillips 2009), I also expect more liberal states to pass legislation regardless of divided government. Therefore, I add an interaction term that looks at the role of citizen ideology and divided government. This tests Hypothesis 5.

State political factors are controlled for by using data obtained from Klarner (2012). The dummy variable *Term Limits* and *Term Length*[7] are included as controls to account for their influence on executive behavior. No expectation exists for their effects. State ideology is controlled for with *Citizen Ideology*[8] and *Government Ideology*.[9] Citizens within a state are progressively more liberal as Citizen Ideology increases. This is expected to increase the probability of issuing executive orders. Similarly, Government Ideology is a measure that takes into account the state's two dominant political parties in both legislative chambers and gubernatorial ideology. Governments are more liberal as Government Ideology increases. No expectation is made for Government Ideology because more liberal governments are expected to increase the likelihood of adopting statutes— making executive orders unnecessary. Finally, the dummy variable *Sexual Orientation Law* was created using Taylor et al. (2012). Sexual Orientation Law is coded 1 in the year that a state adopts a sexual-orientation-inclusive law and in each year after. States with sexual-orientation-inclusive nondiscrimination statutes are expected to be more likely to adopt gender-identity-inclusive executive orders.

Results

The results support all of the hypotheses. Table 7.2, which provides cross-tabulations of gubernatorial action following a change in officeholder, shows that partisanship is strongly connected to the use of executive orders. The second hypothesis is strongly supported because Democratic governors were responsible for issuing executive orders in all twelve cases of executive expansion of protections. Complementary to that and in support of Hypothesis 1, Republican governors (Kentucky and Ohio) ended protections for transgender employees in both instances where governors removed existing protections. Of additional note is the special case of Iowa. In 1999, Iowa governor Tom Vilsack was the first governor to issue an executive order to protect transgender employees. However, these protections were quickly removed by Iowa's Supreme Court as an overextension of executive power.

Considering change in partisan control of the executive supports the electoral incentives argument. Hypothesis 3 argues that there should be more executive orders issued when control of the executive changes from Republican to Democratic. Table 7.2 provides evidence in support of this argument. All of the governors who issued executive orders were Democrats. Eight of the executive orders were issued by Democrats whose predecessors were Republican. The remaining four executive orders were issued by Democrats whose predecessors were Democrats. However, these results should be interpreted with caution because the analysis covers a limited time frame and public opinion regarding the LGBT population is changing much more rapidly than most executive terms (Brewer 2008). These preliminary findings also support Hypothesis 1. Not only did Republican governors remove protections in both of the cases of revocation but no Republican added protections.

The event history analysis (table 7.3) holds similar findings. Model 1 contains all observations from 1999 to 2010. It shows that Democratic governors are more likely to issue executive orders protecting gender identity. The variable Democratic Governor is positive and statistically significant ($p < 0.01$). In fact, the probability of issuing an executive order increases by over a factor of 15 when a Democratic governor is in office. This suggests that the probability of issuing an executive order is strongly predicated on the partisanship of the executive in office. This was already implied since only Democratic governors have issued executive orders. Thus, Hypothesis 2 is supported. As expected, Citizen Ideology is positive and statistically significant. This means that governors whose constituencies are more liberal are more likely to issue an executive order. The probability

TABLE 7.2. Partisan Utilization of Executive Orders Adding Protections

		Present Governor	
		Democrat	Republican
Previous Governor	Democrat	4	0
	Republican	8	0
	Total	12	0

Removing Protections

		Present Governor	
		Democrat	Republican
Previous Governor	Democrat	0	2
	Republican	0	0
	Total	0	2

Source: Human Rights Campaign (2013); National Gay and Lesbian (2012).

that a governor will issue an executive order increases as the state's electorate becomes more liberal.

The model reveals an interesting relationship regarding political actors. A negative relationship is found with Government Ideology. This is possibly because the legislature is more likely to pass a statute as the ideology becomes more liberal. This certainly would help to explain the effects of divided government. The Divided Government term increases the probability of issuing an executive order by a factor of over 200. Interestingly, the government was divided in eight of the 12 instances that gover-

TABLE 7.3. Event History Analysis of Issuing of Gender Identity–Inclusive Executive Orders from 1999 to 2010

Independent Variable	Model 1		Model 2	
	Coefficient	Odds Ratio	Coefficient	Odds Ratio
Democratic Governor	2.72***	15.13	—	—
	(0.943)		—	—
Republican to Democrat	—	—	1.45*	4.27
	—	—	(0.820)	
Citizen Ideology	0.12***	1.13	0.16***	1.18
	(0.034)		(0.055)	
Government Ideology	−0.05*	0.95	−0.04	0.96
	(0.032)		(0.030)	
Divided Government	5.50***	245	9.24***	10,291
	(1.856)		(3.129)	
Citizen Ideology*Divided Government	−0.08**	0.93	−0.15***	0.87
	(0.033)		(0.056)	
Term Limits	1.56	4.73	1.59	4.89
	(1.032)		(2.215)	
Sexual Orientation Law	−0.31	0.73	−0.74	0.48
	(0.944)		(1.112)	
Constant	−10.35***		−11.61***	
	(1.629)		(4.303)	
Observations	588		98	
Pseudo-R^2	0.206		0.203	
AIC	260.28		67.47	

Source: Berry et al. (2010); Fording (2012); Human Rights Campaign (2013); Klarner (2012); National Gay and Lesbian (2012); Taylor et al. (2012).

Note: * $p < 0.10$, ** $p < 0.05$; *** $p < 0.01$. The dependent variable in a given state/year is coded 1 if a governor issues an executive order to protect transgender employees and 0 otherwise. The first column of each cell entry provides the logistic regression coefficients. Simultaneously estimated standard errors, clustered on the state, are presented in parentheses. The second column for each model is the odds ratio.

nors issued executive orders. These findings provide support for Hypothesis 4. The interaction term Citizen Ideology*Divided Government is negative, but does not necessarily negate the effect of Divided Government. The interaction term's influence on issuing executive orders is mild, but plays a substantial role as Citizen Ideology increases from its minimum to maximum value. Government Ideology is negative and statistically significant at $p < 0.1$. This was anticipated because as the legislature becomes more liberal, we would expect the government to pass a statute, reducing the need for an executive order. However, the Citizen Ideology and Government Ideology must change considerably to have a substantive influence. The term Sexual Orientation Law is negative across the models, but is not statistically significant.

Divided government plays an interesting role in explaining governors' behavior. Figure 7.1 illustrates the predicted probability of governors issuing an executive order as the electorate becomes increasingly liberal during divided and unified government. As was theorized, when the electorate is more conservative, governors under divided government are more likely to issue protections relative to governors under unified government. Figure 7.1 shows that governors under divided government are more likely to issue protections, but this quickly changes as the state becomes more liberal. The predicted probability for a governor to issue an executive order under divided government increases steadily as citizen ideology becomes more liberal. Contrastingly, governors under unified government are unlikely (predicted probability < 0.10) to issue protections until the citizen ideology rises above 50 (larger ideology scores are more liberal). The predicted probability skyrockets as citizen ideology increases from 60 to 80, which causes these governors to be more likely to issue protections relative to governors under divided government. Caution should be taken with these findings. Hypotheses 4 and 5 are supported by the findings, but the certainty of the statistical significance between the predicted probabilities for governors during divided and unified government is partially dependent on citizen ideology.

The second model supports Hypotheses 2 and 3. The second model contains only the first year of an executive's term in office, so approximately a sixth of the observations remain. Although these models are intended to test Hypothesis 3, Hypothesis 2 is further confirmed because it indicates that Democratic governors that enter office after a Republican governor increase the probability that an executive order will be issued. The Republican to Democrat term is significant in the second model. This provides evidence in support of Hypothesis 3—that governors are more

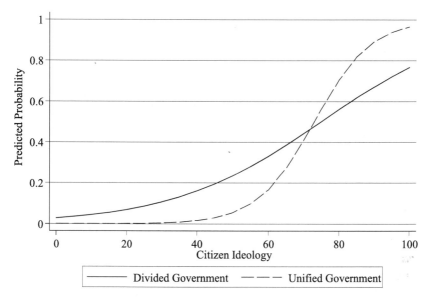

Fig. 7.1. Predicted probability of issuing an executive order. The electorate is more liberal as Citizen Ideology increases. The predicted probabilities were generated for a Democratic governor, the mean government ideology of the states included in analysis, and in a state with term limits and a sexual orientation nondiscrimination statute already in place.

likely to issue executive orders when they enter office after a Republican governor. This is true for the full model and the restricted model that only considers the first year of a governor in office. Model 2 indicates that the probability of issuing an executive order increases by a factor of 4.27 when a Republican governor is replaced by a Democrat. This means that, compared to all other governors, Democratic governors are considerably more likely to issue an executive order during their first year in office if their predecessor was Republican.

The relationships among the nonpartisan variables in Model 2 are similar to Model 1. Citizen Ideology indicates a positive and statistically significant relationship. This suggests that governors whose constituencies are more liberal are more likely to issue executive orders. Although Government Ideology is not statistically significant, the term is negative, which suggests there is an analogous relationship to what Model 1 reveals. Divided Government is again positive and statistically significant, which provides additional support for Hypothesis 4. The odds ratio is even higher, which is notable, but this increase may be an artifact of the few number of executive orders issued. The interaction term Citizen Ideology*Divided Government is once again negative and statistically significant and does not necessarily negate the effects of Divided Government. The interaction term has a mild odds ratio, which suggests that it does little to change the likelihood of issuing executive orders in a governor's first year in office, unless Citizen Ideology changes considerably.

Discussion and Conclusion

Partisanship and strategic position taking appear to play roles in determining whether governors issue or revoke executive orders protecting transgender public sector employees. Understanding why governors issue these executive orders helps to explain partisan politics and the present level of transgender-inclusive legal protections. The electoral incentive for governors to change the status quo varies by state, but there are some shared patterns. To add or remove protections contributes to a governor's overall social policy stance and to public knowledge about any given executive. Adding transgender-inclusive protections is a signal to the public that the governor supports more socially liberal policies, which is attractive to more liberal constituencies. Governors in more liberal states are more likely to issue executive orders. Further, Democratic governors are more likely to issue protections, whereas some Republicans removed protections upon entering office. This suggests that governors act strategically in their deployment of executive orders. Adding protections can win LGBT allies. Not all Democratic governors have a motivation to issue protections, but electoral incentives to do so exist for governors in more liberal states. However, issuing transgender protections is still unappealing to Republican governors whose base is often composed of more socially conservative voters. Republican governors have little to gain, and possibly a lot to lose, from issuing executive orders that protect transgender employees.

As expected by my hypotheses, Democratic governors were more likely to add protections for transgender individuals and Republicans were the only ones to remove protections. In all of the cases, only Democratic governors added protections. The event history analysis shows that Democratic governors are more likely to issue executive orders protecting gender identity. The first model finds that having a Democratic governor increases the likelihood of issuing executive orders by over a factor of 15. Also, support for the third hypothesis is found. Model 2 indicates that the Republican to Democrat term is positive and statistically significant. Shifting from Republican to Democratic control of the executive branch increases the probability of issuing executive orders by more than a factor of four. The results also provide insight into the political factors that contribute to issuing an executive order. Citizen Ideology is positive and statistically significant in both models, while Government Ideology is negative and only statistically significant in Model 1. Yet both terms only marginally change the probability of adopting policies. The most notable effect was Divided Government, which greatly increased the probability of issuing executive orders and is statistically significant across both models. As noted in Hypothesis 4, this was expected.

Protections via executive orders are less durable than passing statutes, so upcoming years will be particularly telling as the governors who issued the original executive orders are replaced. Will future governors keep or repeal these orders? Extension of this project would be especially helpful to understanding policymaking on LGBT rights. Similar executive orders have been issued to prohibit discrimination in public employment based on sexual orientation. Taken together, these two types of nondiscrimination policies are meant to protect individuals that break gender norms, so considering governors' behavior regarding both forms of executive orders would shed further light on the topic. Additionally, considering the interaction of the governor with the legislature would help to elucidate how partisanship and divided government influence the outcome of LGBT public policy.

Issuing or removing protections via executive orders is not random. Partisanship plays a significant role in whether or not governors issue executive orders. Democratic executives have electoral incentives to add protections, but Republicans currently do not. The choice is clear for Republicans: their partisan base does not advocate for transgender protections and their prospective constituency does not exert enough pressure to override their partisan base. Adding protections is not called for, but the partisan base and possible support from the prospective constituency is reason to remove protections. Although all of my hypotheses are supported, a reminder of context and generalizability is important. As public attitudes on LGBT issues become more supportive (e.g., Brewer 2008), Republicans might have some incentive to issue these types of orders in the future. Additionally, the first transgender-inclusive executive order was not issued until 1999 (Iowa), and data analysis only covers the period between 1999 and 2010. Most states' term limits make it possible for governors to be in office for eight years, so turnover is a relatively slow process (Klarner 2012). The upcoming years will be informative as executives are replaced. Governors who issued protections will be leaving office and these protections are not assured, especially considering the split partisan makeup of the states under analysis.

This chapter raises some interesting questions regarding the role of partisanship in creating protections for LGBT individuals. Clearly, Democratic governors are more likely to issue protections. Conventional wisdom suggested that, but this chapter reveals more about governors and their motivations to issue executive orders. Divided government considerably increases the likelihood that governors will issue an executive order. Additionally, it is odd that an increasingly liberal government reduces the probability of issuing executive orders. There are two possible reasons for this finding. First, the governor might issue executive orders when government is divided because they anticipate gridlock or flat-out failure of legislation. Since partisanship is linked to adding protections, passing a nondiscrimination statute would be more challenging with a divided government. Governors might view executive orders as the best option available. Another possible explanation is that a governor in a unified government can play a larger role in setting the agenda or is better able to pass legislation, similar to how the president can do so on the national level (Binder 2003). This chapter finds that as Government Ideology increases (becomes more liberal), the probability of issuing an executive order decreases. A governor might not feel the need to issue an executive order if he or she believes that stronger and more permanent protections can be passed. This is plausible, since the only state to pass a statute while an executive order was in place is Massachusetts. The governor may focus efforts in the legislative arena in an attempt to carry out campaign promises or policy preferences. Further research should consider the effects of divided government on LGBT rights.

The findings support the theoretical argument. Governors are more likely to issue protections based on the prospective electorate and partisan base. A caveat should be made: proxies are used for both the prospective electorate (citizen ideology) and partisan base (partisanship of governor). Still, the results support the idea that governors strategically use executive orders to appeal to voters. Although the effect of Citizen Ideology on issuing an executive order is small, governors are more likely to issue an executive order in more liberal states. These findings also highlight the role of partisanship. Governors can be viewed as appealing to their bases. Democratic governors only added protections, whereas Republicans removed protections. Additionally, Democratic governors who succeed Republicans are more likely than other governors to issue protections in their first year in office. These findings suggest that, until nationwide protections are offered, partisan politics will continue to creep into efforts to secure transgender protections for the foreseeable future.

NOTES

I would like to thank my professors and colleagues at the University of Florida, as well as Donald Haider-Markel and Jami Taylor for their feedback. Their suggestions helped greatly with the development of this chapter.

1. Prospective constituency refers to all voters, except for extreme opposition partisans, that is, those who will potentially support their reelection (Bishin 2000).

2. Statute adoption refers to the year that the state passes a bill into law. It may differ from the year that the law goes into effect.

3. Although 1999 was the year chosen, two alternative start years (1981 and 1993) were tested for robustness. The first sexual-orientation-inclusive statute was adopted in 1981 and the first gender identity-inclusive statute was adopted in 1993 (Taylor et al. 2012). Neither model starting from 1981 or 1993 showed substantive differences in results. The year 1999 was chosen because it was the first year a state-level executive order was issued that included gender identity.

4. Hypothesis 1 cannot be tested because there are an insufficient number of observations. Results would be further biased because governors tended to add protections toward the start of their tenure. While it is possible for the same executive to add, and then remove, protections, this is not expected. Any solution to this problem further reduces the number of observations.

5. An independent variable to control for gender-identity-inclusive laws cannot be included in the models because it predicts failures perfectly. To account for these laws, states are dropped from the risk set once they pass a gender-identity-inclusive nondiscrimination statute.

6. There is a high correlation (0.53) between the terms Democratic Governor and Republican to Democrat. In order to avoid multicollinearity problems, only Republican to Democrat is used in Model 2. The governor's party affiliation is dropped.

7. Term Length was included in initial analysis, but is dropped from the models because it predicts failures perfectly.

8. This measure was originally created for Berry et al. (1998), but the revised 1960–2010 citizen ideology series is used (Berry et al. 2010).

9. This measure was also created for Berry et al. (1998). It is the updated Nominate measure of state government ideology (Berry et al. 2010).

REFERENCES

Berry, William D., Richard C. Fording, Evan J. Rinquist, Russell L. Hanson, and Carl Klarner. 2010. "Measuring Citizen and Government Ideology in the American States: A Re-appraisal." *State Politics & Policy Quarterly* 10 (2): 117–35.

Berry, William D., Evan J. Rinquist, Richard C. Fording, and Russell L. Hanson. 1998.

"Measuring Government Ideology in the American States, 1960–93." *American Journal of Political Science* 42 (1): 327–48.

Binder, Sarah A. 2003. *Stalemate: Causes and Consequences of Legislative Gridlock.* Washington, DC: Brookings Institution Press.

Bishin, Benjamin G. 2000. "Constituency Influence in Congress: Does Subconstituency Matter?" *Legislative Studies Quarterly* 25 (3): 389–415.

Brewer, Paul Ryan. 2008. *Value War: Public Opinion and the Politics of Gay Rights.* Lanham, MD: Rowman and Littlefield.

Button, James W., Barbara A. Rienzo, and Kenneth D. Wald. 1997. *Private Lives, Public Conflicts: Battles over Gay Rights in American Communities.* Washington, DC: CQ Press.

Campbell, Angus, Philip E. Converse, Villen E. Miller, and Donald E. Stokes. 1960. *The American Voter.* Chicago: University of Chicago Press.

Donovan, Todd, Christopher Z. Mooney, and Daniel A. Smith. 2011. *State and Local Politics: Institutions and Reform.* Boston: Wadsworth.

Downs, Anthony. 1957. *An Economic Theory of Democracy.* Ann Arbor: University of Michigan Press.

Edsall, Thomas B. 2006. *Building Red America: The New Conservative Coalition and the Drive for Permanent Power.* New York: Basic Books.

Fording, Richard C. 2012. "State Ideology Data." Accessed November 22, 2012, http://rcfording.wordpress.com/state-ideology-data/.

Gasper, John T., and Andrew Reeves. 2010. "Governors as Opportunists: Evidence from Disaster Declaration Requests." Paper presented at the annual meeting for the American Political Science Association, Washington, DC, September 2–5.

Geer, John Gray. 1996. *From Tea Leaves to Opinion Polls: A Theory of Democratic Leadership.* New York: Columbia University Press.

Greenberg, Jack. 1994. *Crusaders in the Courts: How a Dedicated Band of Lawyers Fought for the Civil Rights Revolution.* New York: Basic Books.

Haider-Markel, Donald P. 2000. "Lesbian and Gay Politics in the States: Interest Groups, Electoral Politics, and Public Policy." In *The Politics of Gay Rights,* by Craig Rimmerman, Kenneth Wald, and Clyde Wilcox, 290–346. Chicago: University of Chicago Press.

Human Rights Campaign. 2006. "Kentucky Governor Gives Green Light to Discrimination on Self-Proclaimed 'Diversity Day.'" Accessed December 12, 2012, http://www.hrc.org/press-releases/entry/kentucky-governor-gives-green-light-to-discrimination-on-self-proclaimed-di.

Human Rights Campaign. 2012. "U.S. Federal Government Employment Policies." Accessed November 12, 2012, http://www.hrc.org/resources/entry/u.s.-federal-government-employment-policies.

King, James D. 2001. "Incumbent Popularity and Vote Choice in Gubernatorial Elections." *Journal of Politics* 63 (2): 585–97.

Klarner, Carl. 2012. "Klarner Politics." Accessed December 22, 2012, http://www.indstate.edu/polisci/klarnerpolitics.htm.

Lax, Jeffrey R., and Justin H. Phillips. 2009. "Gay Rights in the States: Public Opinion and Policy Responsiveness." *American Political Science Review* 103 (3): 367–86.

Lublin, David. 2005. "The Strengthening of Party and Decline of Religion in Explaining

Congressional Voting Behavior on Gay and Lesbian Issues." *PS: Political Science & Politics* 38 (2): 241–45.

Mayhew, David R. 1974. *Congress: The Electoral Connection.* New Haven: Yale University Press.

Milburn, Michael A. 1991. *Persuasion and Politics: The Social Psychology of Public Opinion.* Pacific Grove, CA: Brooks/Cole Publishing.

National Gay and Lesbian Task Force. 2012. "Home Page." Accessed November 6, 2012, http://www.thetaskforce.org/ (accessed November 6, 2012).

Partin, Randall W. 2001. "Campaign Intensity and Voter Informatio: A Look at Gubernatorial Contests." *American Politics Research* 29 (2): 115–40.

Schaffner, Brian F., and Matthew J. Streb. 2002. "The Partisan Heuristic in Low-Information Elections." *Public Opinion Quarterly* 66 (4): 559–81.

Soule, Sarah A., and Jennifer Earl. 2001. "The Enactment of State-Level Hate Crime Law in the United States: Intrastate and Interstate Factors." *Sociological Perspectives* 44 (3): 281–305.

Stone, Amy L. 2009. "Like Sexual Orientation? Like Gender? Transgender Inclusion in Nondiscrimination Ordinances." In *Queer Mobilizations: LGBT Activists Confront the Law,* ed. Scott Barclay, Mary Bernstein, and Anna-Maria Marshall, 142–57. New York: New York University Press.

Stryker, Susan. 2008. *Transgender History.* Berkeley: Seal Press.

Taylor, Jami K., Daniel C. Lewis, Matthew L. Jacobsmeier, and Brian DiSarro. 2012. "Content and Complexity in Policy Reinvention and Diffusion: Gay and Transgender-Inclusive Laws against Discrimination." *State Politics & Policy Quarterly* 12 (1): 75–98.

Wilcox, Clyde, and Carin Robinson. *Onward Christian Soldiers? The Religious Right in American Politics.* Boulder: Westview Press, 2011.

Zaller, John R. 1992. *The Nature and Origins of Mass Opinion.* New York: Cambridge University Press.

Mitchell D. Sellers and Roddrick Colvin

8 | Policy Learning, Language, and
Implementation by Local Governments
with Transgender-Inclusive
Nondiscrimination Policies

Between 1975 and 2000, only 40 local governments in the United States adopted transgender-inclusive nondiscrimination policies. However, from 2001 to 2011, that number nearly quadrupled—to 154 (fig. 8.1). This dramatic increase was due, in part, to the more aggressive, explicit, and outspoken policy-adoption strategies of LGBT rights advocates. By 2001, most national LGBT organizations had agreed to support nondiscrimination legislation if it was sexual orientation and transgender inclusive (McCreery 2001). Previously (as explored in this volume's chapter on advocacy coalitions), transgender-inclusive provisions had sometimes been jettisoned in order to smooth the passage of legislation protecting lesbians and gay men. Advocates, who believed that any progress was better than none, acquiesced to laws that excluded transgender safeguards; now these same organizations fought attempts to remove such protections. And rather than support just any nondiscrimination policy, they sanctioned only those that outlined explicit administrative processes and protections for claimants—a major shift in approach.

This chapter explores those components of nondiscrimination policies that can influence their implementation and enforcement—specifically, the precise language used to define the protected class (in this case, transgender individuals), the authority vested in implementation agencies, and the safeguards afforded to claimants.

We begin with a review of the literature on workplace nondiscrimination protections, the role of language in policymaking as well as its role in implementation and enforcement, and policy learning among communities. We then discuss policy frameworks and mechanisms that are useful

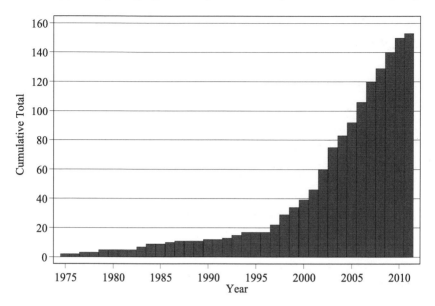

Fig. 8.1. Adoption of local transgender-inclusive policies from 1975 to 2011. This graph includes only policies that remained in place as of 2011. Additionally, Pine Lake, Georgia, is omitted from the cumulative total. The policy was adopted in the 1990s, but the exact year is unknown. (Data from Colvin 2007; Sellers 2012.)

in understanding the policymaking process. We argue that policies that dictate explicitly how to implement policies and that state what explicit protections are available to claimants are more effective than policies that do not. Since more recently adopted policies are more explicit in their language and policy direction, we argue that newer adoptions should be more comprehensive in part because of policy learning and reinvention based on the experiences of early adopters. We recognize that advocates' strategies gradually shifted over time, but we argue that policy adoption tactics had evolved by 2000 and that, if policy reinvention occurred, newer policies should therefore be more comprehensive. We have attempted to determine whether policies developed after 2000 are, in fact, more comprehensive than those written in the earlier period. We use ordered logistic analysis to assess the relationship between policy elements that contribute to implementation and the enforcement of nondiscrimination policies.

We found evidence that policies developed after 2000 are more comprehensive than those of early adopters (i.e., those developed between

1975 and 2000). While we have not yet formalized our conclusions about the precise role of time on policy adoption, this finding supports our central thesis: policies created by later adopters are more likely to be more comprehensive than those created by early adopters. This was likely a result of a gradual evolution toward explicit policies and suggests that advocates' political decision to support only transgender-inclusive policies did in fact influence the policies that were adopted.

The Importance of Work and Nondiscrimination Protections

Although LGBT-supportive legislation has elements of morality policy (Mooney and Lee 1995, 1999), at their core these policies are economic— they provide job security and economic stability for LGBT workers (Hunt 2012). Advocates and lawmakers have pursued economic justice through employment nondiscrimination laws as a means of securing social justice. Such laws are the most common form of local codified transgender-inclusive protections (Sellers 2014). The belief in economic opportunity as a route to social integration and the "American dream" has roots in the civil rights movement of the 1950s and 1960s (EEOC 2012). By prohibiting and preventing harassment and discrimination in the workplace, governments promote economic security, which in turn improves opportunities in housing, health care, education, and credit.

As the broader lesbian and gay rights movement has grown more successful, the struggle for transgender equality has become more overt. However, despite over 35 years of transgender-inclusive policy adoption, there is strong evidence that employment discrimination, harassment, and violence based on gender identity and expression remains pervasive in the workplace (Grant et al. 2011).

Discrimination, Harassment, and Violence Based on Gender Identity and Expression

As previous chapters have noted, transgender people routinely face harassment, violence, and discrimination due to either prejudice or misunderstanding. Minter and Daley (2003) found that nearly 50 percent of their 155-person sample of transgender people experienced employment discrimination based on gender identity. The most recent and most comprehensive study of gender-nonconforming individuals offers an even bleaker picture. In the National Transgender Discrimination Survey of

2011,[1] 90 percent of the 6,450 transgender and gender-nonconforming people surveyed experienced harassment, mistreatment, or discrimination on the job (Grant et al. 2011).

Discrimination occurs when governments, institutions, or individuals treat people differently based on their personal characteristics rather than their merit (Supateera and Kleiner 1999). Since gender identity and expression are among the least understood personal characteristics, discrimination against transgender and gender-nonconforming individuals is especially pervasive (Green 2000). Such discrimination can take a number of forms, including direct discrimination, indirect discrimination, and harassment.

Direct or de jure discrimination is a policy or law that explicitly authorizes unequal treatment. The ban on transgender people serving in the U.S. military is an example of direct discrimination. Indirect or de facto discrimination occurs where the effect of certain requirements, conditions, or practices has a disproportionately adverse impact on a specific group. Indirect discrimination occurs when a requirement that applies to everyone can be met only by a considerably smaller proportion of people from a particular group, thereby disadvantaging them. For indirect discrimination to occur, this biased policy cannot be justified as necessary to operations (Tobler 2005). An example of indirect discrimination based on gender identity or expression might be found in an employer's dress code. For instance, a rule that women must wear skirts in the workplace might adversely affect those transgender employees for whom pants are an important expression of gender identity (Colvin 2007). Harassment is behavior that "has the purpose or effect of creating an intimidating, hostile, offensive, or disturbing environment" (Guerin 2010, 175). Derogatory remarks or jokes contribute to a hostile environment.

Most local nondiscrimination laws and policies address direct discrimination. More recently, discrimination against gender-nonconforming and transgender people has been addressed at the federal level via administrative rulings. For example, in April 2012, in *Macy v. ATF*, the Equal Opportunity Employment Commission held that discrimination based on gender identity, gender transition, and gender expression are all forms of sex discrimination, which is prohibited under Title VII of the Civil Rights Act of 1964 (EEOC 2012). The Commission's decision strengthens the claims of plaintiffs who sue for discrimination related to gender identity. Harassment protections, while not as common in laws and policies, are also being implemented via court and administrative rulings. There are few laws or policies aimed at eliminating indirect discrimination;

where they do exist, such policies are usually organization-level initiatives rather than governmental efforts.

Transgender-Inclusive Language and the Law

Legislation is one way to reduce the harassment and discrimination faced by transgender people. There are several variables that will determine its effectiveness, including the language used to define "transgender" and where that definition is placed in the legislation. Localities have employed a range of terms to protect transgender and gender-nonconforming people. For example, Boulder, Colorado, uses the term "gender variance"; Seattle originally used "transsexuality" in its local ordinance. Seattle later revised the language because "transsexuality" proved too narrowly understood to effectively protect transgender individuals and gender nonconformists. As noted by Marsha Botzer, head of the Seattle Commission on Sexual Minorities, "Every few years, there's a new word. When we passed the law in the eighties, 'transgender' wasn't [a word] anyone used. With all these 'words of the week,' the real objective is to find the most inclusive" (Currah and Minter 2000, 38).

A law's language must be broad enough to safeguard all the people that it is meant to protect. Clearly written policies ensure proper interpretation by employers, the local human rights commission, and the courts. Currently, "gender identity" and "gender expression" are commonly used to articulate legal protections for transgender and other gender-nonconforming individuals. According to the National Center for Lesbian Rights (2010), the best transgender-inclusive nondiscrimination language includes definitions that

- Acknowledge someone's identification as male or female ("gender identity")
- Describe external manifestations or expressions of gender identity via clothing, appearance, demeanor, and personality ("gender expression");
- Discuss how others might perceive someone's gender identity and/or gender expression despite his or her biological sex.

The addition of protections for transgender people to existing nondiscrimination legislation has been handled in three different ways:

1. Lawmakers added "transgender" as a new, freestanding category of protected persons, as San Francisco, California, did in 1994.

2. Transgender-inclusive terminology was included in the definition of sexual orientation, as Toledo, Ohio, did in 1989.

3. Transgender-inclusive terminology was added to the definition of sex or gender, as Santa Cruz, California, did in 1992.

Advocates and scholars disagree on the best approach to ensuring protections for transgender and gender-nonconforming people (NCLR 2010), although the National Transgender Discrimination Survey's report recommends a freestanding category (Grant et al. 2011). Advocates have been strategic, favoring whichever approach is likeliest to lead to trans-inclusive policy adoption. As long as the provision contains broad, inclusive language, advocates can argue for a transgender-inclusive interpretation in any future conflict. Currently, there is not very much empirical research into which strategy is the most effective approach, but innovation and implementation policy frameworks provide models for improving that understanding.

Innovation, Learning, and Reinventing of Policy

The innovation literature suggests that diffusion or spread of public policies can occur spatially and temporally in a systematic pattern (Walker 1969; Gray 1973; Berry and Berry 1990; Mooney and Lee 1995; Pankratz, Hallfors, and Cho 2002). According to Walker (1969), policies can diffuse geographically from one state to other states, or through local jurisdictions. The diffusion of policy relies on policymakers' social learning. The central idea of social learning is that an individual (or community) learns from another through observational modeling (Rogers 2003).

Gray (1973) builds upon Walker's work, suggesting that policy diffusion can occur over time in much the same way as spatial diffusion. In such a scenario, one or two states or localities adopt a policy; others wait to observe the impact of the policy before acting. After a few innovators adopt the policy, others follow. Adoptions then taper off as a few latecomers act. The cumulative number of adopters graphs as an S-curve, with leaders at the beginning, a larger number of second-generation or "2.0" adopters, and then a few laggards. Late adopters benefit from fewer legal challenges, as the innovators' policies will have been vetted by the courts. Furthermore, later adoptions produce more comprehensive policies because gaps in previous adoptions will have been identified and can be addressed.

As policy innovation diffuses across governments, the policy's design evolves (Hays 1996). While each government reinvents the policy, the policy innovation's original goal remains intact. Although Hays finds that these reinventions do not necessarily lead to more comprehensive policies or improved outcomes, policy learning should lead to the promotion of policies that better reflect a community's values. Indeed, the policy reinvention literature argues that policy changes occur systematically (Mooney and Lee 1995; Rogers 2003). Once an economic policy is judged sound, for example, it often moves to another jurisdiction.

In contrast to innovation and reinvention, Gray (1973) notes that some policies, such as civil rights legislation, would *never* have been adopted by certain states. The prima facie case for Gray's argument is marriage equality for same-sex couples. While a number of states have become early adopters, others have not only lagged but actively attempted to prevent innovation through restrictive legislation, constitutional amendments, or both. As with other civil rights, innovation in marriage equality might have to be imposed by court decisions or innovation at higher levels of government.

Walker (1969) and Gray (1973) pioneered spatial and temporal research for the diffusion of policy innovation. However, their work evaluated only *how* the diffusion occurs—not its subject or why it is being disseminated (Colvin 2007; Taylor et al. 2012). The most recent literature on policy variation thoroughly explores the internal and external determinants or characteristics of innovative units. Political, social, and economic factors are the internal determinants (Gray 1994; Berry 1999). The external determinants are the characteristics outside the community that either aid or hinder innovation. Sabatier (1987, 672) defines policy-oriented learning as "alterations of thought or behavioral intentions that result from experience"—a major determinant of policy innovation or change. Policy-oriented learning occurs as policy networks (or, as Sabatier writes, "advocacy coalitions") begin to draw on past experiences in order to better realize their core goals.

Finally, Osborne and Brown (2011) offer a model of policy networks based on Walker's work to explain innovations (which need not be jurisdiction-to-jurisdiction innovation) among entities. Policy ideas or innovations may move through any policy actor regardless of location or sector. Members of the policy network can reside in the public, private, nonprofit, community, or professional realm. For transgender-inclusive legislation, LGBT advocacy organizations or other policy actors—members of the business community, for example—offer ideas and innovations to policymakers whose time, expertise, and experience are limited.

*Policy Design's Influence on the Successful
Implementation of Laws*

Sabatier and Mazmanian (1980) construct a framework for understanding the implementation of policies that have already been adopted; the framework is an ideal model for successful policy implementation. It can be divided into three broad categories: the problem's *tractability*; the *favorability* of the structural environment for the implementation process (i.e., structural factors); and *the political and cultural variables* (nonstructural factors).

A statute or executive order defines the problem and stipulates objectives. Resultant policies can structure the implementation process by providing legal and financial resources to the implementing institution, selecting agency officials supportive of the policy, and regulating the opportunities for participation in the design and implementation process. Sabatier and Mazmanian identify five structural factors that affect implementation:

1. The causality between the problem and the solution as set forth in the statute or executive order;
2. How the policy ranks its objectives and how clearly it lays out the program's importance within the implementing agency;
3. The implementing agency's level of integration into the existing governmental hierarchy;
4. If structural biases can be designed to favor external policy supporters over nonsupporters;
5. In the same way that policies can be designed to harmonize with an agency's existing mission and, they can also be designed for the target group, beneficiaries and semiautonomous agencies.

In addition, adequate funding, minimal clearance points, and a structured decision-making processes will improve the policy's viability.

Theories and Hypotheses

Through trial and error, activists and policymakers have learned to develop better policies. By 2001, nondiscrimination policy expectations had become more detailed and explicit, giving administrators less discretion in and more direction for their implementation and enforcement. Policies also began to include a broader range of desirable features—for example, providing benchmarks for proper implementation or establishing an inspector general to monitor agency administration and policy enforcement.

However, courts ruled in several instances, such as *Underwood v. Archer Management Services, Inc.* (1994), that transgender individuals are not inherently covered by policies that prohibit discrimination based on sexual orientation (Minter 2006). If language matters, then the wording used to provide coverage will affect its future utility. Therefore our first hypothesis is:

> *Hypothesis 1:* Nondiscrimination policies adopted after 2000 will have a greater probability of using the terms "gender identity" and "gender expression" than those adopted previously.

A change in the strategies employed by advocates has affected the implementation and enforcement of transgender-inclusive nondiscrimination employment policies. Sabatier and Mazmanian (1980) argue that ideal policies have provisions for both implementation and enforcement. Therefore, our second hypothesis is:

> *Hypothesis 2:* The features frequently included in nondiscrimination policies adopted after 2000 will be more likely to have features that will enhance the likelihood of successful implementation than policies created in earlier years.

The existence of safeguards for potential claimants can affect whether they actually seek the policy's protections. Policies without such safeguards leave greater discretion to the administrators and greater uncertainty about what could happen to individuals that file claims—possibly leaving the claimants vulnerable to retaliation. More comprehensive policies should provide such safeguards for employees so that employees are more likely to avail themselves via the policies if necessary. Our third hypothesis is:

> *Hypothesis 3:* Nondiscrimination policies created after 2000 are more likely to provide safeguards such as confidentiality, antiretaliation, antiharassment protections, and the ability to sue, than policies created in earlier years.

Policies created after 2000 are more likely to include explicit language that delineates who is protected, how the policy is to be implemented, and the protections they offer to claimants; they should, therefore, be more likely to include *all* of these provisions. The first three hypotheses address policy strength. Combining them allows broader conclusions about their potential effectiveness to be drawn. Our final hypothesis is:

Hypothesis 4: Nondiscrimination policies created after 2000 will have a greater probability of being more comprehensive than policies created in earlier years.

Methodology

To test the hypotheses, an ordered logistic analysis was conducted. Ordered logistic regression capitalizes on the nature of the dependent variable. Rather than using dichotomous dependent variables for each policy feature of interest, indexes were developed that group transgender-inclusive nondiscrimination policy features into four dimensions: explicit language, implementation, protections, and overall policy features. This index permitted the generation of a variable that explains a policy's potential effectiveness in each dimension. Ordered logistic regression recognizes that the order of the dependent variable's values has meaning (i.e., increasing one unit demonstrates the inclusion of one additional policy feature) and uses this information to help predict the most likely outcomes.[2]

We use this ordered logistic approach on a cross-sectional dataset of all 154 local governments[3] that had transgender-inclusive nondiscrimination policies as of 2011.

Four measures of policy strength were used as dependent variables to test each of the hypotheses:

1. Explicit language
2. Implementation
3. Protections
4. Overall

These variables are all indexes, indicating that policies are more comprehensive as their values increase. Our data was generated from Sellers's

(2014) and Colvin's (2007) content analyses of nondiscrimination policies, which include a series of yes-or-no questions about the text of each ordinance. Table 8.1 shows the questions used to create the indexes for each policy dimension. The value of each index is calculated by adding the number of "yes" responses for that particular dimension.

The first index, *explicit language,* looks at the protected class. It asks two questions: Does the policy protect (1) gender identity and (2) gender expression? The possible values range from 0 (neither of these terms is included) to 2 (both terms are used).

TABLE 8.1. Questions Used to Create Indices

Policy Dimension	Question	Frequencies	
		Yes	No
Explicit Language (ranges from 0 to 2)			
	Does the policy protect gender identity?	136	18
	Does the policy protect gender expression?	83	71
Implementation (ranges from 0 to 2)			
	Does the policy designate an enforcement agency?	120	34
	Does the policy delegate autonomy to the implementation agency to enforce decisions?	71	83
Protections (ranges from 0 to 4)			
	Does the policy provide claimants confidentiality in filing claims?	47	107
	Does the policy protect claimants from retaliation?	102	52
	Does the policy protect claimants from harassment?	62	92
	Does the policy allow claimants to sue individuals who are in violation of the policy?	71	83
Overall (ranges from 0 to 8)			
	This is a composite index of all of the above questions.		

Source: Colvin (2007); Sellers (2012).

Note: Each index measures a different dimension of policies; each was created by adding the number of "yes" responses.

The next index, *implementation,* measures the content that helps to implement and enforce the nondiscrimination policies. It is composed of two questions: Does the policy (1) designate an implementation agency and (2) relegate autonomy to the implementation agency for enforcing its decisions? It, too, ranges from 0 to 2. Policies that designate an implementation agency and delegate power to enforce rulings should be more likely to implement and adhere to nondiscrimination policies. Therefore, higher values indicate that a policy is more likely to be implemented.

The variable *protections* assesses the safeguards provided to claimants. It was developed using four questions: Do policies provide claimants with (1) confidentiality in filing claims and (2) the ability to sue violators? Do the policies contain (3) antiretaliation clauses and (4) antiharassment clauses? The value of *protections* ranges from 0 to 4. While this is only a proxy for the possible safeguards that could be provided, these features are among the most common protections (Colvin 2007; Sellers 2014).

The last dependent variable, *overall,* is an index that combines the previously mentioned three variables: Explicit Language, Implementation, and Protections. It was generated by summing those indices. It assesses the policy's comprehensiveness by examining several policy features simultaneously and evaluating differences among the various policies. Its values range from 0 to 8.

The hypotheses are based on the argument that, after 2000, advocates and governments developed policies that were more comprehensive than what might have been expected based on those policies developed previously. A dichotomous variable, *post-2000,* was created to explore the differences between earlier and later policies. *Post-2000* was coded 1 if the policy was adopted between 2001 and 2011; policies adopted prior to 2001 were coded 0. Adoption dates were obtained from the National Gay and Lesbian Task Force (2007), and confirmed using the ordinances themselves. Following past research on LGBT-related policies, the study controlled for demographic and socioeconomic factors within the jurisdiction (Haider-Markel, Joslyn, and Kniss 2000; Mooney and Lee 1995; Sharp 2005). The control variables *population,*[4] *college graduates,*[5] and *same-sex households* were expected to increase the policy's scope, whereas *household size* was expected to be negatively associated with its scope. The percentage of the population that is *white* was used to control for diversity.[6] The controls are obtained from the 2000 and 2010 Census and the American Community Survey. The raw frequencies of the variables are included in the appendix for this chapter.

Results

The findings broadly support the hypotheses that nondiscrimination policies created after 2000 are more comprehensive than those of earlier years. Table 8.2 provides the ordered logistic results for the measures of policy comprehensiveness. While the variable *post-2000* is positive in all the models, as expected, it is not statistically significant across the models. However, the term is statistically significant for the models predicting explicit language and overall policy strength. While the variations are likely a result of gradual change, the probability that nondiscrimination policies will include gender identity and expression as a protected class increases by a factor of 5.29 when comparing policies created after 2000 to those adopted prior to 2000. Further, the *overall* model shows that later policies are more likely to have more comprehensive policies by approximately a factor of three.

Several other features are noteworthy. The model predicting *explicit language* finds that *household size* is statistically significant and negative: jurisdictions with larger households, that is, more families, are less likely to include gender identity or expression in their nondiscrimination laws. The model predicting *implementation* indicates that its relationship with *post-2000* is positive, but not statistically significant. *Population* is positive and statistically significant in the implementation model, which means that having more citizens within a jurisdiction increases the probability that the implementation index will be more comprehensive. As in the implementation model, *population* is the only statistically significant variable in the protections model, which suggests that larger cities are more likely to have more extensive nondiscrimination policies.

The remaining variables' coefficients show similar relationships to the other models in terms of increasing or decreasing predicted values; however, in the *protections* model, the cut points are significant at cut points 3 and 4, indicating a statistically significant difference between the values of protections (with a 95 percent confidence interval).[7] These findings suggest that there are distinct differences between policies, that is, the more extensive policies are more extensive by design, because the model's predicted values of cut points 3 and 4 are statistically significant.

The final model, *overall*, indicates that *post-2000* is positive and statistically significant. It increases the probability of a more comprehensive policy by a factor of almost three. Additionally, *population* increases the probability by a factor of 1.685. *Household size* shows a negative relationship. Cut points 4, 5, 6, and 7 indicate that there is a statistically significant difference between their predicted values and the model's lower values.

TABLE 8.2. Ordered Logistic Results Predicting Policy Comprehensiveness

Independent Variable	Explicit Language		Protections		Implementation		Overall	
	Coefficient	Odds Ratio	Coefficient	Odds Ratio	Coefficient	Odds Ratio	Coefficient	Odds Ratio
Post−2000	1.666***	5.29	0.466	1.593	0.298	1.347	1.09***	2.975
	(0.402)		(0.367)		(0.359)		(0.356)	
Population (log)	0.209	1.232	0.404***	1.498	0.314**	1.369	0.52***	1.682
	(0.150)		(0.146)		(0.135)		(0.137)	
White (%)	−1.345	0.261	−0.441	0.644	1.104	3.018	0.408	1.504
	(1.203)		(1.192)		(1.034)		(1.056)	
College graduates (%)	1.728	5.628	−0.282	0.754	0.9	2.461	1.128	3.089
	(1.211)		(1.055)		(1.035)		(1.024)	
Household size	−2.266***	0.104	−0.208	0.812	−0.306	0.736	−1.166*	0.312
	(0.716)		(0.675)		(0.658)		(0.660)	
Same-sex household	−1.13E-04	1.00	−6.18E-05	1.00	1.69E-05	1.00	−6.45E-05	1.00
	(8.04E-05)		(7.56E-05)		(6.79E-05)		(6.46E-05)	
Cut point 1	−4.399		2.736		2.416		0.882	
	(2.450)		(2.310)		(2.164)		(2.199)	
Cut point 2	−2.276		4.285		3.96		2.739	
	(2.429)		(2.326)		(2.180)		(2.171)	
Cut point 3	—		—		5.149**		3.845	
	—		—		(2.199)		(2.173)	
Cut point 4	—		—		6.667***		4.733**	
	—		—		(2.222)		(2.181)	
Cut point 5	—		—		—		5.665***	
	—		—		—		(2.197)	
Cut point 6	—		—		—		6.881***	
	—		—		—		(2.221)	
Cut point 7	—		—		—		8.612***	
	—		—		—		(2.274)	
χ^2	24.43		17.02		10.12		23.34	
McFadden R^2	0.08		0.05		0.02		0.04	
Observations	154		154		154		154	

Source: Colvin (2007); Sellers (2012); U.S. Census (2000); U.S. Census (2010).

Note: * $p < 0.10$, ** $p < 0.05$; *** $p < 0.01$; The first column of each cell entry provides the ordered logistic regression coefficients. Standard errors are presented below in parentheses. The second column of each model is the odds ratio.

The McFadden-R^2 is a goodness-of-fit[8] measure that suggests a statistical model's ability to explain variation and permits the evaluation of the statistical models. The McFadden-R^2 is low in all of the models, but the *post-2000* term is statistically significant in the *explicit language* and *overall* models. Collectively, the models do not explain much variation in policy strength, but the *post-2000* variable helps to explain outcomes. In short, while governments were more likely to create a stronger policy after 2000, this variable's ability to explain why some policies are more comprehensive than others is very limited.

Figure 8.2 illustrates the effects of the *post-2000* variable, which compares the predicted probabilities of the overall policy strength of nondiscrimination policies created from 1975 to 2000 with those adopted after 2000. Essentially, it contrasts the predicted probability of overall policy strength when the variable *post-2000* equals zero (predicting the years 1975–2000) to when the variable equals one (predicting the years 2001–2011) when all other values are held at their means. The highest predicted probability for the earlier period (~0.25) is three (i.e., the most likely number of features included in earlier policies is three). Clearly, the later years are more comprehensive. The highest predicted probability for policies created post-2000 (~0.21) is five. While the two predicted probabilities overlap considerably, later policies are more likely to be more comprehensive. As table 8.2 indicates, these differences are statistically significant.

Discussion and Conclusion

Policies created after 2000 are more comprehensive than those created prior to 2000. On the whole, the earlier policies contain fewer claimant protections and more suspect-protective language. As expected, governments increasingly included gender identity and expression in the protected class. Moreover, the model gauging overall policy strength supports the argument that policy innovation and learning occurred. With the addition of the claimant-protective language as well as explicit protections for gender identity and expression, policies become less ambiguous, advise employers and employees on acceptable behavior more directly, and establish a protocol for handling claims. Such instructions are vital to the enforcement and implementation of nondiscrimination policies.

Sabatier and Mazmanian (1980) explain that nondiscrimination policies must outline goals and expectations clearly in order to be effective. To ensure adequate implementation, an agency should be designated and be

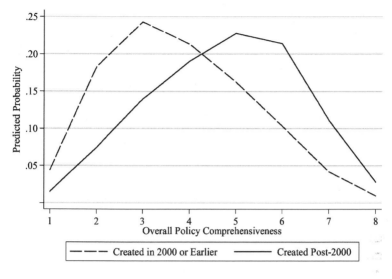

Fig. 8.2. Predicted probability of overall policy comprehensiveness. (Data from Colvin 2007; Sellers 2012; U.S. Census 2000; U.S. Census 2010.)

given enough authority to manifest its decisions. Policies must enumerate claimant protections or claimants might be reluctant to file claims (Colvin and Riccucci 2002). Innovation of these specific protections, along with the consistency in their use, supports the idea that policymakers network and communicate with one another, as Osborne and Brown (2011) suggest. While the models do not indicate that *post-2000* is a statistically significant variable in either the *implementation* or *protections* models, the term is positive throughout all the models and is statistically significant in the overall model, which supports our argument.

There are several limitations to this methodology and these results. Much of the relevant data is neither collected by local governments nor readily available. For example, while documentation of discrimination-related court cases is readily available, initial claims of discrimination and negotiated settlements are not. Since the majority of claims are settled out of court, little is known about the actual use or effectiveness of these policies. More longitudinal data about these policies and their influence on deterring discrimination should be collected. More sophisticated analyses, such as event history analysis, requires much larger amounts of data for numerous time-variant measures.

Given that there are already numerous nondiscrimination policies in place at the state and local levels, adding transgender-inclusive protections is, in fact, more often a mixture of reinvention and innovation than purely innovation (although, considering these adoptions within the framework of innovation is useful). Transgender-inclusive provisions are commonly almost always added to existing nondiscrimination laws. Research that separates new innovations and reinventions would provide a more nuanced picture of the innovation and adoption process. Currently, it is unclear which is more difficult: adding to existing legislation or passing new legislation.

It is not yet possible to fully understand how claimant-friendly provisions affect employees' willingness to make use of nondiscrimination policies. Real-world administration of such policies might vary, and the experiences of transgender claimants could differ greatly across regions, jurisdictions, and time periods. Some of this variability can, however, be attenuated by strongly crafted nondiscrimination policies that use transgender-specific language and robust claimant protections. Nondiscrimination employment policy is more than just social or moral policy; it is also economic policy. Explicit and inclusive policies can have a real impact on the lives of transgender and gender-nonconforming people. A foundation of economic security makes other protections easier to secure. As Grant et al. (2011) underscore, the challenges for transgender people are many and extend beyond employment.

These results suggest that the collective efforts of advocates and activists to pressure policymakers for more extensive, more explicit provisions have had a positive effect on trans-friendly policies. While this study was primarily exploratory, it clearly finds a difference between policies adopted from 1975 to 2000 and those crafted in later years. The evolution toward stronger policies was likely more gradual and complex than this dichotomous term (post-2000) can capture. Nonetheless, this study determined that nondiscrimination policies implemented after the turn of the century are more likely to be more comprehensive. Basically, policies are improving with time.

This is critical for implementation and enforcement of transgender-inclusive policies. Policies unambiguous in their expectations limit administrators' discretion, thereby simplifying enforcement and ensuring proper determinations. Policy learning and innovation at the local level is critical for local governments, but these findings also provide insight for future national legislation. The lessons learned by local governments can be readily applied to state-level legislation as well as the proposed federal

Employment Non-Discrimination Act (ENDA), potentially leading to stronger protections for all employees.

APPENDIX

TABLE 8.3. Summary Statistics

Variable	Observations	Mean	Std. Dev.	Min.	Max.
			Policy Dimensions		
Explicit language	154	1.42	0.69	0	2
Implementation	154	1.24	0.79	0	2
Protections	154	1.83	1.19	0	4
Overall	154	4.49	1.69	1	8
			Independent Variables		
Post-2000	154	0.740	0.440	0	1
Population (total)	154	442,957	925,449	730	8,175,133
White (%)	154	0.688	0.166	0.106	0.960
College graduates (%)	154	0.338	0.150	0.106	0.771
Household size (mean)	154	2.34	0.25	1.52	3.48
Same-sex households (total)	154	1,460	2,771	0	23,118

Source: Colvin (2007); Sellers (2012); U.S. Census (2000); U.S. Census (2010).

NOTES

1. This study was sponsored by the National Gay and Lesbian Taskforce and the National Center for Transgender Equality.

2. The interpretation of ordered logistic coefficients is similar to logistic regression. The positive coefficients indicate that an increase for that variable increases the probability of a higher outcome. Negative coefficients indicate that an increase in the variable decreases the probability of a higher outcome. But the coefficients do not explain linear relationships, so their effects are explained herein by providing the odds ratio and predicted probabilities. Using ordered logistic analysis also requires the use of cut points. These are not independent variables, so they do not affect outcome. Cut points estimate the point at which the dependent variable moves from one value to the next closest value. This is basically an extension of logistic analysis. Both methods try to predict the outcome for a latent dependent variable (the y in an equation). However, unlike binary logistic regression, there are more than two possible outcomes, so it becomes necessary to have cut points that define at what points the dependent variable changes values. The cut points are the estimated value of the latent variable.

3. This dataset includes 117 city policies and 37 county policies.

4. These models employ the log of the total population. This helps to normalize and fit the data better.

5. For all of the models, the AIC and BIC indicate that the percentage of college graduates fits the data better than the percentage of high school graduates.

6. The percentages of the Hispanic or African American populations are not included because these variables would vary inversely with the percentage of the population that is white.

7. Ordered logistic regression predicts values called "cut points" at which the value changes from predicting one outcome to another. For example, cut point 1 can indicate the point where values below cut point 1 is predicted to be 1, while values above the cut point are predicted to be 2. Since the dependent variable is latent, providing exact values at which dependent variable switches from one outcome to the next helps to understand the categories, but should be interpreted with caution. The confidence intervals for each outcome of the dependent variable can overlap. Basically, if the cut points for a given value are statistically significant, then a particular category does not overlap with other values of the dependent variable at a given confidence level.

8. A goodness-of-fit measure is an indicator of how well a model explains variation or predicts outcomes. There are several statistics classified as a goodness-of-fit measure. These measures provide a method for evaluating a model or determining the appropriateness of included variables. The McFadden-R^2 is a statistic that ranges from zero to one, with higher values suggesting the model fits the data better because more variance is explained.

REFERENCES

Berry, Frances Stokes, and William D. Berry. 1990. "State Lottery Adoption as Policy Innovation: An Event History Analysis." *American Political Science Review* 84 (2): 395–415.

Berry, William. 1999. *Theories of the Policy Process.* Theoretical Lenses on Public Policy, edited by Paul Sabatier. Boulder: Westview Press.

Colvin, Roddrick A. 2007. "The Rise of Transgender-Inclusive Laws: How Well Are Municipalities Implementing Supportive Nondiscrimination Public Employment Policies?" *Review of Public Personnel Administration* 27 (4): 336–60.

Colvin, Roddrick A., and Norma M. Riccucci. 2002. "Employment Nondiscrimination Policies: Assessing Implementation and Measuring Effectiveness." *International Journal of Public Administration* 25 (1): 95–108.

Currah, Paisley, and Shannon Minter. 2000. *Transgender Equality: A Handbook for Activists and Policymakers.* San Francisco: National Center for Lesbian Rights; Washington, DC: National Gay and Lesbian Task Force Policy Institute.

Equal Employment Opportunity Commission (EEOC). 2012. "Pre-1965: Events Leading to the Creation of EEOC." http://www.eeoc.gov/eeoc/history/35th/history/pre1965/index.html.

Grant, Jaime M., Lisa A. Mottet, Justin Tanis, Jack Harrison, Jody L. Herman, and Mara Keisling. 2011. *Injustice at Every Turn: A Report of the National Transgender Discrimination Survey.* Washington, DC: National Center for Transgender Equality and National Gay and Lesbian Task Force.

Gray, Virginia. 1973. "Innovation in the States: A Diffusion Study." *American Political Science Review* 67 (4): 1174–85.

Gray, Virginia. 1994. "Competition, Emulation, and Policy Innovation." In *New Perspectives on American Politics*, ed. Lawrence C. Dodd and Calvin Jillson, 230–48. Washington, DC: Congressional Quarterly.

Green, Jamison. 2000. Introduction to *Transgender Equality: A Handbook for Activists and Policymakers*, by Paisley Currah and Shannon Minter. San Francisco: National Center for Lesbian Rights; Washington, DC: National Gay and Lesbian Task Force Policy Institute.

Guerin, Lisa. 2010. *The Essential Guide to Workplace Investigations: How to Handle Employee Complaints and Problems*. New York: Nolo Press.

Haider-Markel, Donald P., Mark R. Joslyn, and Chad J. Kniss. 2000. "Minority Group Interests and Political Representation: Gay Elected Officials in the Policy Process." *Journal of Politics* 62 (2): 568–77.

Hays, Scott P. 1996. "Patterns of Reinvention: The Nature of Evolution during Policy Diffusion." *Policy Studies Journal* 24 (4): 551–66.

Hunt, Jerome. 2012. *A State-by-State Examination of Nondiscrimination Laws and Policies*. Washington, DC: Center for American Progress Action Fund.

McCreery, Patrick. 2001. "Beyond Gay: 'Deviant' Sex and the Politics of the ENDA Workplace." In *Out at Work: Building a Gay-Labor Alliance*, edited by Kitty Krupat and Patrick McCreery, 31–51. Minneapolis: University of Minnesota Press.

Minter, Shannon Price. 2006. "Do Transsexuals Dream of Gay Rights? Getting Real about Transgender Inclusion." In *Transgender Rights*, edited by Paisley Currah, Richard M. Juang, and Shannon Price Minter, 141–70. Minneapolis: University of Minnesota Press.

Minter, Shannon, and Christopher Daley. 2003. "Trans Realities: A Legal Needs Assessment of San Francisco's Transgender Community." San Francisco: National Center for Lesbian Rights. http://www.nclrights.org/publications/transrealities0803.htm.

Mooney, Christopher Z., and Mei-Hsien Lee. 1995. "Legislative Morality in the American States: The Case of Pre-*Roe* Abortion Regulations Reform." *American Journal of Political Science* 39 (3): 599–627.

Mooney, Christopher Z., and Mei-Hsien Lee. 1999. "The Temporal Diffusion of Morality Policy: The Case of Death Penalty Legislation in American Courts." *Policy Studies* 27 (4): 766–81.

National Center for Lesbian Rights (NCLR). 2010. "State-by-State Guide to Laws That Prohibit Discrimination against Transgender People." San Francisco: NCLR.

National Gay and Lesbian Task Force (NGLTF). 2007. "Years Passed between Sexual Orientation and Gender Identity/Expression." Reports and Research. http://www.thetaskforce.org/downloads/reports/fact_sheets/years_passed_gie_so_7_07.pdf.

Osborne, Stephen, and Louise Brown. 2011. "Innovation, Public Policy, and Public Services Delivery in the UK: The Word That Would Be King?" *Public Administration* 89 (4): 1335–50.

Pankratz, M., D. Hallfors, and H. Cho. 2002. "Measuring Perceptions of Innovation Adoption: The Diffusion of a Federal Drug Prevention Policy." *Health Education Research* 17 (3): 315–26.

Rogers, Everett M. 2003. *Diffusion of Innovations*. 5th ed. New York: Free Press.

Sabatier, Paul A. 1987. "Knowledge, Policy-Oriented Learning, and Policy Change: An Advocacy Coalition Framework." *Science Communication* 8 (4): 649–92.

Sabatier, Paul, and Daniel Mazmanian. 1980. "The Implementation of Public Policy: A Framework of Analysis." *Policy Studies Journal* 8 (4): 538–60.

Sellers, Mitchell. 2014. "Discrimination and the Transgender Population: Analysis of the Functionality of Local Government Policies that Protect Gender Identity." *Administration & Society* 46 (1): 70–86.

Sharp, Elaine. 2005. *Morality Politics in American Cities*. Lawrence: University Press of Kansas.

Supateera, C., and B. H. Kleiner. 1999. "Discrimination in Government." *Equal Opportunities International* 18 (5–6): 78–82.

Taylor, Jami K., Daniel C. Lewis, Matthew L. Jacobsmeier, and Brian DiSarro. 2012. "Content and Complexity in Policy Reinvention and Diffusion: Gay and Transgender-Inclusive Laws against Discrimination." *State Politics & Policy Quarterly* 12 (1): 75–98.

Tobler, Christa. 2005. *A Case Study: Introducing the Development of the Legal Concept of Indirect Discrimination under European Community Law*. Social Europe Series. Antwerp, Belgium: Intersentia Press.

Underwood v. Archer Management Services, Inc. 1994. 857 F. Supp. 96, 98.

Walker, Jack. 1969. "The Diffusion of Innovation among the American States." *American Political Science Review* 63 (3): 880–99.

Beyond Nondiscrimination Policy

Ryan Combs

9 | Key Issues in Transgender Health Care Policy and Practice

Many transsexual, transgender, and gender-nonconforming people interact with health care providers as they look to understand and adapt their lives and bodies to their gender identity. The needs of this group vary, and the decision to work with health care professionals—such as therapists, general practitioners, endocrinologists, speech therapists, and surgeons—is a personal one. Depending on individual circumstances, some transgender people enter the health care system for the express purpose of pursuing a social and physical transition, taking medical steps to align their bodies with their inner sense of self. Others are unsure about what their feelings mean or what to do, so they wish to speak with an expert who can help them to understand their situation. Transgender people may not seek medical intervention for various reasons. Among them, a doctor or counselor may have advised against it, or the individual may worry about the impact of a gender transition on work, family, and social life (Schilt and Wiswall 2008; Israel 2004). Others are content with their bodies as they are, and they feel that medical involvement is unnecessary.

The aim of this chapter is to shed light on several important aspects of transgender health and to position these issues in relation to health policy. For this purpose, I define "transgender community"[1] as a loosely constructed collective of people accessing gender reassignment services. They may or may not have ties to a particular transgender or LGBT sociopolitical movement, or have access to social support networks. In the main, this chapter will remain narrow in scope by focusing specifically on the situation of transgender people in the Western, English-speaking context.

This chapter draws on the existing transgender studies literature and an empirical study of transgender patients in the United Kingdom. Transgender people's health needs are examined by looking at the community's demography and their demands on a health care service. I will discuss the composition of the transgender community and explore the group's heterogeneity. I will also present data regarding the number of people estimated to access services. Finally, the chapter explores what gender transition means in practice and the ways in which gender identity can affect other areas of health.

The chapter then takes an in-depth look at the care provided through the United Kingdom's publicly funded National Health Service (NHS). The principal focus of this section is on the experiences of transgender patients and their health care providers, examining their views about the systems through which care is delivered and the level of care provided. I will discuss the power dynamic between health care funders, clinicians, and patients. Additionally, the chapter examines the systemic constraints that can obstruct the delivery of gender reassignment services. I will also investigate what patients and professionals have to say about the nature of gender and gender identity, as well as the extent to which patients feel empowered within the current system. This will be followed by a discussion about the data as interpreted through the health policy literature. The chapter concludes by considering the question of what these data tell us about the viability and sustainability of transgender health care services.

Transgender Health Care Needs

Transgender: Diversity of the Category

Conceptualizations of "transgender" vary across academic disciplines. The understandings proposed by the fields of biology, sexology, psychology, sociology, feminist theory, queer theory, and the law demonstrate that gender and gender identity are complex, and that definitions used to describe gender are debatable and malleable (Greenberg 1999; Whittle 2002; Nestle, Howell, and Wilchins 2002; Rudacille 2006; Combs 2010). Definitions of gender also differ widely across geographic locations because atypical gender presentations are interpreted through the lens of cultural norms. Definitions of gender variance have also changed substantially over time. As such, transgender has no single agreed-upon definition.

Several groups position themselves under the transgender "umbrella" in the Western context. Transsexual people seek medical intervention to change their bodies' primary and secondary sex characteristics, by means such as hormone therapy and surgery. They are arguably the most well known in the public consciousness. Transsexual people usually seek to live fully and permanently as members of a sex other than that assigned to them at birth (i.e., transitioning from male to female or female to male). The term transgender is generally used in two ways. First, it is used as an umbrella term, and second, it denotes people who live in a gender role other than that assigned to them at birth, but who do not pursue surgical and hormonal intervention. Transgender people may change their gender presentation to reflect their gender identity by adapting their name, pronoun, and mode of dress. Genderqueer and other gender nonconforming people actively resist the predominant view of gender categories as a male/female binary and assert a third gender or nongendered identity and presentation (Bornstein 1994, 2000; Nestle, Howell, and Wilchins 2002). There are still others who cross-dress or live in a different gender role, or do both, on a part-time basis, often referred to or self-identifying as a transvestite or cross-dresser. They may still identify primarily as the gender associated with their birth sex or have a dual identity. This list is not exhaustive. The conceptualization and labeling of transgender identities changes rapidly and the definitions are often contested.

In sum, the transgender category represents an extremely diverse collection of people who grapple in some way with their gender identity and its disconnection with their birth sex. It contains people who are comfortable conforming to binary notions of male and female, and others who actively resist binary gender and campaign for the right to be free of gender. Transgender people as a community, and as a patient group, are heterogeneous and, at times, inharmonious. Although the transgender umbrella has arguably been useful in building alliances among people of different identities and creating a louder political voice, it may have also made it more difficult to find consensus on advocacy strategies. This immense diversity leads to a great deal of ambiguity in the transgender policymaking context.

Demography

Gathering accurate demographic information about the transgender population proves challenging for several reasons. In addition to the transgender community's immense variation, it lacks cohesive social and political legitimacy, constituting a significant barrier. Methodological issues inhibit cross-study comparison and there are difficulties in agreeing what constitutes a transgender individual in light of worldwide differences (World

Professional Association for Transgender Health 2011). There have been efforts recently by national agencies such as the UK's Equality and Human Rights Commission to create and test questions for use in data collection (Balarajan, Gray, and Mitchell 2011). However, there are currently no formal mechanisms for collecting gender identity information in large national datasets like censuses. Taking these factors into consideration, it comes as little surprise that no large-scale demographic or formal epidemiological studies have accurately calculated the incidence and prevalence of transgender identities in the population (Zucker and Lawrence 2009).

The studies that exist are predominately Western European in origin and concern the medical category of transsexual people, who are generally the easiest to trace owing to the existence of medical, and sometimes legal, records. However, even if the number of transsexual people was accurately gauged, the figure would fall well short of the total number of gender nonconforming people. Indeed, it is much more complicated to count "hidden" transgender people such as those who do not access medical clinics, those who transitioned several years ago, and those who live in a gender role other than that assigned to them at birth but have not changed their documentation. Another difficulty is that many transgender people are not "out" about their gender identity/gender history. To some extent, the Internet has been useful in reaching this group (Rosser et al. 2007).

Of the demographic estimates that exist, what are they and what do they tell us? Primarily they show that "gender dysphoria"—the contentious term for the medical diagnosis of having a cross-gender identity—is rare relative to other medical conditions. A 2007 review of worldwide prevalence studies found that the figures of people with gender dysphoria ranged from 1 in 100,000 males (MTF, or male to female) and 1 in 400,000 females (FTM, or female to male) in a 1968 Swedish study, to 1 in 2,900 males and 1 in 8,300 females in a 1988 Singaporean study (De Cuypere et al. 2007; Pauly 1968; Tsoi 1988). It also found that there are many more trans women (MTF) than trans men (FTM) in Western Europe while the reverse was true in Eastern Europe, pointing to cross-cultural variability in who pursues a medical transition (De Cuypere et al. 2007). A study by Rosser et al. (2007) found that compared with the general U.S. population, the transgender population was more likely to be younger, white (non-Hispanic), single, more educated but with less household income, living in small towns to medium-sized cities, and less affiliated with traditional Christian denominations. Unfortunately, there are few international comparators.

Accessing Transition Health Care: What Does Transition
Mean in Practice?

Gender dysphoria is arguably rare, but evidence shows that the number of people who medically transition has risen considerably since the mid-20th century (Rudacille 2006; Kuyper 2006). Data from the United Kingdom show that the number of people accessing gender reassignment services is rising substantially year after year (Reed et al. 2009).[2] The availability of new information technology over the past twenty years has improved public access to information about gender identity and the possibility of medical intervention (Whittle 2002; Rudacille 2006). It has also been argued that transgender people are more aware of their legal rights and more likely to use legal mechanisms to claim those rights (Whittle, Turner and Al-Alami 2007). The transgender community is likely bigger, better connected, and more informed than ever.

Nonetheless, geo-cultural factors result in an inconsistent delivery of transgender health care. Studies have shown that transgender people face discrimination and prejudice when obtaining health care services (Lombardi 2001; Whittle et al. 2008; McNeil et al. 2012). In Western countries, medical treatment[3] for transgender people who want their bodies to correspond with their gender identities is considered suitable in many cases (Oriel 2000). While there are debates about gender identity treatments, many physicians affirm that medical interventions for the facilitation of a gender transition are suitable under the supervision of appropriately trained professionals (World Professional Association for Transgender Health 2011). The picture in the developing world is patchy and evidence is lacking.

In practice, a gender transition can involve several medical, legal, and social components. Transgender people can struggle acutely with their gender identity prior to approaching doctors (Jones 2005). In the United Kingdom, for example, there are a number of ways to medically transition, but patients are typically put onto a similar pathway of treatment once their feelings of gender dysphoria are identified. A general practitioner (GP) is usually the first professional that an individual approaches about their gender. GPs normally send the patient to see a local psychiatrist who assesses their mental state and determines whether or not they have genuine gender dysphoria rather than other conditions or states of being that can be mistaken for a transgender identity. The individual is then referred to a gender identity clinic where they begin assessment. Treatments for transgender people can include, where indicated, hormone therapy, surgery, speech, and language therapy, and hair removal (Jones 2005). The World Professional Association for Transgender Health regularly reviews best practice and updates treatment guidelines in their Standards of Care (WPATH 2011).

Shedding Light on Health Care Systems and Power:
A Qualitative Study in the United Kingdom

The publicly funded National Health Service[4] in England routinely provides treatment to adults in cases where gender reassignment is considered necessary. However, the literature demonstrates a widely held view that significant inequalities exist and that the care provided is inadequate to meet transgender people's needs (West 2004; Whittle, Turner, and Al-Alami 2007; Fish 2007; McNeil et al. 2012). For example, West (2004) argues that systemic issues limit equitable access to specialists and McNeil et al. (2012) finds low levels of satisfaction with gender clinics that impact patient well-being and their sense of empowerment.

The following sections present qualitative data about transgender experiences in a large health care bureaucracy. Its aim is to shed light on positive and negative aspects of health practice by eliciting the views of transgender service users and the clinicians who provide specialist care. It then discusses systemic issues from a health policy perspective and briefly offers possible explanations for the current situation.

Methodology

Using an inductive technique, this qualitative study explores questions about transgender health care provision (Combs 2010). It is concerned with the construction of knowledge about transgender health care within the wider sociopolitical context. The work is informed by social constructivist[5] and feminist[6] perspectives on both gender and medicine. A qualitative approach was chosen for a number of reasons. First, it allows under-explored questions to be studied flexibly (Braun and Clarke 2006). Second, it is pragmatically advantageous because a large amount of in-depth data can be generated from a relatively small sample ($n = 42$).

Data for the study were gathered from a sample of two stakeholder groups: focus groups of transgender patients ($n = 30$) and interviews with specialist professionals ($n = 12$). The first group, patients, was recruited through the national advocacy organization Press for Change, local support groups, and via snowball sampling techniques. The inclusion criteria specified that participants (a) identified on the transgender spectrum, and (b) had undergone or intended to undergo medical treatment related to their gender identity through the NHS in England. They participated in focus groups conducted in five locations: London, Manchester, Nottingham, Leeds, and Exeter. The groups were asked questions about their experiences of treatment and support, their views about the NHS's current approach, their opinions about gender dysphoria's etiology and classification, and recommendations for systemic improvement (if warranted). The focus groups lasted between 60 and 75 minutes. They were audio recorded and transcribed verbatim.

The second group, specialist NHS professionals, participated in in-depth semistructured interviews. The professionals in the sample had transgender expertise as well as treatment responsibility or decision-making power. Participants were recruited to the study by direct invitation from Professor Stephen Whittle OBE, project manager for the Department of Health's Mapping Project (Combs, Turner, and Whittle 2008). Discrete questions relating to this study were embedded in the Mapping Project interviews. The questions related to the origin of gender dysphoria, perceptions of transgender treatment in their profession, and the strengths and weaknesses of current health care provision. The interviews lasted between 45 and 60 minutes, and were audio recorded and transcribed verbatim. The professionals held the following positions (some overlapping): five lead clinicians, four consultant psychiatrists, two sexual health physicians, a psychosexual therapist, a clinical psychologist, a consultant in sexual medicine, a Primary Care Trust (funding) manager, and a speech therapist.

The data were analysed using a thematic analysis that involves identifying, describing, comparing/contrasting, refining, and naming and defining themes (Braun and Clarke 2006). The process was heavily informed by the tradition of grounded theory method (Glaser and Strauss 1967; Strauss and Corbin 1990; Charmaz 2006). Grounded theory method was originally developed to strengthen the analytic rigor and legitimacy of qualitative research by producing theory through a systematic inductive data analysis technique (Glaser and Strauss 1967). This approach sits in opposition to deductive, hypothesis-testing models most often used by political scientists;[7] however, the grounded theory method is used widely in the social sciences and medicine (e.g., Charmaz 1990; Morse and Johnson 1991; McAllister 2001; Calman 2006) and has been chosen to examine questions related to gender and sexuality (e.g., Robertson 1992; Wilson, Hutchinson, and Holzemer 1997; Tilley and Brackley 2005). The results of the study are reported over the next several sections.

Clinicians' Perspectives: Professional Experiences

> For most services, people—doctors, nurses—move into an area and expect that their work will be supported, recognized, and not criticized. One of the things I find quite hard when I trained and when I opened this clinic was a torrent of criticism and complaints against medicine generally and about the provision of gender services. . . . Of course it's right for campaign groups to shout loud, but you can't be battered by it.
> —Consultant in sexual medicine and clinic lead

The clinicians interviewed as part of the study were generally strongly committed to the welfare of their patients, and aimed to provide a responsible and high-quality service. However, the context in which they delivered care is difficult because of several professional challenges to working in the gender identity specialty. Clinicians perceived criticism of their work from all quarters. According to some, the specialty is held in low regard when compared with other areas of medicine. A few GPs, who are responsible for referring transgender people to gender specialists, were also said to be hostile to the gender service and its aims. Additionally, services provided by health care funders were variable according to the patient's area of residence. Patients also expressed dissatisfaction about systemic issues over which clinicians felt they have little control, such as long waiting lists and times. Furthermore, clinicians perceived that funding decision makers are covering fewer and fewer treatments because of cost cutting, justified in part by the low priority attached to gender treatments. Political controversy and negative media coverage may also play a role in this classification, although attitudes were said to have improved in recent years.

There are concerns about support for gender specialists and the sustainability of the current system. Transgender patient referrals have risen, and there are not enough specialists to cope with the demand. Professionals perceived that the amount of time spent on bureaucracy and administration is high, which reduces the time they can spend with patients. Practitioners were anxious about current clinical availability and capacity. These individuals characterized the resource allocation as "strained."

Some practitioners also expressed concern about the legacy of their services once they retire, because there is no formalized training program in the specialty and there are few opportunities to share knowledge with peers. The process of standardizing national protocols has been fraught, in part because of differences in ethos between professional disciplines and competing interests. The consensus in this set of interviews was that the NHS was not facilitating a good service in large part because bureaucratic and systemic roadblocks inhibit the specialists' work.

Clinicians' Perspectives: Etiology and Treatment Arrangements

> I think [gender dysphoria] is multifactorial. I look on it as a medical condition that requires medical treatment and that's how I would explain it to family members who were anti, because they are usually looking on it as a choice. I think the origin is still unclear. We know lots about what it isn't, rather than what it is.
> —Psychosexual therapist and clinic lead

Professionals discussed the nature of transgender as a phenomenon, giving an interesting insight into the beliefs that underpin their work. Surprisingly, they said that discussions about the etiology of transgender identities do not take place widely within the profession. The mixture of opinion about etiology was dominated by biological, genetic, and hormonal explanations. A few clinicians said that gender dysphoria's cause is unknown, and therefore it has little bearing on treatment. Some pointed out that a definitive etiological discovery may have a negative effect on those whose histories do not fit the dominant theory. In all cases, specialists rejected the proposition that gender dysphoria is a choice. To some extent, this undercuts assertions that transgender health care is elective, giving some credence to the argument for better access to treatment.

In the United Kingdom, gender identity services currently fall within the responsibility of psychiatry but endocrinology and surgical services are often utilized. The data found tensions around the question of whether transgender care should be under the auspices of psychiatry. In the interviews, psychologists and sexual health physicians contested this as a matter of principle. All of the clinicians interviewed believe that gender dysphoria is not pathological per se, but they were split over who should evaluate patients, and to what extent. This is part of a broader worldwide debate about depathologization (e.g., Ault and Brzuzy 2008).

Information about etiology might help to pinpoint which specialties (psychiatry, sexual health, endocrinology, and so on) should be involved in treatment. The psychiatrists interviewed for this study believed that most transgender people were essentially "normal" but they did not want treatment to be removed from psychiatry. If the current framework was abolished, they said, the medical community would no longer have a basis upon which to treat the condition, nor would funders be willing to pay for transition care. However, one could argue that their reluctance to commit to any particular origin narrative could stem from a concern that the condition will be removed from their professional sphere of activity, undermining their legitimacy as key practitioners.

Transgender Patients' Perspectives: The Impact of Bureaucracy and Delay

> I was referred to a GP who didn't know anything. He looked at me and he went, well, can you tell me what this is? What is being gender dysphoric? I don't know. Should we look it up on Google? And that's what he did; he actually looked it up on Google while I was there.
> —Participant, London focus group

Nearly all focus group participants indicated that there are significant problems with the way transgender people are handled by the health care system. Patient focus group data demonstrate that a lack of understanding, bureaucratic roadblocks, and delay are significant issues in health care provision. Patients want shorter waiting times and fewer hoops to jump through to qualify for hormones and surgery, and they discussed the personal impact of these factors in great depth. For example, participants from across the country reported waiting lists for transgender treatments stretching far beyond government waiting targets. In some cases, it takes years to go through the process. Services were also described as fragmented and patchy. Although there is a gender clinic in London, the large cities of Manchester and Birmingham have no clinics at all, so traveling long distances to appointments is very common.

According to interview participants, patients and doctors lacked basic information about transgender identities and experiences. GPs and patients were frequently unclear about referral pathways, which led to misreferral or stagnant periods without support. This was not helped by communication gaps between funding bodies and frontline practitioners, which delayed appointments.

A couple of years ago, I went to who was then my GP. They gave me a sick note signed up for 12 months and told me to go away and sort it [out]. I kid you not. . . . A sick note dated for 12 months, then said go away and do what you need to do. No letter of referral. . . . that really knocked me back; it's partly why I'm in the position I'm in now . . . it had serious implications, I nearly committed suicide. (Participant, Exeter focus group)

Many patients felt as if no one was in charge of their care and that they had to fight for treatment. A few were angry that they had to assume the burden of educating their doctors. While patients wanted services to be tailored to meet their individual needs and priorities, they found the lack of universally accessible services troubling. The low priority of gender dysphoria treatments and the inequality of treatment between patients in different places had a psychological effect—it prompted resentment and, at times, competitiveness among patients.

Participants believed their situation should be taken more seriously because it is recognised as a medical condition in UK case law (*R v North West Lancashire HA Ex P A, D and G* 1999). As with the professionals' data presented earlier, patients perceived that decisions taken about trans health care had, at times, been motivated by politics or public opinion. Although legal residents in the United Kingdom are covered by the NHS, some transgender people decided to pay for private treatment because they were concerned about the long waiting lists. The prominent narrative about private treatment, even from those who did not have direct experience with it, was that it was desirable because it was faster and gave the patient more power to chart their own path. It seemed to frustrate participants that they could not receive similar treatment through the NHS.

By contrast, there were many positive and encouraging narratives about service provision itself. The majority of participants relayed positive personal experiences in primary care despite the lack of knowledge among GPs. For example, a Nottingham focus group participant said, "I was very lucky with my GP. Though he knew nothing about this . . . he was on board with me all the way and still is." GPs were able to build valued, trusting relationships with their patients by affirming their gender identities, using correct names and pronouns, being open about treatment, and helping them navigate through the system. An interesting aspect of this dynamic was the attribution of positive personal experiences with GPs to luck and good fortune, which suggests that patients entered the system with low expectations. In another discussion, respondents reported mixed views about the quality of surgical provision. Although some expressed dissatisfaction with surgical outcomes and aftercare, there were some indications that surgery results had improved over time.

Transgender Patients' Perspectives: Systemic Disempowerment?

> At that stage, I didn't want very much medical intervention. I very much wanted to do it myself, I wanted to learn how to self inject and I wanted to be in control of this because I was aware at that point that I wasn't in control and that other people were making decisions for me
> —Participant, Manchester focus group

The topic of pathologization and classification is one of the most salient debates in transgender health. Predictably, it was a central focus of discussion throughout the focus group portion of the research. The prescriptiveness of gender reassignment treatment protocols and utilization of a mental illness paradigm, consistent with World Health Organisation and American Psychiatric Association categorizations, was a source of perceived disempowerment. Patients expressed frustration with the number of evaluations that they underwent, some of which they believed to be unnecessary or redundant. The evaluations, designed to minimize the chances of regret by a few, were considered by some to come at the expense of the majority.

Gender dysphoria is usually self-diagnosed, meaning that transgender people explore their gender to a greater or lesser extent before approaching doctors for treatment. Some objected to the doctor's role as gatekeeper because it meant that doctors' opinions were prioritized over a transgender person's lived experience. The participants universally expressed the view that treatment in psychiatry was inappropriate unless comorbid psychiatric conditions were evident. Nevertheless, psychiatric assessment was the service most consistently offered to them.

Psychiatric diagnoses were considered stigmatizing and disempowering. By placing gender treatments under the purview of psychiatrists, it insinuated that transgender people were incapable of making decisions about their bodies. Interviewees who had undertaken a great deal of introspection about their gender seemed especially frustrated with the length of time spent undergoing evaluation. Participants wanted more of a voice in this process. Some spoke of experiencing distress and depression, but this was rarely considered evidence of a mental illness. Instead, some respondents believed that stigma, arduous gatekeeping processes, inappropriate medical treatment, and mistreatment in society were responsible for symptoms of poor mental health among some transgender people.

Despite objections to psychiatric classification, many transgender people still require access to appropriate, informed mental health support. The suicide attempt rates in the transgender population are high (Clements-Nolle, Marx, and Katz 2006; McNeil et al. 2012), so some people are likely to need urgent interventions. The focus group data show that some patients benefited from having someone to talk to and wanted an advocate to help guide them through the system. Participants generally believed that a brief professional assessment to rule out mental illness was acceptable, but they remained opposed to having their gender identity "diagnosed" as a mental illness. Respondents felt that counseling services should be optional, yet accessible.

The data suggest that a mental health rather than mental illness paradigm is better suited for this group. Accordingly, mental health professionals could serve three roles: to establish competency and rule out mental illness; to support trans people who experience depression, anxiety, or who are at risk of suicide; and to facilitate a trans person's overall well-being. In sum, participants want evaluation and treatment moved away from a pathological, mental illness model toward a more holistic, patient-empowered, community-based model. For the NHS, this means changes to the clinical pathways are recommended.

Discussion

Transgender people constitute a small, diverse population. Despite well-evidenced health needs and specialist practitioners, information about transgender people is often lacking on the front lines (World Professional Association for Transgender Health 2011; Combs 2010). Medical care, along with social and legal recognition, is a very important component of gender transition. The literature shows that adequate health policy for transgender people is difficult to achieve because the group is underresearched and there is no consensus about the policy objectives of transgender people. The research presented in this chapter demonstrates that doctors and patients contend with complex and fraught circumstances. Professionals and patients hold mixed views on the system's efficacy in addressing transgender health needs. Doctors feel disempowered because of

Professionals' Concerns	Shared Concerns	Patients' Concerns
• Lack of professional support (e.g. training, peer support, and legacy planning. • Contrasting / incongruent treatment philosophies (e.g. psychiatry vs. psychology).	• Lack of knowledge among non-specialist healthcare providers • Hostility towards specialism (e.g. politics, public opinion, and media representation) • Debates about pathologization, mental health support • Bureaucratic roadblocks (e.g. unclear funding, referral, and communication pathways) • Waiting lists due to rising numbers of patients, service cuts • Service inequality, no national protocols	• Disempowerment (e.g. feeling like have to "fight" for treatment, jump through hoops) • Dependence on private treatment to provide care

Fig. 9.1. Professionals' and patients' concerns with transgender health care in Britain

high demand for services and a lack of support, and patients feel disempowered due to long waiting times and a lack of agency in the transition process. The two groups have several overlapping concerns (see fig. 9.1).

The Health Policy Context

Transgender health care takes place in the broader health policy context. The literature cites several influences on health policy; institutionalist explanations focus on the role of political systems, cultural explanations focus on cultural and historical factors, and functionalist explanations focus on the role of population, wealth, and economics (Blank and Burau 2007). We begin by using an institutional perspective. In unitary health care systems such as the United Kingdom, top-down policies made in Parliament or through precedents developed in legal cases are then applied across the country. As noted earlier in the chapter, nationwide eligibility for gender reassignment services in the United Kingdom came about due to a court ruling (*R v North West Lancashire HA Ex P A, D and G* 1999). But while the unitary system guarantees a level of access, there is no evidence to suggest that the health service actively and promptly addresses transgender patients' systemic complaints. Change may, therefore, rely upon organized, bottom-up advocacy and activism on the part of doctors and patients or another top-down legal decision. Conversely, the U.S. health care system, considered federal and decentralized (Lijphart 1999), generally gives no guarantee of access unless negotiated with and agreed to by health insurance providers in specific insurance plans. Systemic gains are slower, but incremental gains may be easier to negotiate because they are more limited in scope.

Cultural and functionalist explanations of health policy are also helpful in analyzing these data. In the United Kingdom, for example, the publically funded health service derives from an egalitarian philosophy; however, tensions exist due to the contentiousness of transgender medicine. It has been argued in the media and elsewhere that public funds should not be used to pay for gender reassignment (e.g., Condron 2009). To justify their position, functionalist (the group is "too small," the costs are "too high") and cultural (treatment is "unnecessary," "elective," or "immoral") arguments have been used. The data suggest that negativity in the public sphere unsettles health professionals and funders, having consequences for care. Some interviewees believed that they have been treated unfairly. There is, however, evidence of political will among policymakers to protect transgender health (e.g., HM Government 2011). These policy debates will continue on national and international levels, but to be effective this must also involve educating and changing social attitudes.

Policymaking

Zahariadis (2003, 168) writes that "[a]mbiguity is a fact of policymaking. It has drawbacks because it makes policymaking messy, complex, and less comprehensible." He argues that more information will not resolve ambiguity, but can make the situation more comprehensible to policymakers, allowing them to make informed decisions. The transgender case provides an interesting example of ambiguity in a developing area of policy. The competing definitions of sex and gender, the as yet incongruent policy objectives, the heterogeneity of the transgender population, and the lack of demographic information all pose challenges for clinicians, researchers, and policymakers.

The absence of a clear evidence base about the transgender community's size and demographics complicates policymaking. Where identity categories cannot be demarcated from one another, it becomes difficult to assess the number of people with a particular identity, to determine their exact needs, and to adequately plan services. Poor or nonexistent data may result in an underestimation of the size and scope of transgender concerns by policymakers. It also makes it harder for stakeholders to quantify and qualify areas of policy need, to convey legitimacy, and to put transgender issues on the agenda. Finally, the existence of statistical data can help establish evidence of systemic discrimination in court (Stone 1997). Thus, the lack of data may reduce the ability of transgender people to seek legal recourse where necessary.

As Stone (1997) writes, "policy debate is dominated by the notion that to solve a problem, one must find its root cause or causes" and that "in politics, we look for causes not only to understand how the world works but to assign responsibility for problems" (188–89). She adds that stories about causation are used as political tools to decide the winners or losers of policy decision making. Thus, debates about transgender etiology will inevitably have policy consequences. This is especially relevant because gender reassignment treatment is contentious and causation stories influence whether or not transgender people are portrayed as legitimate recipients of publicly funded health care services. The data demonstrating both etiological ambiguity, negative patient experiences with bureaucracy, persistent delay, and potential systemic disempowerment suggests that the causation narrative has not been settled, at least not in a way favorable to transgender patients. If the story shifted solidly toward transgender people as a legitimate and worthy patient group, we can hypothesize that their experiences of health care would improve considerably.

Conclusion

This chapter has looked at some key issues in transgender health care policy and practice. It has examined data about the needs of transgender patients and communities, the systems through which health care is delivered, and the power dynamics inherent in the relationships between funders, patients, and clinicians. Health policy in this area takes place in the context of an increasing demand for services, changing social attitudes, greater connectedness between, and information for, transgender people, and political organizing toward depathologization. Political science literature on ambiguity in policymaking (Zahariadis 2003) and the attribution of causation (Stone 1997) has helped us to better understand the terrain. The evidence presented in this chapter adds to the growing body of knowledge about transgender experiences generally, and transgender policy and practice specifically.

Research on transgender health, such as the qualitative study presented in this chapter, is important. Not only does it shed light on a particular group's experiences, it also helps policymakers to better understand, and better respond to, a nascent area of policy. The literature and research data establish that the transgender category is diverse and complex. The needs of transgender people will not be fully met until (a) we understand more about the population and (b) there is a more coherent narrative about transgender policy goals. This requires a multipronged approach. Quantitative and longitudinal studies are needed to get a sense of the bigger picture and to understand more about the generalizability of the existing findings. Continued qualitative work is required to understand the richness and depth of the topic. However, researchers must be careful to not reduce the transgender experience to crude binary categories. To do so would miss the point. Transgender communities are diverse due to the nature of gender identity; generally, those contained within it will not fit easily into boxes.

Relationships of power have been an important theme in this chapter. In the British system, power appears to manifest itself in several ways. Doctors may feel disempowered because their treatment decisions are hamstrung by restrictive funding bodies, and because their peers undervalue their professional expertise. Patients may feel disempowered because of the stigmatization of a mental illness diagnosis, the strict assessment requirements, and the absence of a strong voice in the policymaking process.[8] The funding bodies may feel disempowered because of the potential for public backlash if they approve so-called elective services. The exact mechanisms of power are likely to vary according to context, but the discussions highlight that many interesting dynamics take place.

So, what do these data tell us about the viability and sustainability of transgender health care services? Although interest in, and knowledge about, transgender health is increasing, questions remain about whether professionals and health care systems will be able to cope with the growing demand for services. In the British context at least, the specialty is likely to struggle because of the lack of institutional support such as formalized training programs, standardized protocols, and opportunities for knowledge exchange between peers. In the short term, these deficiencies could result in increased waiting times and, consequently, more dissatisfaction among service users. In the long term, deficiencies could result in unsustainability and clinic closures. Also, there is still a wide gulf between specialists' knowledge about transgender health and the lack of knowledge held by many policymakers, general practitioners, and members of the public. This restricts and marginalizes transgender health in the policy context. However, there are opportunities to close some of the education gaps by focusing academic efforts on continuing qualitative, and increasing quantitative, research.

The literature and the qualitative analysis show us that there is a difference between providing a service and providing a service well. Systemic disempowerment experienced in health care runs counter to modern public administration's focus on community empowerment and customer satisfaction. The data demonstrate clearly that transgender people are looking for more control over their health care and over their lives. They can face serious social and financial consequences for socially and medically transitioning, but many proceed, despite the personal risk, to live a more authentic life. In these circumstances, it seems prudent for health care systems to make space for transgender people by ensuring adequate funding for treatments, education, and staff. It also seems reasonable that funders and clinicians should avoid further stigmatization by being overly prescriptive about gender or by pathologizing gender-variant identities.

NOTES

1. More accurately, this could be understood as "communities" (plural), as there is a lack of consensus among trans people about who should or should not be included within it.

2. It is important to consider transgender health care needs that are unrelated to gender reassignment, but that is outside of the remit of this piece.

3. A word on discourse: It is perhaps ill fitting to refer to the facilitation of gender transition as the "treatment of a condition" due to its tendency to push the multiplicity of transgender identities into the medical model. Its use within this chapter consistent with its current framing in policy literature; however, it should be acknowledged that the language currently utilized is likely to change as understandings about transgender identities evolve.

4. The discussions about NHS care for transgender people should not be misconstrued as reflecting NHS services as a whole. Although any strengths and deficiencies of the health service are likely to filter through to transgender care, this study is limited in scope and did not examine wider debates.

5. Social constructivism (as opposed to positivism) is a paradigm in which knowledge is understood to be constructed through social interaction, integrated with existing knowledge, and interpreted subjectively.

6. In brief, feminist theory seeks to understand gender inequality. It problematizes rigid binary gender classifications, questions power, and challenges patriarchy (e.g., Foucault 1976; Butler 1990; Lorber 2000).

7. There is an ongoing debate in political science about quantitative and qualitative methodologies, but it is outside of the remit of this chapter. For an interesting review piece on this topic, see Thomas 2005.

8. For literature that examines the effect of policy design on clients see, for example, Soss 1999 and Mettler 2002.

REFERENCES

Ault, Amber, and Stephanie Brzuzy. 2008. "Removing Gender Identity Disorder from the Diagnostic and Statistical Manual of Mental Disorders: A Call for Action." *Social Work* 54 (2): 187–89.

Balarajan, Meera, Michelle Gray, and Martin Mitchell. 2011. *Monitoring Equality: Developing a Gender Identity Question.* Manchester: Equality and Human Rights Commission.

Blank, Robert H., and Viola Burau. 2007. *Comparative Health Policy (2nd Edition).* New York: Palgrave.

Bornstein, Kate. 1994. *Gender Outlaw: On Men, Women and the Rest of Us.* New York: Routledge.

Bornstein, Kate. 2000. "Naming All the Parts." In *The Social Construction of Difference and Inequality: Race, Class, Gender, and Sexuality,* ed. T. Ore. Mountain View, CA: Mayfield.

Braun, Virginia, and Victoria Clarke. 2006. "Using Thematic Analysis in Psychology." *Qualitative Research in Psychology* 3 (2): 77–101.

Butler, Judith. 1990. *Gender Trouble: Feminism and the Subversion of Identity.* New York: Routledge.

Calman, Lynn. 2006. "Patients' Views of Nurses' Competence." *Nurse Education Today* 26 (8): 719–25.

Charmaz, Kathy. 1990. "'Discovering' Chronic Illness: Using Grounded Theory." *Social Science & Medicine* 30 (11): 1161–72.

Charmaz, Kathy. 2006. *Constructing Grounded Theory: A Practical Guide through Qualitative Analysis.* London: Sage Publications.

Clements-Nolle, Kristen, Rani Marx, and Mitchell Katz. 2006. "Attempted Suicide among Transgender Persons." *Journal of Homosexuality* 51 (3): 53–69.

Combs, Ryan. 2010. "Where Gender and Medicine Meet: Transition Experiences and the NHS." PhD thesis, University of Manchester.

Combs, Ryan, Lewis Turner, and Stephen Whittle. 2008. *Gender Identity Services in England: The Mapping Project Report.* London: Press for Change.

Condron, Stephanie. 2009. "Sex Change Ops on the NHS Have Trebled Since the Procedure Became a 'Right.'" *Daily Mail,* June 27. http://www.dailymail.co.uk/health/article-1196024/Sex-change-ops-NHS-trebled—procedure-right.html.

De Cuypere, G., M. Van Hemelrijck, A. Michel, B. Carael, G. Heylens, R. Rubens, and S. Monstrey. 2007. "Prevalence and Demography of Transsexualism in Belgium." *European Psychiatry* 22 (3): 137–41.

Fish, Julie. 2007. *Reducing Health Inequalities for Lesbian, Gay, Bisexual and Trans People—Briefings for Health and Social Care Staff.* London: Department of Health.

Foucault, Michel. 1976. *The Will to Knowledge.* London: Penguin Books.

Glaser, Barney, and Anslem Strauss. 1967. *The Discovery of Grounded Theory: Strategies for Qualitative Research.* Chicago: Aldine Publishing.

Greenberg, Julie A. 1999. "Defining Male and Female: Intersexuality and the Collision between Law and Biology." *Arizona Law Review* 41 (265): 261–328.

HM Government. 2011. *Advancing Transgender Equality: A Plan for Action.* London: Home Office.

Israel, Gianna. 2004. "Supporting Transgender and Sex Reassignment Issues: Couple and Family Dynamics." *Journal of Couple & Relationship Therapy: Innovations in Clinical and Educational Interventions* 3 (2–3): 53–63.

Jones, Lynne. 2005. *Guidelines for Health Organisations Commissioning Services for Individuals Experiencing Gender Dysphoria and Transsexualism.* London: Parliamentary Forum on Transsexualism.

Kuyper, Lisette. 2006. "Seksualiteit en Seksuele Gezondheid bij Homo- en Biseksuelen." In *Seksuele gezondheid in Nederland,* ed. F. Bakker and I. Vanwesenbeeck, 167–88. Delft: Eburon.

Lijphart, Arend. 1999. *Patterns of Democracy.* New Haven: Yale University Press.

Lombardi, Emilia. 2001. "Enhancing Transgender Healthcare." *American Journal of Public Health* 91 (6): 869–72.

Lorber, Judith. 2000. "The Social Construction of Gender." In *The Social Construction of Difference and Inequality: Race, Class, Gender, and Sexuality,* ed. T. Ore. Mountain View, CA: Mayfield.

McAllister, Marion. 2001. "Grounded Theory in Genetic Counseling Research." *Journal of Genetic Counseling* 10 (3): 233–50.

McNeil, Jay, Louis Bailey, Sonja Ellis, James Morton, and Maeve Regan. 2012. *Trans Mental Health Study.* Edinburgh: Scottish Transgender Alliance.

Mettler, Suzanne. 2002. "Bringing the State Back in to Civic Engagement: Policy Feedback Effects of the G.I. Bill for World War II Veterans." *American Political Science Review* 96 (2): 351–66.

Morse, Janice M., and Joy L. Johnson, eds. 1991. *The Illness Experience: Dimensions of Suffering.* London: Sage.

Nestle, Joan, Clare Howell, and Riki Wilchins. 2002. *Genderqueer: Voices from beyond the Sexual Binary.* New York: Alyson.

Oriel, Kathleen A. 2000. "Clinical Update: Medical Care of Transsexual Patients." *Journal of the Gay and Lesbian Medical Association* 4 (4): 185–94.

Pauly, Ira B. 1968. "The Current Status of the Change of Sex Operation." *Journal of Nervous and Mental Disease* 147 (4): 60–71.

R v North West Lancashire HA Ex P A, D and G. 1999. *Lloyd's Law Reports Medical* 399.

Reed, Bernard, Stephenne Rhodes, Pieta Schofield, and Kevin Wylie. 2009. *Gender Variance in the UK: Prevalence, Incidence, Growth and Geographic Distribution.* Ashtead: GIRES.

Robertson, M. M. 1992. "Lesbians as an Invisible Minority in the Health Services Arena." *Healthcare for Women International* 13 (2): 155–63.

Rosser, B. R. Simon, J. Michael Oakes, Walter O. Bockting, and Michael Miner. 2007. "Capturing the Social Demographics of Hidden Sexual Minorities: An Internet Study of the Transgender Population in the United States." *Sexuality Research and Social Policy* 4 (2): 50–64.

Rudacille, Deborah. 2006. *The Riddle of Gender: Science, Activism, and Transgender Rights.* New York: Pantheon.

Schilt, Kristen, and Matthew J. Wiswall. 2008. "Before and After: Gender Transitions, Human Capital, and Workplace Experiences." *B.E. Journal of Economic Analysis & Policy* 8 (1). DOI: 10.2202/1935-1682.1862.

Soss, Joe. 1999. "Lessons of Welfare: Policy Design, Political Learning, and Political Action." *American Political Science Review* 93 (2): 363–80.

Stone, Deborah A. 1997. *Policy Paradox: The Art of Political Decision Making.* New York: W. W. Norton.

Strauss, Anselm, and Juliet Corbin. 1990. *Basics of Qualitative Research: Grounded Theory Procedures and Techniques.* Newbury Park, CA: Sage.

Thomas, George. 2005. "The Qualitative Foundations of Political Science Methodology." *Perspectives on Politics* 3 (4): 855–66.

Tilley, Donna, and Margaret Brackley. 2005. "Men Who Batter Intimate Partners: A Grounded Theory Study of the Development of Male Violence in Intimate Partner Relationships." *Issues in Mental Health Nursing* 26 (3): 281–97.

Tsoi, W. F. 1988. "The Prevalence of Transsexualism in Singapore." *Acta Psychiatrica Scandinavica* 78:501–4.

West, Persia. 2004. *Report into the Medical and Related Needs of Transgender People in Brighton and Hove: The Case for a Local Integrated Service.* Brighton: Spectrum.

Whittle, Stephen. 2002. *Respect and Equality: Transsexual and Transgender Rights.* London: Cavendish.

Whittle, Stephen, Lewis Turner, and Maryam Al-Alami. 2007. *Engendered Penalties: Transgender and Transsexual People's Experiences of Discrimination.* London: PFC/Equalities Review.

Whittle, Stephen, Lewis Turner, Ryan Combs, and Stephenne Rhodes. 2008. *Transgender EuroStudy: Legal Survey and Focus on the Transgender Experience of Healthcare.* Brussels: ILGA-Europe.

Wilson, Holly S., Sally A. Hutchinson, and William L. Holzemer. 1997. "Salvaging Quality of Life in Ethnically Diverse Patients with Advanced HIV/AIDS." *Qualitative Health Research* 7 (1): 75–97.

World Professional Association for Transgender Health (WPATH). 2011. *Standards of Care, 7th Version.* http://www.wpath.org/documents/IJT%20SOC,%20V7.pdf.

Zahariadis, Nikolaos. 2003. *Ambiguity and Choice in Public Policy: Political Decision Making in Modern Democracies.* Washington, DC: Georgetown University Press.

Zucker, Kenneth, and Anne A. Lawrence. 2009. "Epidemiology of Gender Identity Disorder: Recommendations for the Standards of Care of the World Professional Association for Transgender Health." *International Journal of Transgenderism* 11 (1): 8–18.

Jami K. Taylor, Barry L. Tadlock,
and Sarah J. Poggione

10 | Birth Certificate Amendment Laws and Morality Politics

Few people understand the importance of birth certificate amendment laws better than Ohio's Jacob Nash. Jacob was born a girl in Massachusetts in 1964. Thirty-eight years later and in accordance with the state laws where he was born, Jacob was able to amend the sex designation on his birth certificate. About this time, Jacob was living in the Midwest and he had fallen in love with a woman. However, this occurred during an era during which much attention was given to gender, particularly as it related to marriage. During the 1990s and 2000s prohibitions on same-sex marriage were enacted in the majority of states via constitutional amendments and legislation. His new state of residence enacted this type of ban and it also did not allow transsexual persons to amend their birth certificates in the event of sex reassignment. Even though he was not seeking to marry a man, the intersection of state policies on birth certificates and same-sex marriage caught Jacob in a legal crossfire.

Jacob was born as a female named Pamela Ann McEloney. In 2002 and in accordance with Massachusetts law, he applied for an amended birth certificate. Jacob received it because he had undergone gender reassignment surgery. This seemingly positive development was turned on its head when he sought to marry a woman in his then state of residence, Ohio. In 2004, Ohio voters passed Issue 1, a constitutional amendment that bans the state from recognizing or performing marriages or civil unions between same-sex partners. Additionally, and because of a judicial ruling in the 1980s, it forbade the amendment of birth certificates in the event of sex reassignment. The clerk's office in Trumbull County refused to issue a marriage certificate to Jacob and Erin Barr, his fiancée. On the couple's first application, Jacob neglected to list his first marriage, when he was still Pamela, an omission that he claims was due to negligence on his part. On the second application, the marriage was listed. During the time period between the two applications, a search revealed to the court the fact that Jacob had formerly been named Pamela. At the hearing regarding the second application, Jacob refused to answer questions about his sex reassignment surgery. His attorney argued that the questions were irrelevant since Jacob had a valid birth certificate from Massachusetts, on which Jacob's sex was recorded as a male. Both the trial court and two of three judges on a state Court of Appeals panel rejected claims that Jacob was being denied equal treatment under the law and that Ohio was neglecting to give "full faith and credit," as required by the U.S. Constitution, to the Massachusetts birth certificate (*In re Application for Marriage License for Nash* 2003).

As shown by Jacob's story, identity documents are of great importance to transgender individuals. When transitioning, individuals obtain identity papers (e.g., driver's license) that reflect a legally changed name or sex, or both. One of the fundamental identity documents is the birth certificate. At birth, individuals are commonly classified as male or female according to their external genitalia (Bishop and Myricks 2004). This sex classification, along with the other facts of birth, is registered according to the appropriate state's vital records law. Individuals use this birth certificate to gain access to public education and to obtain other forms of identification (e.g., driver's license, Social Security records, and passport).

As of 2013, 25 states have laws that specifically allow individuals who have undergone medical treatment related to transsexualism to amend their birth certificates to show the adopted sex. Of the remaining 25 states, only Tennessee explicitly bans birth certificate amendment in the event of sex reassignment (Tennessee Statute 68-3-203). Three states appear to have an administrative process that promulgates regulations for birth certificate amendment while New York has a two-tiered system that gives New York City authority to issue regulations independently of how they are issued elsewhere in the state. The other 20 states have a *general* statute allowing birth certificate amendment. While many of these states amend birth certificates in the event of sex reassignment, the lack of direct statutory authority to do so is problematic. In such states, some courts have ignored these amended birth certificates (e.g., *Littleton v. Prange* 1999; *In re Estate of Gardiner* 2002). Additionally, the lack of *direct* statutory authority has kept at least one state, Ohio, from amending the birth certificates of transsexual persons (*In re Ladrach* 1987).

The ability to change one's birth certificate has important implications given that a majority of states continue to ban same-sex marriage and because of the federal Defense of Marriage Act (DOMA). A recent Supreme Court's decision, *United States v. Windsor* (2013), struck down a provision of DOMA that barred the federal government from recognizing same-sex couples. As such, the federal government will provide equal benefits to married couples of the same sex. However, the Court's narrow decisions in *Windsor* and *Hollingsworth v. Perry* (2013) did not address all state-level same-sex marriage bans.[1] In fact, the decision in *Windsor* noted that marriage law was a state concern. Therefore, depending on state of residence, a transsexual person's marriage rights are still likely dependent on his or her legal sex.

In the aftermath of *Windsor* and as noted in the immigration case *In re Jose Mauricio Lovo-Lara* (2005), the federal government must treat marriages with deference to state birth certificate policies. A practical implication of this is that where explicit birth certificate amendment laws exist, a postoperative male-to-female transsexual person with appropriate documentation would likely be legally viewed as a female and could thus marry a male. However, in the states that lack direct statutory guidance and that restrict the rights of same-sex couples, the marriage rights of transsexual individuals are less clear and are open to more legal challenges. In some of these states, courts have not respected birth certificates that were changed under general amendment laws (*Littleton v. Prange* 1999; *In re Estate of Gardiner* 2002; Greenberg and Herald 2005). Additionally and as shown in Jacob Nash's story, some states refuse to recognize the amended birth certificates of other states (*In re Application for Marriage License for Nash* 2003). This occurs despite the U.S. Constitution's full faith and credit clause that requires states to extend full recognition to the public acts, records, and court proceedings of other states. States that take such stances argue that the refusal to accept the amended birth certificates qualifies as a public policy exception to the full faith and credit clause (Greenberg 2005; Greenberg and Herald 2005). Where states have taken this position, it appears that a postoperative male-to-female transsexual woman would be allowed to marry a genetic female. This would be true despite the transsexual woman holding a driver's license and U.S. passport with female sex designations, and being recognized as female by the Social Security Administration.

Despite the importance of birth certificate laws, these statutes have received little attention in the political science and public administration literature. Most LGBT rights research has focused on hate crimes laws, nondiscrimination statutes, and constitutional amendments and laws banning same-sex marriage (e.g., Haider-Markel 2001). A consistent take away from this body of work is that conservative states are less likely to enact pro-LGBT rights laws than are liberal states (e.g., Lax and Phillips

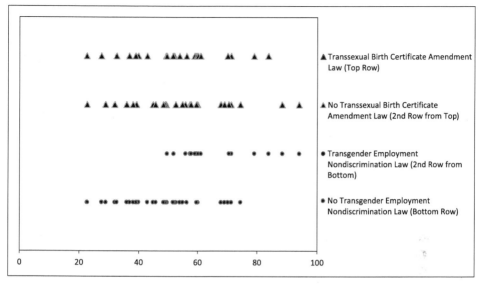

Figure 10.1. Ideological comparison: States with transsexual birth certificate amendment laws vs. states with transgender employment nondiscrimination laws. The *x*-axis is the Berry et al. (2006) citizen ideology measure. Higher scores are more liberal. (Data compiled by the authors.)

2009). However, for birth certificate amendment laws, this relationship does not appear to hold. Figure 10.1 compares the ideological distribution of citizens in states having transsexual birth certificate amendment laws with those having transgender-inclusive employment discrimination laws. The states having transgender-inclusive nondiscrimination laws are more liberal on average than those that do not have such measures. This is consistent with the typical morality politics that is often associated with LGBT rights. In contrast, there appears to be little relationship between ideology and the adoption of transsexual birth certificate amendment statutes. Why? In this chapter, we show that state adoption of these birth certificate laws was influenced by vertical diffusion of policy and that this was conditioned on bureaucratic professionalization.[2]

Policy Diffusion and Bureaucratic Professionalism

As noted in early chapters of this book, LGBT rights are often classified as a type of morality politics, where policy networks combine with internal state political and social factors, including citizen ideology, to determine policy outcomes (Mooney and Lee 1995, 1999; Boushey 2010). However, given the distribution of states with these birth certificate laws (fig. 10.2), morality politics explanations are likely insufficient. After all, we find these policies in conservative states that should be less receptive to a policy that has implications for marriage law and that benefits a negatively constructed group (Boushey 2010). Policy diffusion (Gray 1973; Karch 2007) research provides an alternative explanation for the rather puzzling distribution of states with these laws. From the policy diffusion perspective, significant influences in innovation stem partly from sources external to the state (Gray 1994). These external factors are experienced through social learning from other state governments (Berry and Berry 1990), localities (Shipan and Volden 2006), and from the federal government (Allen, Pettus, and Haider-Markel 2004; Welch and Thompson 1980). Such learning is more likely to occur on complex technical policies, such as regulatory affairs, rather than on higher salience, lower complexity governance or morality policies (Boushey 2010). Additionally, states learn from state, regional, and national policy networks (Kirst, Meister, and Rowley 1984; Gray 1994). For birth certificate amendment laws, the federal government might be an important source of policy learning.

The National Center for Health Statistics was formed in 1960 for the purpose of "inter-governmental data sharing" and to foster the spread of standards and procedures (CDC 2011). The development of the National Center for Health Statistics reflected an emphasis on efficiency and on the rational and technical components of legislation. Ultimately, these twin emphases led the Centers for Disease Control and Prevention (CDC) to issue model vital records statutes (1977 and 1992) that could be emulated by the states (CDC 1997).[3] These policy recommendations included provisions for birth certificate amendment for individuals who had undergone medical treatment for gender identity disorder. We argue that these model records statutes recommended by the CDC were likely to produce vertical policy diffusion as states moved to adopt these best practices. However, states may not have been equally likely to respond to these vertical influences. Given the technical nature of birth certificate law, state administrators, particularly those serving in professionalized bureaucracies, might be more intimately familiar with the existence and nature of the CDC recommendations and more motivated to push for their adoption. These street-level bureaucrats (Lipsky 1980) would have been alerted to gaps in existing policy because of casework with transsexual individuals. As such, their technical expertise and knowledge of new policy challenges could drive agenda setting (Kingdon 2003). We expect that states with more professionalized bureaucracies are more likely to receive and incorporate the information provided by the CDC. Therefore, we expect that these states, responding to vertical influences, are more likely to adopt the recommended policies.

> *Hypothesis 1:* States with higher levels of bureaucratic capacity are more likely to respond to guidance from the CDC's model vital records laws by adopting these statutes.

While most people might consider birth certificate amendment rules to be obscure technical matters, transgender rights have increasingly become a salient policy issue (Taylor 2007). This has likely been affected by the increasing linkage of transgender rights to gay rights. This linkage occurred during the mid-1990s and it stemmed from pressure by transgender activists (Gallagher 1994; Wilchins 2004). Given this increasingly combined LGBT rights advocacy, we expect other cues commonly associated with morality politics, including citizen ideology, to affect legislators' consideration of these protransgender laws (Lax and Phillips 2009). In particular, we expect that states with liberal populations will be more likely to pass these laws. Additionally, elite ideology should also influence passage. Despite mixed evidence concerning the effect of elite ideology on various LGBT issues (Lax and Phillips 2009), we expect that states with liberal political elites will positively influence the passage of these laws.

> *Hypothesis 2:* Those states with relatively higher percentages of liberal elites are more likely to pass a birth certificate amendment law.

> *Hypothesis 3:* Those states with relatively higher percentages of liberal citizens are more likely to pass a birth certificate amendment law.

Data and Methods

We expect that the likelihood of a state adopting a transsexual birth certificate amendment law in a particular year is influenced by the motivation for rational and efficient policy, internal political forces, and a series of commonly used control variables. Given the binary dependent variable, whether a state adopted a transsexual birth certificate amendment law in a given year, and the pooled time series nature of our data (1962–2006), we utilize event history analysis to test our hypotheses. Because we argue that

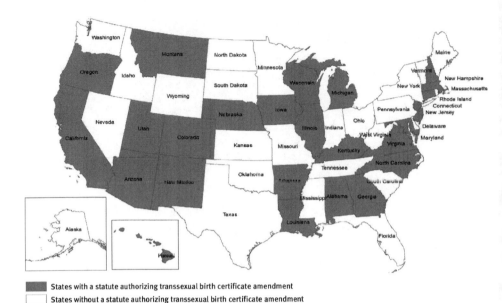

States with a statute authorizing transsexual birth certificate amendment

States without a statute authorizing transsexual birth certificate amendment

Fig. 10.2. Birth certificate amendment statutes by state. Year of adoption by state: IL (1962), HI (1973), NC (1975), NH (1976), CA (1977), MI (1978), LA (1979), VA (1979), AR (1981), MA (1981), NM (1981). OR (1981), UT (1981). GA (1982). CO (1984). MO (1984). NJ (1984), WI (1985), KY (1990), AL (1992), NE (1994), MD (1995), CT (2001), AZ (2004), IA (2006). (Data compiled by the authors.)

the effects of bureaucratic professionalism should differ across time, based on vertical diffusion through information provided by the CDC, we employ the Cox nonproportional hazards model in our analysis (see Box-Steffensmeier, Reiter, and Zorn 2003) with the exact partial likelihood method for resolving tied failures.[4]

Information on whether a state had one of these laws was obtained from the Human Rights Campaign's website. The research team, to the best of its ability, determined the year of adoption through statutory analysis via state legislative websites and LexisNexis. Additionally, we contacted state archives and libraries and relied heavily on this information to clear up ambiguities in our research.[5] The earliest adoption was in Illinois (1962), while the most recent statute was passed by Iowa (2006).[6] Through 2006, 25 states had laws allowing for amendment. Figure 10.2 displays the states with these statutes and the notes provide a chronological order of adoption.[7]

Independent and Control Variables

The independent variables in our analysis include two measures of state bureaucratic professionalism, state political forces and a variety of control variables. To assess the professionalism of state bureaucracy and the resulting interest in rational and efficient policy, we measure state administrative performance using the 2008 Pew Center on the States' review of government performance. This measure of administrative performance captures differences in management capacity across a broad array of administrative agencies and actors in each of the states (see Burke and Wright 2002). Following Burke and Wright (2002) we converted the letter grades assigned by the Pew Center into numeric scores by utilizing indicators in the areas of finance, staffing, infrastructure, and information management. The Pew Center ranks each of the 20 indicators as an area of weakness, average, or area of strength. We converted this to a numeric score by summing the following assigned values: 1 point for a weakness, 3 points for average, and 5 points for an area of strength. The hypothetical range for our measure of bureaucratic performance and professionalization is 20 to 100 while the actual range was 30 to 94. The mean level of bureaucratic professionalization and performance was 60. While this 2008 measure of bureaucratic professionalism is static, it is highly correlated with the Pew Center's earlier but not directly comparable 1997 measure ($r = .70$). This high correlation suggests that although state administrative performance likely varies over time within states, the relative positions of states across time remain somewhat consistent.

However, we recognize the potential weaknesses of a static measure of bureaucratic professionalism and therefore include a dynamic measure of state bureaucratic professionalism, the number of state government health employees as a percentage of state population. This data was obtained from the U.S. Census Bureau.[8] Not only is this measure dynamic, it is also focused specifically on health-related state employees, the people most likely to observe CDC guidelines and advocate for their inclusion in state policy. For example, this measure includes, but is not limited to, state workers employed in jobs related to public health administration, vital statistics, and public health education.

In order to assess the possibility of vertical diffusion of policy, we include multiplicative interaction terms of our measures of professionalized state bureaucracy with a lagged measure of federal influence via the CDC guidelines. The indicator for the CDC recommendations is coded 0 before any guidelines were issued, coded 1 from 1978–92 after the Centers for

Disease Control and Prevention issued the Model State Vital Statistics Act in 1977, and coded 2 for 1993–2006, after the CDC offered revised guidelines in 1992.[9]

Given the demonstrable importance of ideology in morality politics, we assess the role of political forces by using Berry et al.'s (1998) revised 1960–2008 citizen ideology series and their revised 1960–2008 ADA/COPE measure of state government ideology.[10] Based on studies of policy diffusion, we include several control variables. To account for the possibility of policy learning among states, we control for such horizontal diffusion by using the lagged percentage of states within each U.S. Census–defined geographic region that has a transsexual birth certificate amendment law. To account for a state's general orientation toward policy innovation, we include Boushey's (2010) measure of state policy innovation.[11] We control for possible regional influences by using a dichotomous indicator of traditionalistic political culture as compared to either individualistic or moralistic cultures (Elazar 1984). To control for the possibility that more professional legislatures are more likely to adopt new and diffused policies, we include Squire's index (1992, 2007) of state legislative professionalism.

Additionally, we control for three demographic factors that are common in studies of LGBT rights policies: education levels, the percentage of same-sex households in the state, and the percentage of Evangelical adherents in the state. With respect to education levels, our variable measures the percentage of residents who are age 25 or older with a bachelor's degree or higher.[12] The percentage of same-sex households in a state is used as a proxy for gay interest group strength and it is held constant at 2000 levels (Barclay and Fisher 2003).[13] Our measure of Evangelical adherents was obtained from the Association of Religion Data Archives.[14]

Analysis

Given that our theory predicts that the influence of state bureaucratic professionalism on the likelihood of state policy adoption changes over time, we present the results of a nonproportional hazards model as well as the more commonly used proportional hazards model. These are shown in table 10.1.[15] In our nonproportional hazards model, one of the two measures of state bureaucratic professionalism—state administrative performance—is statistically significant and it performs in the expected direction. Additionally, the interaction between state administrative performance and CDC recommendations is statistically significant. The significance of the interaction term suggests that the hazard rate associated with state administrative performance does vary over time. In other words, the relationship between bureaucratic professionalism and the CDC guidelines operates differently before the release of any standards and different after each successive release of standards. These factors provide support for Hypothesis 1.

While we find support for Hypothesis 1 with our state administrative performance variable and its interaction with CDC guidelines, the measure of state government health personnel is not statistically significant. It appears that while overall management capacity in state executive branch agencies is related to state adoption of birth certificate amendment laws, the relative size of the health-related state government workforce has little effect on the likelihood of passing such laws.[16] Because the 2008 Pew Center measure is multidimensional, we believe that it is a better measure of bureaucratic professionalism than is state health employees per capita. In addition, it explicitly addresses items that relate to the concept of professionalism in bureaucracy. These include training and development, strategic workforce planning, and managing employee performance (Pew Center 2008). As such, it is not surprising that this measure better explains which states might be more responsive to CDC guidance. Furthermore, the measure of state health employees includes workers who have no impact over matters related to vital records. Therefore, it fails to capture state capacity related to vital records and statistics.

Additionally in the nonproportional hazards model, government ideology, traditional political culture, and education are statistically significant at traditional levels. The statistical significance and predicted direction of performance for government ideology provides support for Hypothesis 2. With respect to the statistically significant control variables, education has the expected effect. States with higher percentages of college educated adults have an increased chance of policy adoption compared to those with less. However, traditional political culture does not operate as expected. States with traditional political culture are more likely to adopt the policy than those with either moralistic or individualistic culture. It is possible that both the public and elites in states with more traditional culture might view sex reassignment as maintaining traditional gender stereotypes rather than undermining notions of a gender binary and therefore be more inclined to support birth certificate amendment laws. Another possible explanation for this counterintuitive finding lies in the application of traditional gender stereotypes stemming from the 19th and early 20th century understanding of homosexuality. During this period, it was common to view homosexuality as gender inversion—lesbians were masculine while gay men were feminine (Minter 2006). The connection between traditional political culture and birth certificate amendment after sex reassignment might tap into this older view of sexual desire and gender status.

With regard to the other variables, we find that citizen ideology, other state-level demographics, including evangelical adherence and same-sex-

TABLE 10.1. Adoption of Transsexual Birth Certificate Amendment Statutes, 1962–2006

	Cox Model[a]		Cox Model with Time-Based Interactions[b]	
	Coefficient	St. Error	Coefficient	St. Error
Citizen Ideology	−.06*	(.03)	−.05	(.03)
State Govt. Ideology	.04*	(.02)	.03*	(.02)
State Bureaucratic Professionalism				
State Admin. Performance	−.02	(.02)	−.09*	(.04)
State Govt. Health Personnel	−271.95	(556.04)	953.60	(1,326.32)
Time-Based Interactions				
State Admin. Perf.*CDC Guidelines			.08*	(.04)
State Govt. Health Personnel*CDC Guidelines			−1,056.72	(1,187.50)
Control Variables				
Regional Diffusion	−6.96	(3.84)	−6.91	(4.03)
Boushey Index	−.85	(3.80)	−.94	(4.01)
Traditional Political Culture	1.63	(.93)	1.93*	(.95)
Squire's State Legislative Professionalism	−.25	(2.65)	−.16	(2.76)
% Same-Sex Households	−1.47	(2.66)	−1.72	(2.82)
% Evangelical	−3.23	(3.47)	−3.86	(3.54)
% College Educated	.28*	(.11)	.30**	(.12)
Log Likelihood	−70.33		−67.12	
Model χ^2	17.92		24.35*	
N observations	1,655		1,655	

Note: The analysis includes 49 states. Illinois, the first state to adopt such a law in 1,962, is excluded from our analysis. The Illinois adoption provides the opportunity for adoption by other states and consequently determines the start of our time series.

[a]Cell entries present coefficient estimates of the Cox proportional hazard rate model, exact partial method for resolving ties.

[b]Cell entries present coefficient estimates of Cox nonproportional hazard rate model, exact partial method for resolving ties.

+ $p < .10$, * $p < .05$, ** $p < .01$ for two-tailed tests.

partnered households, offer no significant explanatory power. In addition, regional diffusion, Boushey's index of policy innovation, and the professionalism of state legislative institutions are not significantly related to state adoption of birth certificate amendment laws.[17] Thus, in contradiction to Hypothesis 3 and to the findings of the morality politics literature, citizen ideology does not have a statistically significant effect.

To understand the nature of the effects of the significant variables on state policy adoption, we need to consider the change in the hazard rate produced by a marginal change in the independent variable.[18] In general, a hazard rate expresses the probability that a subject of interest will survive or fail at an event during a particular time interval. In our case, the hazard rate expresses the chance that a state without a birth certificate amendment law will adopt such a law during a particular year (or "fail," according to the common interpretation of this particular statistical method). For Hypothesis 2, a one standard deviation increase in elite ideology (becoming more liberal) increases the hazard rate for a state by 106 percent in a given year. This means that states with one standard deviation more liberal government elites are more than twice as likely to adopt this particular transgender policy. Taken collectively, the findings for elite and citizen ideology (Hypotheses 2 and 3) support the claim by Lindaman and Haider-Markel (2002) that position differences held by Democratic and Republican elites do not always lead to party-related issue sorting among the general public.

With respect to Hypothesis 1, the statistical significance of the interaction term for state administrative performance indicates that this particular measure of bureaucratic professionalism does not have a uniform hazard rate. In other words, the impact of bureaucratic professionalism varies over time. In order to fully understand the impact of state bureaucratic performance, we graph the percentage change in the hazard rate of policy adoption that is produced by a marginal increase in each independent variable over time estimated under the nonproportional model. We also include an estimated change in hazard rate under the proportional model for comparison. We present these estimates in figure 10.3.

The solid line in figure 10.3 represents the change in hazard rate due to a one-unit increase in state administrative performance under the nonproportional hazard model. Note that in the earliest period, 1962–77, before the CDC issued any relevant recommendations, a one-unit increase in state administrative performance produced a 9 percent decline in the hazard rate of policy adoption. To put this variable in perspective, a standard deviation increase in state administrative performance would pro-

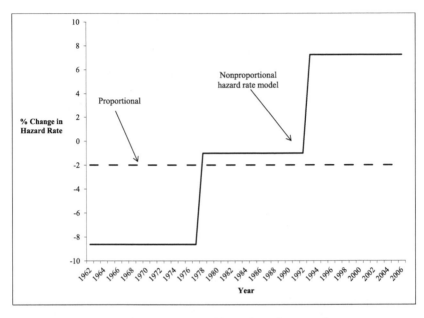

Fig. 10.3. Percentage change in estimated hazard rate for state administrative performance, nonproportional and proportional hazard rate models. (Data compiled by the authors.)

duce about a 69 percent decline in the hazard rate. This suggests that absent any advice from the CDC, states with more professionalized bureaucracies were less likely than states with less professionalized bureaucracies to adopt such policies. Perhaps this represents a reluctance to engage in ad hoc policymaking absent professional consensus.

In the 1978 to 1992 period, after the CDC issued its first recommendation for permitting birth certificate amendment after sex reassignment, the same one-unit increase in state administrative performance resulted in a 1 percent decline in the hazard rate. A one standard deviation increase during this period would produce only a 12 percent decline in the hazard rate. During this middle period, differences in the hazard rates of states with more and less professional bureaucracies become much narrower. In the final period (1993–2006), beginning after the CDC reaffirmed its recommendation for birth certificate amendment laws, the hazard rate increased markedly in response to improved state administrative performance. During this period, a one-unit increase in this measure of bureaucratic professionalism resulted in a 7 percent increase in the hazard rate. A one standard deviation increase in state administrative performance would now yield a 148 percent increase in the hazard rate.[19] This suggests that states with professional bureaucracies, as compared to those with less professional ones, were far more likely to adopt this protransgender statute in any given year in the final time period. Thus, our findings serve to illustrate the difference that exists among issues in the broader LGBT agenda. It suggests that the politics surrounding some of these issues may be determined by a different set of forces and factors than those prevalent in typical morality politics.

Conclusion

This chapter investigated an anomaly in LGBT rights law, states statutorily allowing for the amendment of birth certificates in the event of sex reassignment. Unlike other LGBT rights laws, these policies appear in a number of relatively conservative states. We find that vertical diffusion of policy via recommendations from the CDC affected the adoption of these laws. In 1977 and again in 1992, the CDC promoted these policies as best practices in their model vital records legislation. In states with more professionalized bureaucracies, administrators may have shepherded these guidelines before legislators as part of the agenda setting process. The policies appear to have been treated as low salience technical matters. However, as transgender identity and transgender politics have become more politically salient since the mid-1990s, we have seen fewer states adopting these laws. Hawaii's 1993 same-sex marriage case, *Baehr v. Lewin,* might have given policymakers reason to consider the implications of allowing a person to legally change their sex. Additionally, as the transgender movement has become increasingly attached to gay rights advocacy, transsexual birth certificate amendment proposals might be less likely to be viewed as purely technical concerns. After all, our model demonstrates that political elites respond to this issue in predictable patterns. Conservative elites locate themselves in opposition to these policies while liberal elites are more likely to offer support. As such, it is likely that the factors affecting the adoption of transsexual birth certificate policies and other transgender rights issues might increasingly resemble those of other LGBT rights policy. Certainly, the story of Jacob Nash that opened this chapter illustrates how issues that are distinctly transgender related may be intertwined with gay rights in an unexpected and complex fashion.

While we are confident in our findings, it is important to note several limitations in our work. As mentioned in our discussion of the independent variables, one of our measures of bureaucratic professionalization varies across states but is constant over time. Unfortunately, the discipline lacks consistent multidimensional measures of this concept over time and, as such, we might miss how states have professionalized their bureaucracies over the decades. Additionally, given the age of some of these statutes and their technical nature, there remains the possibility that there are flaws associated with our dependent variable. However, we took several precautions. This included checking our list of state laws with sources such as the Human Rights Campaign. Our team also corresponded with officials in many of the states with birth certificate amendment laws. Another possible issue is that our measure of interest groups active on this issue may be incomplete. For example, medical centers or universities engaged in treatment for these gender identity conditions may have pushed state legislators to pass these policies. Unfortunately, we are not aware of any comprehensive listing of such institutions over time. However, we include two variables (evangelical adherents and same-sex partner households) that often serve as proxy measures of interest group strength in this policy domain.

Our research has important implications for the study of LGBT rights. For example, Button, Rienzo, and Wald (2000) note that the "legal successes of gays in the early 1970s were also achieved because of the lack of organized resistance." Thus, it seems reasonable to suggest that the political opportunity structure that was present in many states during the 1975–95 time period was such that the rights of some transgendered individuals—in the case of birth certificate amendment laws—could be advanced without engendering debilitating opposition. Furthermore, a sufficient number of political elites in these states presumably believed that attention to "best practices" was a wise course of action. Alternatively, the amendment of birth certificates was not a salient political issue. In other words, not very many state legislators were willing to obstruct their state's bureaucracy from following the model provided by the CDC. Indeed, we demonstrate that gains in transgender rights can occur by means of public policy that is mediated through bureaucratic structures. Thus, we echo Wald (2000) in highlighting another possible way in which LGBT rights activists can successfully advance their cause.

However, our findings also raise a difficult question. Has the association of transgender rights with the lesbian and gay rights movement, at least over the past 20 years, damaged the prospects for legal recognition of a transsexual person's sex? While the association of transgender persons with the gay and lesbian rights movement was not done solely for prospective policy gains, the increased salience of transgender identities may have expanded the scope of conflict. Given the public's conflation of LGBT identities and the various communities' common problems associated with the stereotyping of gender, it is plausible that there have been negative ramifications that have received insufficient scholarly attention. In a related point, if same-sex marriage ever becomes a nationwide policy in the United States, will the policy relevance of the sex marked on a transsexual person's birth certificate decline as a matter of public importance? Another point of inquiry concerns the interesting relationship between traditional political culture and these transsexual birth certificate amendment laws. Might these statutes be associated with the protection of traditional gender norms, including a binary understanding of gender? While these questions are beyond the scope of our research, our work has contributed to a fuller understanding of transgender politics and we have suggested a number of new and interesting questions for future research. Our work also shows that even in conservative states, the blockage of transgender rights policy advances is not a foregone conclusion.

NOTES

1. *United States v. Windsor* (2013) did not address the constitutionality of Section 2 of the Defense of Marriage Act. Section 2 granted states the power to avoid legal recognition of same-sex marriages conducted in other states. *Hollingsworth v. Perry* (2013) addressed Proposition 8, a California ban on same-sex marriage. The decision held that supporters of the Proposition 8 campaign did not have legal standing to defend this provision in court. California's elected officials had declined to do so and a federal district court had declared Proposition 8 to be unconstitutional.

2. This chapter is an updated version of Taylor, Tadlock, and Poggione (2014).

3. The Bureau of the Census issued earlier versions of a Model Vital Records Act in 1907 and 1942. In 1959, the Department of Health Education and Welfare issued new recommendations. The 1977 revision by the CDC was a major change from its predecessors and called for increased centralization of records keeping and reporting. There was an emphasis placed on efficiency and effectiveness (Centers for Disease Control and Prevention 1997). While we have not investigated whether the 1959 version of the Model Vital Records Act contained provisions for amendment in the event of sex reassignment, we consider the existence of such a recommendation as unlikely given that the first publicized case of medical sex reassignment of an American was Christine Jorgensen in the early 1950s. It is plausible that sex reassignment might have made an appearance in the initial National Center for Health Statistics' Model State Vital Statistics Regulations (issued in 1973). While we have not explored that possibility, we note that regulations do not require a new action by the legislature.

4. We estimated the model using the more common Breslow method for resolving

tied failures (not reported). The results are strikingly similar and not particularly sensitive to the choice of method. Given the greater accuracy of approximating the partial likelihood with the exact partial likelihood method (Box-Steffensmeier and Jones 2004), we present only these results here.

5. The authors thank Susan Brace of the University of Toledo for her many hours of dedicated assistance in data collection. We also express thanks to Ryan Combs of the University of Manchester and Donald Haider-Markel of the University of Kansas for their constructive comments.

6. The early adoption of a transsexual birth certificate amendment law in Illinois was confirmed in two separate self-reports. The statute was also referenced in a 1974 case about criminalized cross-dressing that was before the Illinois Supreme Court in 1978 (*City of Chicago v. Wallace Wilson et al.*, 75 Ill. 2d 525; 389 N.E.2d 522, 1978 Ill. LEXIS 402; 27 Ill. Dec. 458). As a result, we begin our analysis in 1962. We assume, as Berry and Berry (1990) do, that other states were then "at risk" for adopting such a law given that one state had done so. As the first state to adopt such a law, Illinois is effectively eliminated from the analysis. However, given that the second adoption by a state did not occur until a decade later, we also estimated a model beginning in 1972 (not reported). The results from the analysis beginning in 1972 are remarkably consistent and substantively identical to the results beginning with 1962. As a result, we report only the results of analysis beginning in 1962.

7. Of the remaining 25 states, three of these (Maine, Nevada, and Washington) appear to give administrators latitude to promulgate regulations while a fourth state, New York, allows New York City to have a separate system. However, the choice to give such decisions to other governmental actors in no way limits the legislature from adopting such laws. We estimated a model that excludes these four states, assuming that the existence of their administrative procedures eliminated their risk for adoption. The results of this supplemental analysis (not reported) are strikingly similar to the findings we report. As a result, we report only the findings from the analysis that includes these four states.

8. U.S. Census Bureau records contain state health full-time equivalent (FTE) employee data for the years 1962, 1967, 1972, 1977, 1980–95, and 1997–2006. Our measure is computed by dividing state health employee FTEs by state population. Missing data was interpolated. The data base ("Annual Survey of State and Local Government Employment and Census of Governments") is an internal file of the U.S. Census Bureau (the Employment and Benefit Statistics Branch) and is shared with outside data users upon request.

9. Each of these recommended best practices contained provisions allowing for the amendment of birth certificates in the event of sex reassignment (1977 Section 21(e); 1992 Section 21 (d)).

10. Available from Richard Fording's website at the University of Alabama: http://www.bama.ua.edu/~rcfording/stateideology.html.

11. The decision to use Boushey's (2010) overall state innovation index rather than one of his indices for regulatory or morality politics was driven by the difficulty of classifying birth certificate statutes dealing with sex reassignment in a single policy category. Boushey focuses on three types of policy innovation (regulatory, morality, and governance). These birth certificate amendment laws are part of a larger regulatory scheme (model vital records policies) that requires private actors to collect data for the state (like

regulatory policy). It is technical and low salience. However, we focus on the narrow sex reassignment provision that might also harken to morality policy given that it concerns transgender individuals and it has implications for state marriage policy. We ran separate models with Boushey's overall policy innovation index, his regulatory index, and his morality policy index. Our core findings are not dependent on which policy innovation index is chosen. We also tried a model using Walker's (1969) state innovation measure (with missing values for Hawaii and Alaska assigned at the mean); in both a proportional and a nonproportional model, the Walker variable was significant.

12. To construct this annual measure, we interpolated between statistics available in the 1962 and 2011 editions of Statistical Abstract of the United States.

13. This statistic was not collected prior to 1990.

14. Following Erikson, Wright, and McIver (1993), we include members of the Church of Jesus Christ of Latter-Day Saints in our evangelical measure given their similar views on public policy matters. We use the Association of Religion Data Archives 1990 estimate of evangelicals and hold this constant because of variation in data collection methodology. Particularly problematic is that the 2000 Association of Religion Data Archives estimates do not include congregation data for historically African American denominations (Association of Religion Data Archives 2010).

15. See Taylor, Tadlock, and Poggione (2014) for a full discussion of the Cox proportional hazards model. Our results support the conclusion that the proportional hazard model is suboptimum, because it assumes that the impact of state bureaucratic professionalism on the hazard rate operates in a uniform fashion across our time period of interest. As a result, we focus our attention on the nonproportional hazards model.

16. To address the possibility that state health personnel per capita was too narrow of a measure of state bureaucratic professionalism, we also estimated the model using U.S. Census Bureau statistics on the total number of state employees relative to the state population (not reported). Our results were similar to those reported for state government health personnel. In both cases, the employee-based measure of state bureaucratic professionalism and its interaction with the CDC recommendations were not statistically significant.

17. To account for the possibility that more professional legislatures might also respond to vertical diffusion through the CDC's communication of best practices, we estimated the model including the interaction of Squire's index of state legislative professionalism and the CDC recommendations. Neither of the coefficients for state legislative professionalism or its interaction were significant at traditional levels. Given the technical nature of this policy area, professionalism of state bureaucratic institutions rather than legislative institutions appears to be the necessary factor for states to modernize their vital records laws.

18. The percentage change in the hazard rate associated with a one unit increase in X is $(e^b - 1)*100$.

19. For comparison, consider the dashed line in figure 10.3, the estimated percentage change in the hazard rate under the proportional hazards model. Under the proportional hazards model, a one-unit increase in state government performance always produces about a 2 percent decline in the hazard rate regardless of whether or not the CDC has issued any recommendations. Even a one standard deviation increase in state government performance only yields a 23 percent decrease in the hazard rate. Not only are both the coefficients for state administrative performance and its interaction not statisti-

cally significant under the proportional hazards model, the estimated substantive impact of state administrative performance is quite small. This demonstrates how the conclusions regarding the impact of bureaucratic professionalism on state adoption of such laws differ significantly between the nonproportional and proportional hazards models. The nonproportional hazards model shows the process of vertical diffusion at work through the advice of the CDC and the attention of professional bureaucracies in a way that is not apparent in the proportional hazards model.

REFERENCES

Allen, Mahalley, Carrie Pettus, and Donald P. Haider-Markel. 2004. "Making the National Local: Specifying the Conditions for National Government Influence on State Policy Making." *State Politics & Policy Quarterly* 4 (3): 313–44.

Association of Religion Data Archives. 2010. "Sources of Religious Congregations and Membership Data." http://www.thearda.com/mapsReports/RCMS_Notes.asp (accessed March 11, 2011).

Barclay, Scott, and Shauna Fisher. 2003. "The States and the Differing Impetus for Divergent Paths on Same-Sex Marriage, 1990–2001." *Policy Studies Journal* 31 (3): 331–52.

Berry, Frances Stokes, and William D. Berry. 1990. "State Lottery Adoptions as Policy Innovations: An Event History Analysis." *American Political Science Review* 84 (2): 395–415.

Berry, William D., Evan J. Ringquist, Richard C. Fording, and Russell L. Hanson. 1998. "Measuring Citizen and Government Ideology in the American States, 1960–1993." *American Journal of Political Science* 42 (1): 327–48.

Bishop, E. P., and Noel Myricks. 2004. "Sex Reassignment Surgery: When Is a He a She for the Purpose of Marriage in the United States?" *American Journal of Family Law* 18 (1): 30–35.

Boushey, Graeme. 2010. *Policy Diffusion Dynamics in America.* Cambridge: Cambridge University Press.

Box-Steffensmeier, Janet M., and Bradford S. Jones. 2004. *Event History Modeling: A Guide for Social Scientists.* New York: Cambridge University Press.

Box-Steffensmeier, Janet M., Dan Reiter, and Christopher Zorn. 2003. "Nonproportional Hazards and Event History Analysis in International Relations." *Journal of Conflict Resolution* 47:33–53.

Burke, Brendan, and Deil Wright. 2002. "Reassessing and Reconsidering Reinvention in the American States: Exploring Administrative Performance." *State and Local Government Review* 34 (1): 7–19.

Button, James W., Barbara A. Rienzo, and Kenneth D. Wald. 2000. "The Politics of Gay Rights at the Local and State Level." In *The Politics of Gay Rights,* ed. Craig A. Rimmerman, Kenneth D. Wald, and Clyde Wilcox, 269–89. Chicago: University of Chicago Press.

Centers for Disease Control and Prevention (CDC). 1977. *1977 Revision of the Model State Vital Statistics Act and Model State Vital Statistics Regulations.* http://www.cdc.gov/nchs/data/misc/mvsact77acc.pdf (accessed March 20, 2011).

Centers for Disease Control and Prevention (CDC). 1992. *1992 Revision of the Model*

State Vital Statistics Act and Model State Vital Statistics Regulations. http://www.cdc. gov/nchs/data/misc/mvsact92b.pdf (accessed March 21, 2011).

Centers for Disease Control and Prevention (CDC). 1997. *U.S. Vital Statistics System*. http://www.cdc.gov/nchs/data/misc/usvss.pdf (accessed March 21, 2011).

Centers for Disease Control and Prevention (CDC). 2011. *Celebrating 50 Years*. http://www.cdc.gov/nchs/about/50th_anniversary.htm (accessed January 1, 2012).

Elazar, Daniel. 1984. *American Federalism: A View from the States*. 3rd ed. New York: Harper & Row.

Erikson, Robert S., Gerald C. Wright, and John P. McIver. 1993. *Statehouse Democracy: Public Opinion and Policy in the American States*. Cambridge: Cambridge University Press.

Gallagher, John. 1994. "For Transsexuals, 1994 Is 1969: Transgendered Activists Are a Minority Fighting to Be Heard within the Gay and Lesbian Community." In *Witness to Revolution: The Advocate Reports on Gay and Lesbian Politics, 1967–1999*, ed. Chris Bull. Los Angeles: Alyson Books.

Gray, Virginia. 1973. "Innovation in the States: A Diffusion Study." *American Political Science Review* 67 (4): 1174–85.

Gray, Virginia. 1994. "Competition, Emulation, and Policy Innovation." In *Perspectives on American Politics*, ed. Lawrence C. Dodd and Calvin Jillson, 230–48. Washington, DC: CQ Press.

Greenberg, Julie. 2005. "When Is a Same-Sex Marriage Legal? Full Faith and Credit and Sex Determination." *Creighton Law Review* 38 (2): 289–307. Retrieved December 7, 2006, from LexisNexis Academic database.

Greenberg, Julie, and Marybeth Herald. 2005. "You Can't Take It with You: Constitutional Consequences of Interstate Gender-Identity Rulings." *Washington Law Review* 80 (4): 819–85. Retrieved March 1, 2006, from LexisNexis Academic database.

Haider-Markel, Donald P. 2001. "Policy Diffusion as a Geographical Expansion of the Scope of Political Conflict: Same Sex Marriage Bans in the 1990s." *State Politics & Policy Quarterly* 1 (1): 5–25.

Hollingsworth v. Perry, 133 S.Ct. 2652 (2013).

In re Application for Marriage License for Nash, 2003-Ohio-7221.

In re Estate of Gardiner, 42P.3d 120 (Kan. 2002).

In re Jose Mauricio Lovo-Lara, 23 I&N Dec. 746 (BIA 2005). http://www.usdoj.gov/eoir/vll/intdec/vol23/3512%20.pdf (accessed December 14, 2005).

In re Ladrach (1987), 32 Ohio Misc.2d 6, 513 N.E.2d 828

Karch, Andrew. 2007. *Democratic Laboratories: Policy Diffusion among the American States*. Ann Arbor: University of Michigan Press.

Kingdon, John W. 2003. *Agendas, Alternatives, and Public Policies*. 2nd ed. New York: Addison Wesley.

Kirst, Michael W., Gail Meister, and Stephen R. Rowley. 1984. *Policy Issue Networks: Their Influence on State Policymaking*. Stanford: Stanford University.

Lax, Jeffery R., and Justin H. Phillips. 2009. "Gay Rights in the States: Public Opinion and Policy Responsiveness." *American Political Science Review* 103 (3): 367–86.

Lindaman, Kara, and Donald P. Haider-Markel. 2002. "Issue Evolution, Political Parties, and the Culture Wars." *Political Research Quarterly* 55 (1): 91–110.

Lipsky, Michael. 1980. *Street-Level Bureaucracy: Dilemmas of the Individual in Public Service*. New York: Russell Sage Foundation.

Littleton v. Prange, 9 S.W.3d 233 (Tex. App 1999).

Minter, Shannon Price. 2006. "Do Transsexuals Dream of Gay Rights?" In *Transgender Rights,* ed. Paisley Currah, Richard Juang, and Shannon Price Minter, 141–70. Minneapolis: University of Minnesota Press.

Mooney, Christopher Z., and Mei-Hsien Lee. 1995. "Legislating Morality in the American States: The Case of Pre-*Roe* Abortion Regulation Reform." *American Journal of Political Science* 39 (3): 599–627.

Mooney, Christopher Z., and Mei-Hsien Lee. 1999. "Morality Policy Reinvention: State Death Penalties." *Annals of the American Academy of Political and Social Science* 566:80–92.

Pew Center on the States. 2008. "Grading the States 2008." http://www.pewcenteron thestates.org/gpp_report_card.aspx (accessed March 11, 2011).

Shipan, Charles, and Craig Volden. 2006. "Bottom-Up Federalism: The Diffusion of Antismoking Policies from U.S. Cities to States." *American Journal of Political Science* 50 (4): 825–43.

Squire, Peverill. 1992. "Legislative Professionalization and Membership Diversity in State Legislatures." *Legislative Studies Quarterly* 17 (1): 69–79.

Squire, Peverill. 2007. "Measuring Legislative Professionalism: The Squire Index Revisited." *State Politics & Policy Quarterly* 7 (2): 211–27.

Taylor, Jami K. 2007. "Transgender Identities and Public Policy in the United States: The Relevance for Public Administration." *Administration Society* 39 (7): 833–56.

Taylor, Jami, Barry Tadlock, and Sarah Poggione. 2014. "State LGBT Rights Policy Outliers: Transsexual Birth Certificate Amendment Laws." *American Review of Politics* 34 (Winter 2013–14): 245–70.

United States v. Windsor, 133 S.Ct. 2675 (2013).

U.S. Census Bureau. 1962, 1967, 1972, 1977, 1980–1995, 1997–2006. *Annual Survey of State and Local Government Employment and Census of Governments.* Washington, DC: Government Printing Office.

Wald, Kenneth D. 2000. "The Context of Gay Rights." In *The Politics of Gay Rights,* ed. Craig A. Rimmerman, Kenneth D. Wald, and Clyde Wilcox, 1–30. Chicago: University of Chicago Press.

Walker, Jack L. 1969. "The Diffusion of Innovations among the American States." *American Political Science Review* 63 (September): 880–99.

Welch, Susan, and Kay Thompson. 1980. "The Impact of Federal Incentives on State Policy Innovation." *American Journal of Political Science* 24 (4): 715–29.

Wilchins, Riki Anne. 2004. *Queer Theory Gender Theory: An Instant Primer.* Los Angeles: Alyson Books.

Jami K. Taylor and Donald P. Haider-Markel

11 | Conclusion and Future Directions in Transgender Politics and Policy

The transgender community is a stigmatized and diverse collection of identities that are organized around the individual-level concepts of gender identity and gender expression; it also contains many people who have been politically, economically, and socially marginalized. Although there are no reliable estimates about the prevalence of transgender identities in the population nor are such figures collected by governmental agencies, it is highly likely that the trans community is a smaller minority group than are the gay and lesbian communities. Yet, despite its small size and lack of resources, the transgender rights movement has grown and it has made a series of impressive policy gains. With an empirical approach, the authors in this volume have explored this topic. In this final chapter, we review these findings and compare them to what we know about gay civil rights.

At the level of national policy, transgender-inclusive policies have been adopted in a diverse range of countries, including some in Latin America, Europe, North America, and Asia. Within the U.S. context and during the Obama administration, transgender activists obtained their first major legislative victory at the federal level. They were named as a protected class in a fully LGBT-inclusive hate crimes prevention law. Also within the United States, the number of localities and states with transgender-inclusive nondiscrimination laws has rapidly expanded. Although there has been significant diffusion of these policies, these laws are not exact replicas of each other; there is considerable variation in what and who is covered. As policymakers and activists learn from experience, many of these nondiscrimination policies are becoming stronger and easier to implement via the use of more inclusive language and by containing more substantive enforcement mechanisms.

The victories do not stop with the passage of fully LGBT-inclusive laws. There have also been a number of transgender-inclusive executive orders at the state level. State and federal bureaucracies have increasingly become mindful of trans constituents with their policies and regulations. For instance, the U.S. Department of State has made policies that more easily allow trans individuals to amend the sex marker on their passport. The Centers for Disease Control and Prevention has included provisions for birth certificate amendment by transsexuals in their model state vital records act. Trans individuals and their legal allies have also successfully obtained shelter under Title VII of the Civil Rights Act in a ruling by the U.S. Equal Employment Opportunity Commission. Of course, this ruling followed on the heels of decisions by several federal district and appellate courts that noted that discrimination against trans individuals can be a prohibited form of sex based stereotyping.

Transgender Policymaking and Gay Rights

One of the important advances for the trans movement was coalescing around the notion of transgender. This decision brought together many distinct and disparate identities and there was an increase in organized transgender advocacy in the 1990s. This increase in activity came in reaction to a series of high-profile crimes and social, economic and political deprivation. The concept of transgender allowed activists to focus on gender identity and gender expression rather than a little understood medical condition or an activity like cross-dressing. Therefore, it provided trans rights advocates a better way to argue for inclusion in gay rights advocacy. Trans activists were able to show how their concerns were similar to those of other sexual minorities. After all, everyone has a gender identity and a gender expression. Attaching transgender advocacy to the gay rights movement has given the small number of trans activists the ability to leverage the superior resources of gay rights groups. This incorporation of transgender rights occurred during the mid-1990s through the early 2000s (after years of marginalization by gay and lesbian communities) and it has heavily contributed to the trans community's policy gains since that time. When transgender inclusion has been packaged with gay rights, as in states such as Oregon and Iowa, it has been far easier to obtain rights. Where states have passed stand-alone gay rights measures, as in the Massachusetts, there is often a very long delay in "coming back" for transgender people. This is due to the defensive advantage held by opponents, the small size of the trans community, a lack of resources, competing LGBT policy priorities, and the attitudes of policymakers and their constituents.

When acting alone, transgender rights advocates have a very difficult time getting their concerns on the agenda of legislatures.

The incorporation of transgender activism with gay rights advocacy was facilitated because of many of the similarities in gay and transgender policymaking. Both gay and transgender rights advocates share many of the same policy goals. This includes laws combatting discrimination, policies against bullying in schools, or statutes that address hate crimes. Additionally, some transgender people are caught in the crossfire over same-sex marriage and they face some of the same challenges in family law. As such, much joint-LGBT advocacy can be framed by activists in terms of a desire for economic and social equality. Correspondingly, many of the same political and social factors contribute to the passage of gay and transgender-inclusive policies. On average, Democrats are more supportive of LGBT rights than are Republicans. Constituent ideology often matters in LGBT policymaking and conservatives are commonly in opposition. Included in common opposition to most LGBT rights measures are fundamentalist "traditional values" oriented interest groups like the Family Research Council or the American Family Association. Thus, it is not surprising that large, diverse, cosmopolitan cities are more likely to pass fully LGBT-inclusive ordinances than are more homogeneous rural localities. LGBT-inclusive statutes and ordinances are also rarely found in the American South. Congress is also a difficult policymaking venue for LGBT rights given its institutional rules and the composition of its membership.

Given similarities in many goals and some of the factors that affect policy adoption, LGBT rights advocates have many opportunities for combined advocacy. This is of course facilitated in the U.S. context by the federal system and separation of powers. Thus, LGBT activists, like advocates in other policy areas, engage in substantial amounts of venue shopping. This activity is performed by the large number of national advocacy groups that are fully LGBT inclusive as well as a network of state and local interest groups. These groups often compete with one another for resources and they must find an ecological niche where they must specialize. Some of these groups focus on particular states or cities. Other groups focus their efforts on the media, Congress, or the courts. There are also transgender focused groups such as the National Center for Transgender Equality. While the groups use different tactics, favor different policymaking venues, and focus on different jurisdictions, they generally share the same policy goals. As such, there is much sharing of political and technical information within this advocacy coalition.

Depending on the favorability of the political environment, this coalition of LGBT groups switch their advocacy efforts between the federal, state, and local levels and between the different branches of government. At the municipal level, if there are substantial home rule powers and a lack of state policy direction, localities can choose to engage in compensatory policymaking by passing fully LGBT-inclusive ordinances. This is more likely to occur when cities have mayor-council governments, a well-organized LGBT lobby, and a political environment that is nontraditional. Similarly, and in the face of legislative inaction, governors can become a lobbying target for LGBT activists. Unless the state has a particularly conservative electorate, Democratic governors will sometimes use executive orders to engage in position taking and to advance the interests of an electoral constituency. This is particularly true when control of the governor's mansion switches from Republican to Democrat.

Departures from Gay Rights?

Despite all of the similarities between gay and transgender advocacy, this volume has identified some important differences. Because the public is generally less familiar with transgender issues, proponents must spend more time using education frames with the public and with lawmakers. This lack of familiarity occurs not just in the United States but also in Latin America. Additionally, opponents of transgender rights have seized on the "bathroom issue" to develop a potent security/safety frame to attack policy proposals. This has made full transgender inclusion quite challenging in some jurisdictions.

The security/safety frame has been apparent even in more progressive states such as California. In 2013, that state's lawmakers adopted a law that would allow transgender students to join sports teams and clubs, as well as use restrooms, based on gender identity rather than assigned sex. Conservatives in the state charged that the measure threatened the safety of children and they immediately began the process of trying to repeal the measure at the ballot box (Megerian 2013).[1]

Despite the occasional opposition, and at least with respect to the passage of nondiscrimination laws, trans inclusion seems to occur at a less piecemeal pace than does gay rights lawmaking. Although fewer states protect trans individuals, once a state goes down that path, it tends to do so fully. This might be due to gay rights policy being driven by typical morality policy forces while transgender nondiscrimination might be viewed as an expansion and reinvention of existing policy toward sexual minorities. At present, no U.S. state or locality has chosen to explicitly protect trans individuals from discrimination or hate crimes without concurrently or previously protecting sexual orientation.

Within the LGBT advocacy coalition, there are sometimes disagreements over policy goals and over tactics. In states such as New York and Maryland, gay activists and their legislative allies have sometimes excluded transgender protections from bills. Such strategic decisions on legislation are sometimes arranged to help improve the likelihood of passage. Many policymakers and activists view this as part of the give and take of the legislative process and there is a strong desire by some people in the advocacy coalition to accept a partial victory. And indeed, anecdotal evidence finds that legislators are less familiar with and are more uncomfortable with transgender identities, making the arguments of some activists appear prudent.

In the face of legislative resistance, removal of trans-inclusive protections from a bill is facilitated by the comparatively small amount of transgender participation in LGBT advocacy coalitions and related interest groups. There are few trans board members, staffers, or key decision makers in many LGBT interest groups. Trans individuals also contribute fewer organizationally relevant resources (money, access, time, and labor) than do their gay peers. There are distributional concerns over the costs and benefits of combined LGBT advocacy. The lack of transgender power within the LGBT coalition is often more fully exposed when transgender *exclusive* legislation is enacted. When that occurs, it is common for the advocacy coalition to move to additional goals, such as same-sex marriage, rather than "coming back" for trans inclusion. A very recent example of this happened when Delaware adopted broad gender identity nondiscrimination protections and a transgender-inclusive hate crime law in 2013 *only after* banning sexual orientation based discrimination (2009), enacting civil unions (2011), and then legalizing same-sex marriage (2013). We have seen similar patterns in Massachusetts, New York, and Maryland. Yet, in the past decade, this has become less common. More states are passing fully inclusive LGBT nondiscrimination laws.

Beyond those differences and issues, there are also policy goals that the gay and transgender communities do not fully share. Access to specialized health care services is an important policy goal for many trans people. Even where a nation's health care system provides for treatment of transgender people, as in the case of the United Kingdom, substantial challenges remain in regard to adequate resources, knowledge about trans identities, and the continuing debate about the medical pathologizing of trans identities. Gay rights advocacy was advantaged by removing homosexuality from the Diagnostic and Statistical Manual of Mental Disorders (DSM) in 1974 but the pathologizing of gender identity dysphoria remains. However, without this type of formalized diagnosis, obtaining medical treatment related to gender identity becomes difficult. Such is the conundrum for transgender rights activists.

Changing the sex marker on identity documents like drivers' licenses, passports, and birth certificates are also significant policy concerns for the trans community. With perhaps the exception of same-sex parents desiring to avoid a mother and father classification on their child's birth certificate, vital records law is likely an afterthought for most gay people. Interestingly, states, including many in the South, have passed statutes allowing for birth certificate amendment by some trans individuals. Policymaking in this area does not resemble typical morality policy because many conservative jurisdictions have embraced these trans rights policies. Most of these laws were passed before the substantial incorporation of transgender advocacy into the gay rights movement. It appears that passage of these statues was driven in part by vertical diffusion of federally recommended best practices and was likely facilitated by more professionalized bureaucracies. At present, this policy area appears to be a real anomaly in the study of LGBT politics. However, the attachment of trans issues to gay rights advocacy might make this policy area respond in more typical fashion in the future.

Future Considerations

The stutter steps of progress made by the trans community aside, to us it appears that we are entering a new phase of the LGBT political movement where the T is no longer just an afterthought or "something we'll address later." Thus, we hope that the publication of this volume can serve as a cornerstone for future empirical research on transgender politics and policy.

The authors in this volume have contributed significantly to shedding empirical light on the study of transgender politics and policy. The included chapters use mainstream social science theory and empirical methods to help us understand the politics and processes involved in the consideration and adoption of laws protecting against discrimination, policies that allow for changes in sex on official documents, as well as the strategic framing efforts of political actors in these processes.

Although we make a substantive contribution to the literature, this volume does not address all of the empirically motivated research questions that we would currently like to answer regarding transgender politics and policy. And as with all movements for equality it is never entirely clear which direction the movement or its politics might take in coming years and how these developments might pose new research opportunities. Given these limitations, we speculate as to some potentially fruitful avenues for empirical research.

Although some chapters in this volume examine the role of institutions, few researchers have examined the role of institutional rules and design on LGBT politics generally (but see examples in Lewis 2011a, 2011b or Smith 2005). As the salience of transgender issues grows in the United States and throughout the world, we believe that researchers should theorize more about how political systems and institutional design affect policy outcomes. Fruitful avenues to explore might include federal versus nonfederal systems, direct democracy (Lupia et al. 2010), the scope of bureaucratic rule-making authority, or the role of executive orders in national as well as subnational jurisdictions.

Just as we have little good data on how many transgender people there are, we also still know very little about their policy attitudes, their likelihood of involvement in LGBT politics, or even their political orientations. Like the broader LGB community, the transgender community is a very difficult and expensive population to survey in a random probability sample. Nevertheless, this is an important missing piece of the empirical puzzle of transgender politics. We can ask, for example, are there widespread, shared policy goals in the community? Does the community feel as though it is part of the broader LGB movement? Do movement political goals coincide with the daily lives of trans people?

Likewise few general population surveys ask respondents specifically about attitudes toward transgender people or policies. As noted throughout this volume many researchers use measures of attitudes toward gays and lesbians as surrogates for attitudes toward transgender people or policies, but we have little empirical evidence that these measures are anything better than crude proxies. For example, although support for nondiscrimination laws protecting trans people might be similar to support for nondiscrimination laws protecting gays and lesbians, would support for parenting rights or adoption be the same (Becker 2012)?

Given the problems with polling the trans community, we also know very little about their actual political participation, whether it be with interest groups, in the voting booth, or contacting elected officials. We know much more about these things in the LGB population (see Bailey 1999,

2000; Egan 2012; Hertzog 1996). For example, it is likely true that many trans individuals identify as Democrats and perhaps even liberals, but would those figures approach the 65 percent we observe in the LGB community (Bailey 2000; Egan 2012; Hertzog 1996; Pew Research Center 2013)? If not, what does that mean for movement cohesion and goals?

Although there is some evidence that more transgender candidates are running for public office at the state level in the United States (Haider-Markel 2010), most transgender candidates have run for local offices, and we have collected no systematic evidence about how they fare in these contests or how they represent the trans community (or the broader LGBT community) if elected. As with the policy goals of the LGBT movement, the trans candidates often tend to follow the electoral successes of the gay community. For example, a Minnesota-based transgender candidate for Congress in 2013 declared that she was running only because voters in the state had blocked a same-sex marriage ban in 2012 (Magan 2013). In addition, as the chapter on Latin America suggests, transgender candidates in Latin American countries have become more visible, suggesting a greater need for empirical investigations of transgender candidates and officials outside of the United States.

Finally, transgender advocacy might offer insight into how technology facilitates activism and how it affects policy diffusion. Because of the small and dispersed nature of the trans community, technologies like the Internet likely played a role in connecting this network of activists. The costs of communication have decreased and this has likely facilitated the sharing of policy information within countries and across the globe. Additionally and given the stigma associated with trans identity, there is at least a limited veil of anonymity online that is not available in most public forums. We call for more research in this area.

Concluding Remarks

Through the mid-2000s, the disciplines of political science and public administration had given little thought to transgender rights or policy. During that era, an author associated with this project asked a colleague about whether research on transgender policy was viable. The answer questioned whether transgender issues and policy were an appropriate topic of study for a political scientist. The individual felt that it was something better addressed by gender studies, doctors, psychiatrists, and lawyers; he hinted that it was activism run amok. Interestingly, this opinion was similar to the views of some political scientists about the study of gay and lesbian politics in the 1990s.

The social science views about the study of trans politics and policy began to shift as the 2000s wore on. The excellent edited collection *Transgender Rights* (Currah, Juang, and Minter 2006) was published by the University of Minnesota Press. Additionally, respected peer-reviewed journals such as *Administration & Society,* the *Review of Public Personnel Administration,* and *Social Science Quarterly* published transgender-focused pieces. Although some of these articles were normative in approach, others were empirical.

Of course, the publication of books and articles on trans policy and politics was helped by the expansion of transgender rights via the political system. This increase in policy activity is perhaps where we can connect the divides between empiricists and theorists and between those who believe that social scientists should approach topics in a neutral manner and those who believe that scholars should be more critical of societal injustice (Novkov and Barclay 2010). The empirical study of anything, transgender rights included, requires a reality to study. Empirical social scientists need data. For instance, they need information about advocacy groups. They need events to occur, such as bills being sponsored and voted on; and of course they need policies to be enacted in at least some jurisdictions. One cannot neutrally study a phenomenon that has not happened.

At the same time, the policy activity needed by neutral empiricists often does not occur without the dedicated work of scholars and activists. Those normative actors shed light on the injustices faced by marginalized groups, like trans people, through narratives, argument, and documentation. By doing so, these more critical scholars help to generate part of the reality that empiricists study, even as they are trying to explain that reality themselves. We hope that this volume helps to document the realities generated by activists and theorists in an objective manner that contributes to their efforts. Hopefully, additional social scientists will join this volume's authors in this endeavor.

NOTES

1. Opponents failed to collect enough signatures to place the issue on the ballot for 2014.

REFERENCES

Bailey, Robert W. 1999. *Gay Politics, Urban Politics: Identity and Economics in an Urban Setting*. New York: Columbia University Press.

Bailey, Robert W. 2000. *Out and Voting II: The Gay, Lesbian, and Bisexual Vote in Congressional Elections, 1990–1998*. Washington, DC: Policy Institute of the National Gay and Lesbian Task Force.

Becker, Amy B. 2012. "What's Marriage (and Family) Got to Do with It? Support for Same-Sex Marriage, Legal Unions, and Gay and Lesbian Couples Raising Children." *Social Science Quarterly* 93 (4): 1007–29.

Currah, Paisley, Richard Juang, and Shannon Price Minter, eds. 2006. *Transgender Rights*. Minneapolis: University of Minnesota Press.

Egan, Patrick J. 2012. "Group Cohesion without Group Mobilization: The Case of Lesbians, Gays, and Bisexuals." *British Journal of Political Science* 42 (3): 597–616.

Haider-Markel, Donald P. 2010. *Out and Running: Gay and Lesbian Candidates, Elections, and Policy Representation*. Washington, DC: Georgetown University Press.

Hertzog, Mark. 1996. *The Lavender Vote: Lesbians, Gay Men, and Bisexuals in American Electoral Politics*. New York: New York University Press.

Lewis, Daniel C. 2011a. "Bypassing the Representational Filter? Minority Rights Policies under Direct Democracy Institutions." *State Politics & Policy Quarterly* 11 (2): 198–222.

Lewis, Daniel C. 2011b. "Direct Democracy and Minority Rights: Same-Sex Marriage Bans in the U.S. States." *Social Science Quarterly* 92 (2): 364–83.

Lupia, Arthur, Yanna Krupnikov, Adam Seth Levine, Spencer Piston, and Alexander Von Hagen-Jamar. 2010. "Why State Constitutions Differ in Their Treatment of Same-Sex Marriage." *Journal of Politics* 72 (4): 1222–35.

Magan, Christopher. 2013. "Eagan Woman Doesn't Want Gender Identity to Define Impending Run for Congress." *St. Paul Pioneer-Press*, August, 11. http://www.twincities.com/dakotacounty/ci_23841229/eagan-candidate-congress-doesnt-want-her-gender-identity.

Megerian, Chris. 2013. "Conservatives Target Law on Transgender Students." *Los Angeles Times*, August 16. http://www.latimes.com/local/political/la-me-pc-california-transgender-students-20130816,0,4950843.story.

Novkov, Julie, and Scott Barclay. 2010. "Lesbians, Gays, Bisexuals, and the Transgendered in Political Science: A Report on a Discipline Wide Survey." *PS: Political Science & Politics* 43 (1): 95–106.

Pew Research Center. 2013. *A Survey of LGBT Americans: Attitudes, Experiences, and Values in Changing Times*. Washington, DC: Pew Research Center.

Smith, Miriam. 2005. "The Politics of Same-Sex Marriage in Canada and the United States." *PS: Political Science & Politics* 38 (2): 225–28.

Contributors

Roddrick Colvin is an associate professor in the Department of Public Management at John Jay College of Criminal Justice. In addition to his interests in employment policy, he is also interested in gay rights, hate crimes, and international human rights policies. He currently teaches courses in public administration, human resources management, and policy analysis.

Ryan Combs is a research associate at the University of Manchester (UK). He has presented his research on transgender health policy to the American Political Science Association and the Political Studies Association. His paper, "Gender Mainstreaming in the European Union: Not for All? The EU's Role in Healthcare Provision for Trans People," won the 2010 Robert W. Bailey Award.

Brian DiSarro is an assistant professor of government at California State University, Sacramento. His research interests include U.S. state political institutions, LGBT politics, federalism, and the judicial process.

Donald P. Haider-Markel is professor of political science at the University of Kansas. His research and teaching is focused on the representation of interests in the policy process and the dynamics between public opinion and policy. He has authored or coauthored over 45 refereed articles, multiple book chapters, and several books on a range of issue areas, including the environment, religion and the culture wars, civil rights, criminal justice, and terrorism. He has been recipient or corecipient of grants from the EPA STAR program, the National Science Foundation, and the American Psychological Foundation.

Matthew L. Jacobsmeier is an assistant professor of political science at West Virginia University. His research deals with public opinion and political behavior and focusses on the effects of race and religion. His work has appeared in *State Politics & Policy Quarterly, Politics and Religion,* and *PS: Political Science and Politics.*

Daniel C. Lewis is an assistant professor of political science at Siena College. He is the author of *Direct Democracy and Minority Rights: A Critical Assessment of the Tyranny of the Majority in the American States.* His research on gay rights policies and direct democracy has also been published in *State Politics & Policy Quarterly* and *Social Science Quarterly.*

Jacob R. Longaker is a PhD candidate in political science at the University of Kansas. He is researching LGBT and abortion-related activism and policy in Latin America.

Anthony J. Nownes is a professor of political science at the University of Tennessee, Knoxville. His research interests include interest group politics, GLBTQ politics, and voting behavior. His most recent book, *Total Lobbying: What Lobbyists Want (and How They Try to Get It),* was published by Cambridge University Press in 2006.

Sarah J. Poggione is an associate professor of political science at Ohio University. Her work on state legislatures and women and politics has appeared in *Legislative Studies Quarterly, Political Research Quarterly, State Politics & Policy Quarterly,* and other outlets.

Mitchell D. Sellers is a doctoral student of political science at the University of Florida. His research interests include government responsiveness, public policy, bureaucracy and LGBT politics. His work on local laws affecting transgender rights has appeared in *Administration & Society.*

Barry L. Tadlock is an associate professor of political science at Ohio University. He is the coeditor (with Ellen D. B. Riggle) of *Gays & Lesbians in the Political Process: Public Policy, Public Opinion, and Political Representation* (1999) and a book chapter concerning the framing of same-sex marriage. His other research interests include welfare reform and congressional election.

Jami K. Taylor is an associate professor of political science and public administration at the University of Toledo. She conducts research related to LGBT rights and on public service motivation. Her work has appeared in *State Politics & Policy Quarterly, Armed Forces & Society, Politics & Policy, Administration & Society, American Review of Politics,* and the *American Review of Public Administration.*

Index

Note: Page numbers in *italics* indicate figures and tables.

Suffredini, Kara, 177
Sullivan, Dan, 146–47
surgery. *See* sex reassignment surgery
Svara, James, 141
Sylvia Rivera Law Project (SRLP), 33, 90–92

Tadlock, Barry, 12, 14, 15, 113, 159
Tanis, Justin, 13
Tapety, Kátia, 73n5
Taylor, Jami, 13, 14, 15, 159–60, 197
Teena, Brandon, 8
Tennessee, 145–46, 253
Thomas More Law Center, 135
Toledo, Ohio, 213
traditional or conventional political climates, 140–41. *See also* morality (traditional values)
Transamerica (film), 28
transgender, concept of, 6–7, 232–33, 274; newspaper articles using term, *38–40*, 41–42; use of term, 29, 52, 212–13
transgender advocacy interest groups, 13, 43–44, 83–104, *85, 91*; backlash against, 99–101, 103; competition for resources, 86–88, 90–96, 103; defined, 84; determinants of founding dates, 87–90, *89*; legitimation, 13, 86–88, 93–96, 105n5; population resurgence, 97–100; population stasis, 96–99, 103; resources and funding, 123–24
Transgender Americans Veterans Association, 16
transgender community: demographics and size of population, 18n1, 98, 118, 120, 233–34, 245–47, 273, 279; policy attitudes, 279–80; poverty and marginalization in, 14, 112, 120, 128, 273
transgender etiology, 6–7, 239, 246
Transgender Law and Policy Institute, 140
Transgender Law Center, 10
transgender military service, ban on, 16–17, 211
transgender nondiscrimination laws, 14, 53, 87–89, 273–77; causality for, 104n4; by component, *172*; event history analysis (1981-2011), *166*; implementation

of, 208–25; language use in, 15, 208, 212–13, 216–25; linked to sexual orientation nondiscrimination, *126*, 155–56, *156*, 257, 266–67; in local governments, 3, 14, 15, 135–50, *143*, 208–26, *209*, *218*, *221*, *223*, *225*; in Maryland, 108–9; policy process and prioritization of, 111–28; safeguards for claimants, 208, 216–25. *See also* LGBT nondiscrimination laws
transgender politics and policy, 1–6, 273–74; linked to gay and lesbian rights, 274–78; research on, 278–81
Transgender Rights (Currah, Juang, and Minter), 281
transgender rights movement, 7–9; linked to gay and lesbian rights movement, 266–67; nontransgender allies, 98. *See also* transgender advocacy interest groups
Transgender Rights Project, 177
Trans Media Watch, 100
Transsexual Empire, The (Raymond), 101
transsexualism and transsexuals, 6–7; newspaper articles on, *35–37,* 41–42; use of terms, 52, 68–69, 232–33
transsexuality, use of term, 69
transvestites, 6, 233
travesti, 63–64, 69–71; use of term, 52

United Kingdom, 277; Equality and Human Rights Commission, 234; National Health Service (NHS), 232, 236–45; transgender health care, 15, 231–48
United Nations Gender Equality Index, 51
United States: health care and insurance system, 7, 245. *See also* states
University of Alaska-Anchorage Justice Center, 147
Uruguay, 54–56
U.S. Census Bureau, 259, 267n3, 269n16
U.S. Congress, 100, 121, 275, 280; LGBT-inclusive hate crimes statute, 4
U.S. Constitution, full faith and credit clause, 254